The Lord, the Giver of Life

The Lord, the Giver of Life

Spirit in Relation to Creation

Aaron T. Smith

LEXINGTON BOOKS/FORTRESS ACADEMIC
Lanham • Boulder • New York • London

Published by Lexington Books/Fortress Academic
Lexington Books is an imprint of The Rowman & Littlefield Publishing Group, Inc.
4501 Forbes Boulevard, Suite 200, Lanham, Maryland 20706
www.rowman.com

6 Tinworth Street, London SE11 5AL, United Kingdom

British Library Cataloguing in Publication Information Available

Library of Congress Cataloging-in-Publication Data

Names: Smith, Aaron T., 1973– author.
Title: The Lord, the giver of life : Spirit in relation to creation / Aaron T. Smith.
Description: Lanham, Maryland : Fortress Academic, [2021] | Includes bibliographical references and index. | Summary: "Reflecting the Third Article of the Nicene Creed, The Lord, The Giver of Life describes God and creation according to the redeeming work of the Holy Spirit. Aaron T. Smith shows that it is not immateriality and materiality, which define 'God' and 'world,' but reflexive capacity for otherness realized in covenantal history."—Provided by publisher.
Identifiers: LCCN 2021011857 (print) | LCCN 2021011858 (ebook) | ISBN 9781978707740 (cloth) | ISBN 9781978707757 (epub)
Subjects: LCSH: Creation. | Holy Spirit. | Covenant theology.
Classification: LCC BS652 .S65 2021 (print) | LCC BS652 (ebook) | DDC 231.7/65—dc23
LC record available at https://lccn.loc.gov/2021011857
LC ebook record available at https://lccn.loc.gov/2021011858

♾™ The paper used in this publication meets the minimum requirements of American National Standard for Information Sciences—Permanence of Paper for Printed Library Materials, ANSI/NISO Z39.48-1992.

I wrote the bulk of this book while in vocational transition from university professor to parish pastor. I could not have finished without the selflessness of my wife, whose fidelity scorns the cynic, and whose unflagging confidence in her husband inspires him to merit it, at least to make earnest effort toward its warrant. Uncomplainingly, she left behind our home in the foothills of the Rocky Mountains, moved to central Pennsylvania, and took on the major responsibilities of our daily lives as I returned to the classroom desk, assumed the mantle of intern, and wrote feverishly in the second bedroom of our subsidized, dormitory apartment. There could be no other to whom this work is dedicated.

For Dawn
Chambersburg, PA, 2021

Contents

Introduction

Professor of the Hebrew Bible, Rolf Rendtorff (d. 2014), writes:

> The Bible does not speak of God "per se," but of what God says, how he acts and how he is experienced. The concern is thus always with God in his relationship to the world and to humans and quite especially to Israel. Thus the first sentence of the Bible . . . does not speak of whether God *is*, or who he is, but expresses the fact that God *acts*. The verb that describes his action appears even before the mention of God himself: "In the beginning *created* God."[1]

Whatever the Bible has to say of "God," including as Creator, it says in the terms of *covenantal relation*. At first blush, this seems circular and presumptive: God the Creator turns out to be the actor already playing Savior in the drama of Israel's history. But it is better to describe biblical portrayal of the divine as *inferential*. That God or the gods was/were involved in creaturely happenings was not a question for the ancient Hebrews any more than it was for the Sumerians, Assyrians, or Egyptians; like with their cultural myths, the Bible assumes God's existence, and assumes it to be relevant for creaturely existence. The question—and it was a lively one—concerned the *character* of God in the light of God's involvement with creation.

How was God to be described in view of God's dealings with Israel? It is in answer to this historically specific interrogative, not in general claims about divine nature, that the Bible speaks of "God." Israel's experience from Egypt to Cana and from Cana to Babylon and back indelibly defined its understanding and speech of the divine. The biblical authors could only give account of God in the terms of deliverance from slavery, sustenance in the wilderness, and restoration from exile.

Thus in turn, the Bible's accounts of God's activity "in the beginning," in creation, take shape with reference to this redemptive framework and further elucidate God's character: creation entails not only sourcing existence but also constantly providing for it, and God's Godness, if I may, is found in the integrated performance of both activities. God is like a farmer who sows the seed of life *and at once* secures the conditions of its developmental health and variety. Indeed, God sources life *by* restraining threats that would drown, choke, or otherwise prevent its appearance and flourishing. The event is so integrated that each aspect may precede the other (either the sowing or the securing). As a farmer sows seed not just in any ground but in soil that has been tilled and freed of weeds, so God brings sun and moon into a reality where darkness has already been separated from light (Genesis 1). Yet conversely, sun and moon regulate or govern the separation—the (re)appearance of sun and moon removes the darkness.[2]

The coordinated act of creating continues, and so creation continues (the world endures). A sovereign commitment to life and corresponding, equal commitment against death go on and on, and "God" takes shape for the biblical author in the experience of this caring sovereignty. God is Giver of Life in human encounter with provision specific to demands of the season.

The God made known to the biblical author through encounter with acts of redemption (through inference from Israel's history, and more widely, as we will later learn from Karl Barth, the existential experience of "revealedness") is better described as *relational event* than as *metaphysical being*. It is the unwavering constancy of life-sustaining order, which supplies the referent "God" with sufficient stability to admit meaningful personalization, to speak of an eternal subject, an always-living *he* or *she*. Against much of the classical Western tradition, it is not the quality of maximal thingness that distinguishes God, but the constancy of characteristic, triadic work: creation-preservation-glorification. In sowing, securing, and harvesting, "he is."[3]

As the first of a two-volume treatment of the doctrine of creation, this book begins an extended effort to retell the biblical narrative and rethink Christian teaching pneumatologically, in terms of existential relation rather than states of being. What makes *spirit* of the biblical Spirit is not immateriality or incorporeality but reflexive capacity for otherness.[4] To say "spirit" is to say readiness-for; the Spirit of God is unconquerable self-determinative power to be-with, an irrefutable prerogative to have and ingrained disposition toward elective communal existence.

A postmetaphysical, pneumatocentric retelling of the Christian story highlights the reality of God's presence in a world not naturally inclined to it. It speaks constructively and, one hopes, compellingly of God's involvement in temporal affairs, neither of necessity nor of supernatural intervention but persistent, charitable companionship and intention. However desolate and weed-infested this world-garden has become—however damaged, diseased, and death-bound the creature finds itself—it is not and will not be godforsaken, for the preservation and fulfillment of its every moment is relevant to God.

We might say that "God" is *the party responsible for sowing and securing the world*,[5] but even that expression turns prematurely from the biblical narrative toward metaphysical speculation (as Being imparts being). Sowing and securing better bespeak a quality of *giving-a-share*; God *is* generous dissemination of life, the Giver of Life and not withholder. God is not the Creator *in potentia*. God would not be God in reserving life (as a possibility to be imparted); God is only God in life's actual allocation and division, *in acto ergo in essentia*.[6] God is *agape*, love (1 Jn. 4:8).

I laid the groundwork for this argument in my previous book, which offered a participatory account of God's creative revelation (I coined the term "Inverberation," as a corollary to *Incarnation*, to describe the way in which God's Word reverberates productively across generations of witnesses, at once generating a redemptive perception of reality and removing godlessness—the work of creating a people in faith is what we call the "Spirit of the Word").[7] In keeping with the generative and formational character of Spirit-Word, I proposed that time itself ought not to be thought of in linear but in existential, or what I would now construe as cynosural terms: as regular, rhythmic progression from and toward an animating center. "The creation" does not refer to the sequential outcome of a once-upon-a-time declaration but to the continuing, dynamic consequence of divine self-determination. As God exists relationally, so a relational other ("creation") exists.

Thinking of creation at the grandest scale, the sequences that comprise quotidian existence must be con-sequences: "seconds" first in the sense of *rank*. The most basic units of space-time must not be thought of as given containers of reality but recurrent opportunities for new life, reiterative instances of love. They are not only registers of rotation around the sun, but more, they are the events of life's becoming—the mutually determinative media of God's self-expression and of creation's opportunity. In this regard, since Einstein we have known that seconds are, paradoxically, measures of the events that make them. They are best described as units of distance-relation, which are given rise by the distances they measure. Motion between points A and B acts determinatively on the length of "a second." Time's originating is at once an act of separating, and vice versa—its separating into quantities originates the chance for spatial relationship, a lifespan or *history*. For all their con-sequence, then, the moments that make up time are not insignificant. They are consequential, momentous. In their mutual determination, "God" and "creation" exist and are known.

As a consequence, the world takes the pattern of *afterward*. Creation involves more than a protological "bang" followed by cumulative idiosyncrasy (gradual accumulation of differentiated entities). Rather, "creation" is resultative *by nature*, manifesting the productivity of divine love in its very constitution.[8] Time's necessity is proportional to its graciousness, its readiness to become *again* the medium of relation in the way of the Creator. Creation's protology must be eschatologically constructed.

Ongoing reaction (read: re-action) really is the only "being" of the world. Creation's essence is in perpetual openness to the event of life. It exists "after" God. It does this not sequentially, for to say that God is "before" anything can only mean that God is precedent (as criterion and means) to that thing. On the contrary, creation is after God in that it *takes after* God—its constitutive processes arise and share in the eternal openness and giving of "God."

As lives which identify themselves in consciousness of a subsistent present, which they project into the future, learning to think and speak of ourselves and our world as perpetually consequent upon *archetypal* (not "prior") divine action takes habituation. Our linear and statically inclined views of being have to be caught up into cynosural and dynamic movement. For, even our language reinforces linear sequence (as here, thoughts are expressed and built by a progression of letters, words, sentences, and paragraphs). Our language itself has to be confronted by an alternative word—opened to new functionality in its old usage.[9]

The *disposition* to linear sequentialism is the real problem. Thought moves uncritically, *impulsively* toward a perception of the world as existing after the creature, as taking form and operation after succession from a certain start to stop. We think of time in terms of our own beginning and ending, birth and death. We give thought of the world over to the banal framework of human chronology, when in fact, the charity determinative of God's life has no chronological beginning and ending, and this charity is more constitutive of creation than any sequential start and stop.[10]

The un-thoughtful forfeiture of thought to the march from a fixed past to future consequent upon self-referenced human being is easily described. Lest things become too abstract too early, it may be worth doing so briefly.

If one observes two objects at a distance—say a basketball 50 yards behind a grapefruit, with an observer standing 100 yards away from the latter (150 yards from the former)—the observer simply perceives two objects of similar size, shape, and color. She may think that she sees identical objects. She deduces that they could be different if there is distance between them, even though they appear to be the same.

Similarly, an observer of the night sky must gather information about shining lights to discern their size and composition, which to the naked eye, sometimes even the eye aided by telescopes, appear the same. By observing certain signature operations, the astronomer may learn that one light is a galaxy and the other a single star, and she may further determine which is nearer and which is farther from her. She may ascertain that the light of the galaxy has had to travel farther to reach her than that of the star. But unlike with basketball and grapefruit, the unscientific observer of the sky rarely takes the distance factor into account (and even with basketball and grapefruit, he has no reason to take into account the distinct *times* of their lights reaching his perception). He simply considers the heavenly lights as equi-distant parts of a total sky-picture. His day/night cycle is structured by multiple, same-ly appearing lights even though his "now" actually consists of the appearance of differing objects in different "pasts."

It takes minimal extrapolation to realize that, although generally unnoticed, the human present is really the subjective rendering of manifold pasts in observation. Or to come at it from the opposite direction, the human observer always stands futurely in relation to the objects about her, even as she, standing as object to another, exists pastly in that other's perception (and each constantly trades perspectives in discourse). Whether communicated by light and the ocular sense, or sound and the auditory, or smell and the olfactory—in truth, of all these together at differing rates and intensities (for, sense deficiency must also play its role in constructing the "now")—reality in human knowing is always a convergence of past and future in a fleeting "present." Temporal existence is merely reiterative perception of flexible relations.

The speed of sense media, especially light and sound, contributes to our unawareness of this reality; they move too quickly for us to be automatically conscious of the present's elasticity. Their rate of intake contributes to an artificial notion of a stable now. We therefore tend to be *naturally* inattentive to the moment's lack of permanence, to the transitory character of the present.

Covenantal God remakes the present by endowing it with *anticipation*, the ongoing movement from *promise* to *fulfillment*. God does this by making time both the object and medium of creation: God reconstructs the now by entering it. God remakes the human impulse to a fixed beginning and ending by making an ever-new *beginning* and *ending* in the Messiah. The history of Israel fulfilled by its recapitulation in the life, ministry, death, and resurrection of the Christ is the ground of the world and the event of "God." This ground and event recur in the experience of faith.[11] In faith, the biblical reader takes part in the divine-human encounter of the biblical author.

Faith structures the temporal alternative; it serves as the means of humanity's spiritual transformation. In faith, the human moves from old *adam* to new *adam*, from the promise of life to its fulfillment. In faith, the human encounters creation in covenantal form, as ongoing redemption. Several claims follow from the fact that faith is the means of the creature's spiritual transformation, and so also the willed condition by which God exists and is known. We will consider each in turn.

TWELVE THESES

Thesis 1. Pneumatocentric theology is biblical theology.

The experience of faith does not entail conversion to general spiritualism but perpetually returning to the specific past-future of the Christ event as the ground of existence. This event fulfills the promise of Israel's history, within which, again, God lives and acts. Movement within the specific time of *Incarnation–Resurrection* structures the transition from the old to the new *adam*. The experience of faith entails ongoing conformity of thought, will, speech, and act to the pattern of life realized in the Christ. Becoming disposed toward this transformation is the consequence of the Spirit of God.

Thesis 2. The Bible does not lay out a general cosmology.

The Bible displays no commitment to a particular cosmology or cosmogony. It freely engages multiple traditions. Genesis 1 depicts creation to take place by the fiat, "let there be," and a creative agency that operates almost independently of its object, that is, a Creator who relates transcendently to creation. Gen. 2–3, on the other hand, understand creation to happen by tactile formation (body sculpted from ground material, woman from the "side" of man), and with this, a creative agency that involves creation itself, as well as a Creator who exists intimately with creation. The latter account, moreover, construes creation as God's temple; as we have begun to see and will discuss more fully in the ensuing chapters, the place of encounter with "God" is the history of creation-preservation-glorification.

Similarly, Ps. 82 portrays God as triumphant judge over rival deities (see v. 1, 6–8; vv. 2–5 interpolated). Together with Pss. 74 and 89, it indicates that creation occurs as victory over threats (Leviathan, Rahab) and mastery over forces (setting boundaries to water and seasons). Psalms 74 and 89 recall the covenant, connecting Israel's adversaries with God's and so depicting the anti-creative (chaotic) threats to continue today (see Ps. 74:1–12, 18–23), staking the very nature of God's legitimacy *as God* upon continuing defeat of these enemies. Gen. 6–9, Job 38, and Isaiah 51 also treat the ancient near eastern theme of *Chaoskampf*, construing creation as occurring, and God as existing, in victorious establishment of ordered relation.

So, the Bible simply does not endorse any single account of the cosmos or its origins. The first statement of faith called forth by confrontation with Scripture is to reject all cosmological and cosmogonic presuppositions.

Thesis 3. Creation in the Bible is intimately bound up with covenant.

A crimson thread of canonical continuity runs through the text's divergent strands of cosmological engagement. Each strand in its peculiar way repairs thought to the covenant. Each hearkens to a divine readiness for otherness as, per se, the condition of being: whether by fiat or by warfare against death, God exists in a relational constitution that forever summons life.

Jon D. Levenson therefore concludes that the Western world in particular has too often read the biblical stories of creation as perspectival tellings of how God made discrete things "out of nothing." I will have more to say about the propriety of the doctrine of *creatio ex nihilo* in chapter 1. For now, I will simply acknowledge that Levenson is correct to turn attention toward active implementation of the covenant as the central motif in the biblical accounts of creation: "the point of creation is not the production of matter out of nothing, but rather the emergence of a stable community in a benevolent and life-sustaining order. The defeat by YHWH of the forces that have interrupted that order is intrinsically an act of creation."[12]

Thesis 4. Christ is the basis, content, and goal of the covenant.

The covenantal testimony of the prophets and apostles orients toward a particular figure: the Christ. In him, the forces of death are restrained and creation emerges, and in his self-giving, the fullness of God as Life-giver is revealed. An actualistic theology of creation is at its core a theology of the cross.

In Jesus of Nazareth, the divinely willed relation between God and creation, in which relation "God" and "creation" exist and are known, is achieved:

> He is the image of the invisible God, the firstborn of all creation; for in him all things in heaven and on earth were created. . . . He himself is before all things, and in him all things hold together. . . . He is the beginning, the firstborn from the dead, so that he might come to have first place in everything. For in him all the fullness of God was pleased to dwell, and in him God was pleased to reconcile to himself all things, whether on earth or in heaven, by making peace through the blood of his cross.[13]

The collective insights of two classical theological figures help to flesh out this thesis. Karl Barth (1886–1968) and Friedrich Schleiermacher (1768–1834) figure prominently in the following pages.

Barth perspicaciously correlated creation and covenant and understood the latter in terms of Christ Jesus. In §41 of the *Church Dogmatics*, he treated "creation as the external basis of the covenant" and "the covenant as the internal basis of creation."[14] Creation supplies the theater, so to speak, of God's covenantal performance, whereas that performance in Christ's life and work supplies the inner rationale, the conceptual basis and teleological form of creation. Although Barth moves in this order, from creation to covenant, the tight correlation between the two suggests that it is equally legitimate, and dogmatically fruitful, to move in the other direction. I am initiating that reciprocal motion here; the second volume of this project completes the turn.[15]

Schleiermacher considered the God-world relation more thematically than Barth did, locating it specifically in the existential event of absolute dependence. He thus also emphasized the actualistic nature of God's defining life-act, the Christ event occurring decisively in the here and now. But as we will see, Schleiermacher introduced an unfortunate break in the event of dependence between "feeling," on the one side, and "knowing" and "doing," on the other, the upshot of which, as I see it (with Barth), is to evacuate the event of Christ and the contemporaneity of the covenant of its specific Incarnation–Resurrection trajectory. Schleiermacher thought of God's determinative relation to creation in terms of a general category of religion rather than the specific content of revelation. I will argue that if we translate Schleiermacher's magisterial contribution into a revelation, rather than religion-centric framework, reading it in terms of Spirit-Word rather than world-spirit, if you like, it offers valuable, enduring resources for contemporary reflection.

Barth foresaw reconciliation with Schleiermacher along the lines of a pneumatocentric theology that retained the objective focal point of divine action in the concrete history of Jesus of Nazareth. Besides being a constructive project in its own right, the present book can be read as at least aiming toward such rapprochement.[16]

Thesis 5. Creation cannot be rigorously differentiated from Redemption; neither is the Creator other than the Redeemer.

If the covenant that God makes with creation is not a second action subsequent to the gift of life, but is in fact central to that gift as creation's eternal ground, so that the creature only enjoys existence as she emerges from God's continuing covenantal faithfulness in Christ Jesus, then the nature of the work of creation is the same as the nature of the work of redemption.[17] The latter is *not* mere repetition of the former (now specially endowed with grace), or correction of it (now better informed of creaturely pitfalls), but the structure and means of the former. Furthermore, if we only rightly think

"God" and "creation" in terms of *covenant*, and the covenant is fulfilled in Christ, so that "God" and "creation" exist and are known in him, then the Redeemer just is the Creator. The life-act that determines God's existence in Jesus of Nazareth—the election to God's life of the atoning conditions by which creation comes to fruition—must be determinative of "God" in creating.

Concerning the first (redemption being determinative of creation), "redemption" is transformation, not restoration, of history into right cadence. The hope of the world is not to arrive by progress at a chronologically backward starting point, the return of humankind to paradise, but for each generation to emerge in its own dimensionality (within its own generational situatedness) as God's creative partner. A particular generation materializes, which is to say, authentic creaturely agency is generated, in God's Word, in which Word it also culminates—it becomes a reverberative act of generation. In this, the work of creation is entirely the *achievement* of grace, in both senses of grace's victory and the outcome of grace's application, and it accounts for creaturely pitfalls.[18] Creation involves the continual overcoming of un-creation.

Concerning the second (the Redeemer being determinative of the Creator), the work of the Christ is existentially relevant to the life and character of "God." From all eternity, that work represents a decisive factor in God's life, giving it a definite structure.[19]

To think "God" as *Creator* is to recognize (better, re-cognize, or persistently re-think) the way of self-giving charity in Christ Jesus in its full scope—even unto death on a cross—and in this act of recognition, to be overcome in every alternative impulse, to experience total dependence upon this One. Thinking after Jesus, one confesses that the Creator is not a metaphysical Mystery above and behind creation but a personal, self-relating agency invested in creation. The Creator is *as* illimitable refusal of non-being, darkness, and death, in which life we are graciously granted a share.

Finally, the only basis for triune differentiation between Creator and Redeemer is the same as that for differentiating between creation and redemption: the *relation* of opposition. A first stands opposite a second, but not sequentially. One might make use of the distinct categories, "creative grace" and "redemptive grace" (the latter being subdivided into "justifying" and "sanctifying" grace), as well as "uncreated grace" (divine benevolence) and "created grace" (preaching and the sacraments), so long as one does *not* mean by these terms "supernatural inducements" then "natural inducements," or in any way convey the notion that the one is sequentially precedent in God's work and life to the other. For, the benevolence by which God exists and is known only happens in the faith event of creaturely rebirth, and the Father exists and is known only in the cry of the Son, that is, in existential realization of the Son's dependence.[20]

In fact, looking at reality from the perspective of redemption, all grace is *gratia praeveniens*, "prevenient grace," in that the gift of life derives entirely from the eternal act of divine self-election. Only as God exercises a determinative will, reiteratively placing divine existence in characteristic relation to another, does creation transpire and Creator exist. It is only in continuing renewal of this self-election by way of the covenant, only in the Spirit of Christ, that "God" and "creation" exist and are known. As Barth rightly understood: "it is in the decision in favour of this movement [toward humankind], in God's self-determination and the resultant determination of man, in the basic relationship which is enclosed and fulfilled within Himself, that God is who He is."[21]

Thesis 6. Because redemption is determinative of creation, preservation belongs to the doctrine of creation.

In that, "creation" refers to a continuing work of God to bring a corresponding reality into ordered relation; it encompasses *preservation*.[22] It is heuristically useful to distinguish between origination and conservation, between generation of life and its preservation, in order to maintain the non-divinity of the world: the event of creaturely dependence includes awareness of creation's otherness from God, which awareness is at least partially secured by affirming that unlike God, the world is not eternal. "God" exists in the event of eternal love; "world" exists as *consequence* of eternal love. Hence, the act of creation cannot be collapsed into *eternal preservation* as this ambiguates the status of world relative to God by implying identical non-origination; unlike God, "world" must involve, besides preservation, some kind of origination. Yet as indicated, redemption is constitutive of creation, so the distinction must dialectically be negated. The generation and securing of life, while distinct, comprise one and the same act—of gardening or farming.

It is not that God first originates then preserves. There is a modalism to such account of divine action, which, in view of the reality that God exists and is known only in such action, conjures the historically heretical modalism of being. It is rather that in originating, God at once, without any sequential priority, establishes the conditions of creation's endurance and fulfillment. What happens is that God, in the self-sufficiency by which God is Lord or Spirit, the capacity by which God gives life, elects against every threat to the achievement of God's love, in which gracious electing the world originates. God preserves *in God's self*, within eternal triune relationship, the life that God originates alongside God's self.

That creation entails divine preservation is obviously significant for whatever account we might give concerning the nature and persistence of evil. Once again, Levenson states the connection for the biblical authors with special insight:

The confinement of chaos rather than its elimination is the essence of creation, and the survival of ordered reality hangs only upon God's vigilance in ensuring that those cosmic dikes do not fail, that the bars and doors of the Sea's jail cell do not give way, that the great fish does not slip his hook. . . . Whatever form the warranty takes, it testifies both to the precariousness of life, its absolute dependence upon God, and to the sureness and firmness of life under the protection of the faithful master. The world is not inherently safe; it is inherently unsafe. Only the magisterial intervention of God and his eternal vigilance prevent the cataclysm. Creation endures because God has pledged in an eternal covenant that it shall endure and because he has, also in an eternal covenant, compelled the obeisance of his great adversary. If either covenant (or are they one?) comes undone, creation disappears.[23]

Thesis 7. "Evil" is the anti-Spirit or "flesh," which actively contradicts, interrupts, or otherwise suppresses creation's absolute dependence on God.

The protection that God originate-ly affords the world takes the form of active annulment of the kind of life that would effect independent selfhood. God eliminates the threat of disunity and disharmony, confines the chaos, and thus safeguards against nonexistence. But as Levenson noted, elimination of the threat is not the same as elimination of the threatening agent. God confines the chaos but does not eradicate it. The world-ness of world and God-ness of God take place, at once, in the latter's application of sovereignty *over* every alternative in the occurrence of existential dependence, *over* every self-ruling existent, *over* every would-be god, including, as we will later discuss, the human. Three challenging questions surface.

One, is the basic impulse to independence and self-sufficiency, and thus to divine usurpation, so bound up with the essence of world (as alternative to God) that creaturely achievement in harmony with God always presupposes a measure of disharmony? Or put simply, can the creature *be* creature absent instinctual tension with the Creator? Similarly, two, is assertion of God's own self-sufficiency (as alternative to world) so elemental to the deity of "God" that we must expect rivals to endure forever so that God might have something to rule and, by ruling, *be*? And three, if the Lordship constitutive of God's God-ness demands subordination of every rival, must God *create* rivals just to be, that is, must God give life to the anti-God in order to give "God" life? Again, Levenson: "[YHWH's] victory is only meaningful if his foe is formidable, and his foe's formidability is difficult, perhaps impossible, to imagine if the foe has long since vanished. No emperor will achieve heroic status in the eyes of his subjects if all he forces to march through his streets is a sunken-chested weakling or, worse, if he has no one to force to march."[24] I will address the first question within the context of this thesis and the second and third questions in the next theses.

While disposition to independence lurks within world existence, the tendency may be ended without ending the world. In fact, just this ending preserves the world. What makes primal chaos chaotic and in need of confinement is not propensity to bring forth life from within creation itself. That propensity is in fact the goodness of creation, the share in living given by the Creator. But the world is to take its part in living in *grateful response* to the share it has been given. What is chaotic in creation is the propensity not granted by God to bring forth life *irresponsibly*, without consequential gratitude for the *giving* of life, treating life as if it was a *given*; it is to act without accountability to creation's covenantal character. To seek independence in this sense, the sense of non-dependence on God and unconcern for neighbor, is to give space (in fact, space-time) to evil.

This latter propensity must arise from the former, independent ability from interdependent responsibility; the evil in creation must arise from the good. It can only find animation as a kind of viral imitation and annexation of pro-creation, in that it is inherently self-compromising. Life *is* interdependent. To act otherwise impairs life. The threat to life is intrinsically parasitic, bound for death the instant that the life it assails is compromised, and so, for all its harmfulness, evil cannot be considered a life unto itself. It is anti-life and must be thusly identified and ended. God's self-determinative rule takes hold as the life-cycles of creation manifest the ending of anti-covenantal independence and new beginning of interdependence.

However much the disposition to independence arises from creation's goodness in actually bearing life, it must not be confused with the life-bearing that it apes. It must not be considered essential to the world-ness of the world. Critical identification of evil precisely in its parasitic mimicry is part and parcel of life's achievement. True life resolves to end death.

Thesis 8. God elects to God's self the ending of evil.

We meet true life, God in pure resolve to end death, and encounter true humanity, the creature as accountable participant in life's giving, in the cross and resurrection of Christ Jesus.[25] Because of him, and in response to the second question above, the Lordship of God does not require abstract endurance of rivals. In Christ, God exposes death's nothingness and gives life abundantly.

The psalmist is not misinformed in beseeching YHWH to destroy the wicked.[26] It is not that the psalmist has failed to realize that the sovereignty constitutive of "God" presupposes the endurance of wickedness. Quite the opposite, the psalmist understands that such sovereignty ultimately demands its defeat. For, so long as the wicked alternative threatens, so long as irresponsible independence moves from latency to reality even in the slightest form, even simply as desire or lust,[27] the rule by which God lives and is known comes under assault. The abiding indignation of the creature impugns the dignity of "God."

It is with a view to God's subtle necessity of destroying what is wicked while upholding the creature that we must differentiate between the latency of the evil impulse—temptation—and its realization, most basically in the form of lust; the one is fundamental to humanity and is something to which even Christ is subject (Heb. 4:15) while the other is not. God *can* make existence *apart from* lustful impulse to independence and death. Again, hope in this victory of the creature over its (own) menace, the promise of this active righteousness in the moment-by-moment power of God, forms the basis of true life. How, then, can God make humanity in the promise of its own transformation while destroying wickedness?

In that the wicked impulse is latent in all creaturely existence its defeat must entail new creation from within creation, the assumption of human existence. To combat God's enemies and redeem the creature, God must locate God's self in the midst of the creature's unbecoming, improper animus and end that animus there. God must adopt that life, which is constantly susceptible to temptation, ever ready to fall in upon itself, yet resist the temptation and withstand the fall, thus making a new kind of humanity within humanity. God must make real within the creaturely sphere a human alternative to itself—that is, doubly, an alternative to human falseness and a *genuine* alternative to God—one vulnerable to evil who perfectly resists and defeats it. The Spirit of God must overcome evil in the flesh. This happens in the history of Christ Jesus, as this person lives by the Spirit in perfect conformity to God's will even unto the cross.

Thesis 9. God's temporal self-election is of eternal significance.

If the eschatological ground of creation entails defeat of God's enemies, then, protologically, the work of the Creator is not the source of those threats. Evil takes rise elsewhere. In response to the third question above, the Lordship that makes God of God need not involve generating rivals to defeat.[28]

For God to be God, Lord over the creature in the living constitution of Redeemer and Creator, the creature must find herself in this explicit situation: condemned in the wickedness of her impulse to life absent God, yet befriended and cherished by God, atoned for and recovered to God. She finds herself in this situation as she finds herself in Christ.

The life that God wills *for all time*, in the eschaton, God makes real *in* time. Or, God makes time after the cadence of the creature's redemption. The temporality (con-sequence) of resurrection confronts the temporality of evil—showing and making true its nothingness, thus condemning it—and reveals the divinely intended tempo of life.[29] In creating, God bestows to reality that share of self-determination by which it might gratefully acknowledge him and enter into authentic union with him, and so also by which it might seek its own ends. God gives bona fide latitude to the latter *not*, again, to render it a *legitimate* alternative, but to establish its consummate illegitimacy, to render complete its failure in the more perfect achievement of the covenant. The work of creation supposes the eternal defeat of evil, not its recurrent generation.

God secures *in himself*, once more, the conditions of the covenant that he brings about in time. God actualizes the time of resurrection in the enfleshed Word by the power of the Holy Spirit, which is the same as saying that God makes reality in Word and Spirit. The completeness of evil's threat and corresponding glory of its failure happen together in the triune life of God. The emptiness that threatens creation, the ear-piercing silence of God-abandonment, the futile isolation of life pursued independently of God, is lived out and made actual in God. Thus, however tangible and poignant the threat, the resurrection establishes the reality that its termination is a fait accompli, in encounter with which we are made to turn again in hope, to partake of this promise, to invoke once more the victory of God here and now, indeed, as the ground of here-now.

Thesis 10. It is through human agency that evil and death take rise.

The existence of evil is thus essential neither to the creatureliness of the creature nor to the deity of God. Whence, then, is it?

I have already stated that, by virtue of not being a part of God's creative work, evil is factually *nothing*. It has, as we will later relearn from Augustine, the character of non-being. And so, being of that character, it must arise from nothing. But description accords substance; appellations of "evil," "threat," even the pronoun "it" connote thingness. How, then, can we describe evil's nothingness and non-positive-origin if the descriptive act itself confers thingness and suggests concrete origination? By maintaining studied silence? But would silence toward its reference take seriously evil's tangibility?

"Evil" is not merely an unfortunate linguistic convention. The human does experience its threat: she is tempted and imperiled; she is harmed and defiled; she fails to give thanks for life; she denies life to others and lies about it; she dies.

It is of the essence of evil, exactly as nothing, to obscure its own identity, or conversely, to pursue positive valuation. To become rival to God, evil must be posited in perception as bona fide and confirmable. It must become a factor in the life of the creature, indeed, such a factor as to engender a new order of divine alternative, a life lived for itself and not for God. This evil does, quintessentially, in speech.

"Evil" becomes objectified in speech. In speech, "the serpent tricked me." In speech, "the woman you put here with me, she gave me fruit from the tree" (Gen. 3:12–13). Evil originates in the human action of externalizing the independent impulse. The human names evil without and so enacts it within. She narrates reality in such a way as to exempt herself from the action and consequence of irresponsibility and thus reproduces irresponsibility like a child.[30] In this way, she falsely posits an existence in which "evil" is that which victimizes her, in whatever shape it might come ("natural" or "moral"). Such endowing *is* evil already in exercise; it is annexation of the creature's reflective capacity in service to the nonexistent end of non-covenantal existence.

The human must learn to *confess* (post facto) evil rather than to *describe* (inter facto) evil *as*. More exactly, she must come to perceive that evil is a *contradictio inhaerens* both as she experiences it and as she conceives of it, that is, existentially and conceptually. Evil is not a freestanding power, but at most, so far as cruciform language expresses it, it is a liminal condition, an "in-between" God and creation, which, as neither, has no positive identity or ground. Its conditionality *can be* neutralized or brought back to factual non-being here and now because it *has been* neutralized in God's incarnational life-act. In Christ, the human confesses evil as baseless self-contradiction.[31]

Yet now, regarding the tangible nature of evil in human experience, we must draw a series of conclusions that in every meaningful way stands in dialectical tension with evil's non-reality. Also in the light of the cross, we recognize that in order to establish its factual baselessness as inherent self-contradiction, God gives to evil the most extensive reality possible: he makes himself subject to it.

God gives evil its day. He affords it a time unto itself, a consequential lordship over creation. He allows it to be that alternative, which by itself it is not, a force to be reckoned with. Evil confronts creation as a threat that *needs* to be overcome. It takes rise as a genuine adversary, a rival sovereignty manifested with a ferocity that frightens, a power that actually jeopardizes the divine order of things. Evil actually destroys, actually so damages creation as to make it endangered, actually threatens to unmake it, and in so doing, evil threatens to overtake God's sovereignty and unmake *him*.[32]

Evil appears to carry the day. It becomes a god to humankind. This it does in manifold forms, which the reader hardly requires me to recount—wealth, coercion, unjust gain, exploitative power, terror—as that which, in any case, introduces an interval in the creaturely sphere between the self-giving life of God and creaturely life. Evil interrupts life and culminates in death.

Thesis 11. The end of death has become the beginning of time.

The threat of evil, though creaturely in origin, is not finally realized until the Creator takes death into his life. The history that God lives in Christ Jesus is a time of ultimate confrontation with evil. And by the Spirit, this history moves inescapably toward evil's demise: the Christ event ends in the beginning of the empty tomb. The death that God gives reign meets a higher authority in the Spirit that gives life. The resurrection of Jesus from the dead forms the centerpiece of God's time with us; his self-giving becomes the cornerstone of covenantal existence, the character of that sacrificial love from which new life springs, the hope that grounds creation.

Time is thus made new by God in the defeat of the adversary. In Christ's resurrection, history obtains a grace-filled openness to life, a welcome whereby life that once was bound for death might become something else. Promise and fulfillment become the new order of "the day."

Thesis 12. We must recommence.

It is in obedient, continuous proclaiming, hearing, and reflecting on Scripture that time is newly inaugurated, that resurrection time confronts and defeats the day of evil, and a new generation is made to stand, in authenticity, before its Maker. Pneumatocentric theology never finishes, but must always begin again.

NOTES

1. Rolf Rendtorff, *The Canonical Hebrew Bible: A Theology of the Old Testament,* Tools for Biblical Study 7, trans. David E. Orton (Leiden: Deo, 2005), 586.

2. Light-emitting sources like fire may have suggested to the ancient near eastern observer a property of light that existed independently of the heavenlies, even though it is only the heavenlies that set a cyclical, regulative boundary to it.

3. Catherine Mowry Lacugna makes a cognate claim in her now-classic work, *God for Us: The Trinity & Christian Life* (Chicago: Claretian, 1991; repr. New York: HarperCollins, 1993). Arguing that Christian theology can only give accurate account of the triune life of God in view of God's economy of redemption, she writes, "the economy of creation, salvation, and consummation is the place of encounter in which God and the creature exist together in one mystery of communion and interdependence. . . . God's To-Be is To-Be-in-relationship, and God's being-in-relationship-to-us *is* what God is" (250).

4. Denis Edwards describes the Spirit similarly as "the power of becoming in evolutionary history," and as "ecstatic communion." See, *The God of Evolution: A Trinitarian Theology* (New York: Paulist, 1999), 88–92, 95–100.

5. Slightly modifying Robert Jenson's memorable claim: "To the question, 'Who is God?' the New Testament has one new descriptively identifying answer: 'Whoever raised Jesus from the dead.'" See Jenson, *Systematic Theology Volume I: The Triune God* (Oxford: Oxford University Press, 1997), 44. Jenson rightly contends that this identification simply "verifies" the OT identification of God as "the one who rescued Israel from Egypt" (ibid.). In both cases, "God" is the one who brings life from out of its opposite, in the face of opposition; in this double action, God is life-giver.

6. Again, Lacugna (endorsing Cappadocian contributions to trinitarian teaching): "personhood or relation is 'how' being exists. If God were not personal, God would not exist at all"; *God for Us*, 244.

7. Aaron T. Smith, *A Theology of the Third Article: Karl Barth and the Spirit of the Word* (Minneapolis: Fortress, 2014).

8. We tend to think of creation as the appearance of bodies, beings, or substances; most basically, "nature" refers to the total count of objects, from particles to planets. These entities enter subsequently into relation (attraction, repulsion, orbit). *But in fact, relations are equi-basic with entities.* It is no less correct to say that relations give rise to things as it is to say that things give rise to relations. Orbit, collision, and charge are as basic to an electron as mass and wave properties. As Edwards argues:

> Every entity seems to be constituted by at least two fundamental sets of relationships. First, there are the interrelationships between the components that make up an entity. Thus, a carbon atom is constituted from subatomic particles (protons, neutrons, and electrons). Second, there is the relationship between the entity and its wider environment. So a carbon atom in my body is constituted as part of a molecule, which forms part of a cell, which belongs to an organ of my body. I am part of a family, a human society, and a community of interrelated living creatures on Earth. The earth community depends upon and is interrelated with the Sun, the Milky Way galaxy, and the whole universe (*Breath of Life: A Theology of the Creator Spirit* [Maryknoll, NY: Orbis, 2004], 131).

Many have thought along similar lines. I find a great deal of affinity with the work of John Zizioulas. See for starters, "Relational Ontology: Insights from Patristic Thought," in *The Trinity and an Entangled World: Relationality in Physical Science and Theology*, ed. John Polkinghorne (Grand Rapids: Eerdmans, 2010), 146–56; *Being As Communion: Studies in Personhood and the Church* (Crestwood, NY: St. Vladimir's Seminary Press, 1985). Above all, I commend Zizioulas's insight with respect to modern science that the inherently relational character of world existence invites eschatological completion. The world is "a reality that in its *very relational being calls for a way of being which the world cannot by itself fulfill*. . . . Relational ontology contains in its very nature a dimension of *transcendence*, an *openness* of being, pointing to a *beyond the self*, to *seeking communion with the Other*, an eschatological orientation" ("Relational Ontology," 155; italics in original). I endorse his conclusion, drawn from the Greek Fathers, concerning the non-priority of *substance* in "God":

The manner in which God exercises His ontological freedom, that precisely which makes Him ontologically free, is the way in which He transcends and abolishes the ontological necessity of the substance by being God as *Father*, that is, as He who "begets" the Son and "brings forth" the Spirit. This ecstatic character of God, the fact that His being is identical with an act of communion, ensures the transcendence of the ontological necessity which His substance would have demanded—if the substance were the primary ontological predicate of God—and replaces this necessity with the free self-affirmation of divine existence (*Being as Communion*, 44).

9. Research in neuroscience has identified a linear dimension to the formation of words in the brain. Peter Hagoort characterizes the assemblage of words as "the temporally orchestrated retrieval" of conceptual, phonetic, and syntactical information stored in memory (Hagoort, "The Uniquely Human Capacity for Language Communication: From *Pope* to [po:p] in Half a Second," in *Neuroscience and the Person*, eds. Robert John Russell, Nancey Murphy, Theo C. Meyering, and Michael A. Arbib, Scientific Perspectives on Divine Action [Vatican City State: Vatican Observatory, Berkeley: Center for Theology and Natural Sciences, 2002], 49). "Activation of the syntactic features of [for instance] *pōpe* . . . precedes the retrieval of the onset phoneme of the word [po:p] by about 40 milliseconds. Importantly, the information about a word's phonological form is not available at once, but accrues in a left-to-right order. For words of 3 phonemes (/p//o://p/), it takes maximally 80 milliseconds to retrieve the remaining segments once the word-initial phoneme is available" (ibid., 52).

Language formation occasions linear temporality and no doubt reinforces a more general, linear sense of time. But as Hagoort observes, the act of wording in writing or speaking evinces an orchestral quality; words result from "a cascade of retrieval processes" (ibid., 52) transpiring on the order of milliseconds. Indeed, memory stores the conceptual, semantic, and phonetic qualities of words not as self-contained units, but as potencies. "Information about the meaning of words is stored in memory as a network of connected pieces of information, and not as isolated packages of individual word meanings" (ibid., 50). The being of a word is in its becoming, its readiness to be brought together both again *and anew* as pieces of information are accrued and lost. Language happens as an event and its linearity thus assumes a more basic quality of eventful openness.

10. Insofar as the relationships that constitute existence involve the action of human consciousness toward redemption, that is, the event of a self-awareness that entails other-awareness and especially awareness of God, they invoke reflection on the constructive nature of that consciousness. I intend in vol. 2 to address the character and role of *memory* in creaturely constitution. For a helpful introduction to questions surrounding consciousness and relationship, specifically the "mind's" constructive potency in the light of brain science, see William R. Stoeger, S.J., "The Mind-Brain Problem, the Laws of Nature, and Constitutive Relationships," in *Neuroscience and the Person*, 129–46.

11. As Martin Luther wrote, "faith is the creator of the Deity." See Luther, *Lectures on Galatians 1535: Chapters 1–4*, Luther's Works 26, ed. Jaroslav Pelikan (St. Louis: Concordia, 1963), 227. More fully reflecting Luther's conviction that God

makes us and not the other way around: "faith is the creator of the Deity, not in the substance of God, but in us." This is an oft-quoted phrase of Luther (e.g., Martin Marty, *Martin Luther: A Life* [New York: Penguin, 2008], 39).

12. Levenson, *Creation and the Persistence of Evil: The Jewish Drama of Divine Omnipotence* (Princeton: Princeton University Press, 1988/1994), 12.

13. Colossians 1:15–20. Unless my own translation or otherwise noted, biblical citations are from the New Revised Standard Version.

14. Barth, *Church Dogmatics* III.1, ed. G. W. Bromiley and T. F. Torrance (London: T & T Clark, 2004/1958), 94–329.

15. The reason for reversing direction is straightforward: doing so more clearly grounds creation in *action* and *relation* than in *thingness* and *metaphysics*, which I take to have been Barth's wish all along. It was never Barth's aim to supply a metaphysical account of "God" or "creation."

16. My first book argued that if one was to construct a theology of the Third Article of the Nicene Creed, which confesses the Spirit as "Lord and Giver of Life" in a manner that appreciates Barth's corrective effort not to confuse spirit with merely religious "feeling" (a purely psychological dependence), then one must think "spirit" in the terms of God's defining life-act in Christ Jesus (see Smith, *A Theology of the Third Article*, chs. 1–2). The current project represents constructive application of that argument.

17. The early church already identified the interrelationship between creation and redemption as well as the Creator and Redeemer, specifically under the rubric of *giving life*. Athanasius argues this point in some detail, and I intend to interact with him more fully in subsequent work. For now, see the helpful summary of Athanasius' thinking in Edwards, *The Natural World and God: Theological Explorations* (Adelaide, Australia: ATF, 2017), 381–464.

18. The work of creation is not the building of foliage, rivers, animals, and landscape of sufficient lushness, aesthetic quality, and serenity as to warrant the designation, "product of the divine" (more mythically, "paradise"), which by virtue of two persons' incautious concession to serpentine beguilement was destroyed (paradise by its very nature would seem to exclude beguiling serpents), so that the work of redemption amounts to a protracted process of restoration. That thinking obviously is already *fallen* into the sleepy haze of linear sequentialism, with its problems of temporal artificiality and, in this case, irreverence concerning the Almighty, who allegedly failed to foresee humanity's mistake, or if foreseeing, to correct it, or if correcting, to forgive it.

19. And in turn, because God is Creator and Redeemer, he is Father and Son. The economic Trinity is the basis upon which the immanent Trinity exists and is known. Against St. Thomas, the immanent Trinity is the economic Trinity *and vice versa*; cf. Karl Rahner, *The Trinity*, trans. Joseph Donceel (New York: Herder & Herder, 1970). Lacugna endorses Rahner's axiom with slight qualification at that point where Rahner fails to carry through the full consequences of his thought and returns to speculation about intradivine processions; see *God for Us*, 211–24.

20. The biblical authors (especially the prophets of the OT and the synoptic writers of the NT) depict Christ's experience of dependence on God to be fulfillment

of Israel's experience of the same as God's "son." Jesus fulfills Israel's history by recapitulating the nation's suffering and estrangement from their Father within the arc of his life, culminating on the cross, as well as reconciliation with the Father in the resurrection.

21. Barth, CD II.2, 52.

22. So Schleiermacher: "our immediate self-consciousness represents finite being only in the identity of origination and continuance"; *The Christian Faith*, ed. H. R. Mackintosh and J. S. Stewart (Edinburgh: T & T Clark, 1999), 150. Material from *The Christian Faith* is reproduced with written confirmation of no objection from T & T Clark. "Creation" is a term for the new-making work of God; the term is a verbalizing of our being-made-new, which verbalizing is at once a participation in and description of the new-making. Giving account of creation is to give reflexive expression to redemption, which activity springs naturally from being redeemed. As such, it expresses the unity of redemption, preservation, and creation in the formation of our consciousness.

23. Levenson, *Creation and the Persistence of Evil*, 17.

24. Ibid., 27.

25. This thesis and the next summarize key features of Barth's discussion of evil as *"das Nichtige,"* and the overcoming of it in God's defining life-act; see CD III.3 §50. "God, but he alone, can deal with [nothingness] and has already done so, in accordance with the fact that He transcends it from all eternity in His essence as God. But it must be clearly understood that He has treated it as His adversary, as the No which is primarily and supremely addressed to Himself" (p. 303).

26. For example, Ps. 28:3–5; 37; 73; 92:6–7; 94.

27. So, the Sermon on the Mount: "You have heard that it was said, 'You shall not commit adultery.' But I say to you that everyone who looks at a woman with lust has already committed adultery with her in his heart" (Matt. 5:27–28).

28. Perhaps no one has better lodged the damning complaint against religion that it creates "god" out of attributes cleansed of imperfection and hypostatically reified than Ludwig Feuerbach; see *The Essence of Christianity*, trans. George Eliot (New York: Harper, 1957). If Feuerbach has taught theology one thing, it must be that any kind of systematization vis-a-vis the knowledge of God engenders, by its very nature, idolatry. Neither cataphaticism nor apophaticism, neither the *via eminentiae* nor *negativa*, nor most perniciously the *via analogiae entis*, can be employed without persistent dialectical cancellation of their conclusions. Only such practice can return the theologian to the surer *via apocalypsis in homini Christi*.

29. For more on the time of resurrection confronting fallen time, see Barth, CD I.2, 45–121.

30. Immanuel Kant approached this truth when he construed deviation from ethical duty as the tendency, springing from "self-love," to make exceptions in one's own favor: "if we now attend to ourselves in any transgression of a duty, we find that we do not really will that our maxim should become a universal law . . . but that the opposite of our maxim should instead remain a universal law, only we take the liberty of making an *exception* to it for ourselves (or just for this once) to the advantage of our inclination" (Kant, "Groundwork of the Metaphysics of Morals [1785]," in *Practical*

Philosophy, trans. and ed. Mary J. Gregor, The Cambridge Edition of the Works of Immanuel Kant [Cambridge: Cambridge University Press, 1996], 37–108, 4:424).

The underlying logic for this construal of transgression is found in Kant's famous dictum: "I ought never to act except in such a way that I could also will that my maxim should become a universal law" (ibid., 4:402). Morality is deontological; action promoting my good is just (*Recht*) only insofar as it conforms to principles, which if extended would likewise promote good everywhere and every-when. Idiosyncratically-beneficial, moral dictates are not moral at all, because they may construe as "good" what is in fact evil to the other. Self-excepting inversion of this rule (itself a universal moral principle or maxim) would thus look something like, "I act without consideration of a broader rectitude, but I take exception to others doing the same when it impinges upon my sense of the good." Although I am hardly setting forth an exposition and defense of Kant's deontological ethics, much of this book's logic follows the contours of his concerns about the self-excepting character of self-love.

31. It is true that even biblical speech, to the degree that it is also human description, is subject to the fallibility of hypostatizing evil—of making it artificially objective. Identifying the myth-nature of the biblical description is therefore exegetically critical. If the reader fails to perceive that the aim of the text is to point her once more back to herself, to locate evil's origin here, in deep self-contradiction, and instead gives herself to evil's treacherous obfuscation by finding satisfaction in externalized depiction, so that she mistakenly fixates upon the adversary as a metaphysical agent, perhaps even dedicates herself to defending his being-thus as of the essence, then she will tragically find herself subject to the most sinister evil of all—that which depreciates evil within, and so gives it wider reign.

32. For more along this line of thinking, see Jürgen Moltmann, *The Crucified God: The Cross of Christ as the Foundation and Criticism of Christian Theology*, trans. R. A. Wilson and John Bowden (Minneapolis: Fortress, 1993); see esp. 200–290.

Chapter 1

God and the Human

אֵלֶּה תוֹלְדוֹת הַשָּׁמַיִם וְהָאָרֶץ בְּהִבָּרְאָם בְּיוֹם עֲשׂוֹת יְהוָה אֱלֹהִים אֶרֶץ וְשָׁמָיִם:
וְכֹל שִׂיחַ הַשָּׂדֶה טֶרֶם יִהְיֶה בָאָרֶץ וְכָל־עֵשֶׂב הַשָּׂדֶה טֶרֶם יִצְמָח כִּי לֹא הִמְטִיר יְהוָה
אֱלֹהִים עַל־הָאָרֶץ וְאָדָם אַיִן לַעֲבֹד אֶת־הָאֲדָמָה:
וְאֵד יַעֲלֶה מִן־הָאָרֶץ וְהִשְׁקָה אֶת־כָּל־פְּנֵי־הָאֲדָמָה:
וַיִּיצֶר יְהוָה אֱלֹהִים אֶת־הָאָדָם עָפָר מִן־הָאֲדָמָה וַיִּפַּח בְּאַפָּיו נִשְׁמַת הַיִּים וַיְהִי הָאָדָם
לְנֶפֶשׁ חַיָּה:

This is the account of the heavens and the earth when they were created.
When the LORD God made earth and heaven,
when no shrub of the field was yet on the earth, and no plant of the field
had yet sprouted, for the LORD God had not sent rain upon the earth,
and there was no human to work the ground—
but a spring came up from the earth and watered the whole surface of
the ground—
the LORD God formed a human of dust from the ground, and breathed
into his nostrils the breath of life, and the human became a living being
(Gen. 2:4–7).[1]

Gen. 2–3, and in fact the Bible more broadly, do not plainly indicate what it means for God to create. They do not employ direct speech to describe what this work consists of or supply its content in any detail, but relegate the "how" and "what" of creation to highly pictorial, mythical depictions, which deal with representative, macro-level products (light, sun, water, earth, creatures of air, sea, and land).[2] In the second volume of this project, we will consider the way that the biblical accounts describe the activity of God in relation to other creation narratives of the Ancient Near East, and this will shed some light on the restricted focus of the biblical stories. For now, it suffices to note the restriction, and with it that the text is taciturn about the meaning, that is

to say, the essence or fundamental quality of "God." It presents no prehistory
or antecedent composition of this referent. It offers no anatomy, reports no
idiosyncrasies, quantifies no range of capacities, and attempts no definition of
the term, but like with other ANE accounts, makes arrestingly free use of it.[3]
It proceeds in this way not because it assumes the reader to possess accurate
and thorough knowledge of God already but because it expects God's nature
to emerge through narration of a particular history. Konrad Schmid summarizes both observations:

> It must be grasped above all that the Old Testament knows no substantive
> concept for "creation. . . ." At least for the Old Testament the lack of a unique
> conceptualization is not astonishing. "Creation" comes into the frame of a socio-
> morphic world picture (*im Rahmen eines soziomorphen Weltbildes*), which
> does not fundamentally differentiate between cosmological and sociological, or
> between scientific and theological aspects. . . . That the world in which ancient
> Israel lived was God's creation is a theological statement, which indeed ancient
> Israel foremost developed again and again, but which was reckoned in the time
> of the formative period of the Old Testament as self-evident. How, where, and
> when God was perceptibly present in creation were legitimate questions, but not
> whether he generally was the Creator.[4]

It was of the essence of ancient Israel's world picture that God created the
cosmos; granted as a fact of no less certainty than the existence of the cosmos
itself. Indeed, the assumptive nature of the Israelite world picture concerning the Creator gave character to its accounts of creation: they took shape as
admixtures of cosmology (or, as noted in introduction, cosmologies), sociol-
ogy, "science," and theology.[5] The presumption of interplay between world,
society, nature, and deity yielded a coordinated system of meaning. Each
comes to comprehension in the light of the others. What we know of Creator
and creation is given in the biblical portrait of a unique sovereignty: "God"
is defined in and by a kind of executive relation to what is "not-God." As the
reader is made to comprehend the world's contingencies and interdependencies, God emerges as that plenitude on which all things depend.

To put a fine point on it: the Bible reveals that the creature does *not* know
God, but constantly learns anew who God is and what God intends from
within the narrative of creation and redemption. Understanding of God is
mediated, then, by the reading and hearing of scriptural story. The object of
the story is married, as it were, to the telling insofar as the textual witness reiterates and makes sense of a primal experience, the experience of creaturely
dependence.[6] The text's presentational character presupposes the possibility
of an event, the development of the reader's self-awareness in relation to its
object, or, the reader finding herself constituted in a living relationship with

the textual object—as the subject of his generous provision. In speaking of creation, the biblical text invites the reader into a creative encounter, which event completes the creative depiction.

The Bible "defines" God by failing to invoke or endorse any particular, certainly any metaphysical description but rather by eventful narration.[7] The Bible identifies God with the creature in mutually descriptive relation.[8] The Bible obliges the reader to encounter "God" in and through resonant depiction of life-giving activity.

This chapter argues that "God" and "creation" exist and are known in existential realization of the covenant, which is the same as saying in the creature's experience of dependence and provision as this recurs in the reading and hearing of Scripture. The chapter makes this case first exegetically, then by analytically introducing relevant insights from Friedrich Schleiermacher and Karl Barth.

EXEGESIS OF GEN. 2:4–7

It has been remarked that in the Hebrew Bible, the word בָּרָא (to create) refers to a unique action whereby material existence is brought into being from non-material existence, or more exactly, from the complete absence of materiality. Where there was nothing, by miraculous decree there is now something. This claim seems to follow from the fact that the Hebrew Bible only employs בָּרָא in contexts of divine agency; a special quality of action evidently accrues to the word by virtue of the specialness of its Actor. So, for instance, Karl-Heinz Bernhardt observes that the Bible uses בָּרָא "to express clearly the incomparability of the creative work of God in contrast to all secondary products and likenesses made from already existing material by man."[9] Humanity creates by recombination of given matter. God, as *God*, creates from nothing. But there are two reasons why this observation has to be stringently qualified.

First, בָּרָא is sometimes used in parallel construction with cognate verbs, which carry their meaning over into its meaning and disallow containment of its meaning in rigid isolation. This is the case in poetic passages, with their characteristic parallelisms. For example, Isa. 45:7 reads, "I form (יָצַר) the light, and create (בָּרָא) darkness, I make (עָשָׂה) peace, and create (בָּרָא) evil; I the LORD do (עָשָׂה) all these." The parallel structure forestalls ascription of fixed meaning to בָּרָא, certainly any notion of "bringing forth matter out of non-matter" or "creation out of nothing."[10] Occupying some of the same semantic space as יָצַר (to form or fashion) and עָשָׂה (to do or make), God's "creating" darkness and evil means something like *shaping* or *defining,* more exactly, *shaping relative contrasts to light and peace.* Hence, Bernhardt concedes that "to a certain extent [poetic parallelism] results in a leveling of [the meaning of בָּרָא]."[11]

Gen. 2:4 presents a kindred construction. It treats בָּרָא and עָשָׂה synonymously: "These are the generations of the heavens and earth in the day when they were *created*, when the LORD God *made* earth and heavens."[12] Thus, when 2:4a says, in effect, "this is the story of when the heavens and earth were created," it does not mean "this is the empirical account of when matter came into existence." Leveled by the banal עָשָׂה in 2:4b, בָּרָא simply refers to the shaping of this ordered contrast. Canonically, the verse at once recalls Gen. 1:1f,[13] and looks forward to the forming to be discussed in Gen. 2:5f: the creation of the cosmos and its constituencies just is the enforcing of order in the midst of disorder, bestowing form to formlessness.[14]

Second, there is no special linguistic cue by which we can discern a given aspect or quality of the creative act, which differentiates it as *God's*, or looking at it from the reverse angle, there is no such cue that indicates what must be the character of God's work of *creation*.[15] We do not know what it is that makes this act divine as such or what specifically the divine actor does as such.[16]

The semantic range of the OT terminology relating to *creating* and *making* encompasses a variety of activities, none of which is distinguishable by an evident divine quality.[17] Just as in English, one "creates" not only *things* but also *conditions*, *wealth*, and *a stir*, one "makes" not only *articles* but also *amends*, *magic*, and *a scene*, and one "forms" not only *figures* but also *friendships*, *opinions*, and *habits*, so also in Hebrew there is no single, differentiated category of referent for בָּרָא, עָשָׂה, or יָצַר, or יָסַד (to establish or fix), or כּוּן (to set up or make fast). God "creates" (בָּרָא) the heavens and earth in Gen. 1:1 and a clean heart in Ps. 51:10[12]; God "makes" (עָשָׂה) a helper suitable for the human in Gen. 2:18 and (does) good things for Israel in Ex. 18:9; God "forms" (יָצַר) Leviathan in Ps. 104:6 and Israel as a people in Isa. 43:1; God "establishes" (יָסַד) the earth in Ps. 24:2 and the Babylonians to execute judgment in Hab. 1:12; God "sets up" (כּוּן) his sanctuary in Ex. 15:17 and Solomon as king in 1 Kgs. 2:24.[18]

The individual verbs take a range of direct objects, which objects in context reciprocally influence the drift of the verbs. That is just as much the case in the Genesis accounts of creation as in the *Pickwick Papers* or a biography of James Cone. It is inherent in the nature of language for words to convey a range of senses and to accrue new senses according to usage.

So the Bible does not supply clear indication of what it means for *God* "to create."[19] That is, in thinking with the biblical text about creation we have to warn against subconsciously supplying preconditions by which God operates, the character of the creative act, as well as the nature of antecedent state(s) relative to creation's factual condition (other than in the terms of disorder, threat, chaos, which in any event describe creation's factual condition apart from "God"). What, then, does Scripture say concretely of *God* and *creation*?

Gen. 2:4 places a sovereign subject, called "LORD God," relative to a conditional object, "earth and heavens." It does this in a mutually descriptive way. The sovereignty of the sovereign subject happens in relation to the dependent object. LORD God becomes who he is in taking comprehensive responsibility for earth and heavens. Resonant construal of creation's absolute dependence gives rise to the Creator as living ground of existence. *Primus* relates to *secunda* in an irreversible order: although *primus* is only known, as such, in and by the existential experience of *secunda*, *primus* (God) remains *primus* throughout the relation or the relation collapses.[20] The identity of *secunda*, as such, likewise requires *primus*; however much the identity of *primus* is located in and with *secunda*, that is, however much God's life is determined by the conditions of *secunda*, God remains in this and each instant *primus*, or neither actually exists. "God" is *Lord* among that to which he is *Giver of Life* or there is neither God nor creation (neither could be meaningfully described).

So the subject of 2:4b is not simply אֵל (*el*/"god") or אֱלֹהִים (*elohim*/"gods" or capital-G, "God"), but again, יְהוָה אֱלֹהִים (*yhwh elohim*/LORD God). Nahum Sarna expresses reserve about the significance of this rare double-naming.[21] "The remarkable concentration of these divine names in this narrative and their virtual absence hereafter have not been satisfactorily explained," he writes.[22] Still, he suggests that "the repeated use here may be to establish that the absolutely transcendent God of Creation (*'elohim*) is the same immanent, personal God (YHVH) who shows concern for the needs of human beings."[23]

Other commentators are less reserved. In the main, historical critics take the addition in 2:4b of יְהוָה to אֱלֹהִים, the latter of which is used alone throughout Genesis 1, to signal the beginning of a distinct creation account and a shift from Priestly to Yahwist source tradition.[24] And many see a confessional unity of *Creator* and *Redeemer* indicated by the compound name. So Franz Delitzsch: "while אלהים is the more especially appropriate name of the Creator, יהוה designates more particularly the God of history, and indeed of the history of redemption, hence God the Redeemer. The combination of the two names denotes . . . the oneness of the supermundane God and the God of history, the oneness of God the Creator and the God of Israel, or the God of positive revelation."[25]

Barth, unsurprisingly, is among the least reserved in perceiving this unity. For him, there could be no other actor in creation except the God of redemption. "So close are we here to the history of the covenant which commences after the completion of creation that even in the history of creation God must bear this name."[26] The material history of God's dealings with Israel coalesces, so to speak, with the material construct of "Creator." The God who must come to mind in reading this second creation account—differentiated as a unit encompassing the Creator's initial dealings with the sinner by special use of the compound name, "LORD God"—is strictly the God who reveals himself in Israel's redemptive struggle.[27] "The Israelite who hears or reads about the Creator is to think at once of the One to whom he and his nation owe everything, against whom he and his people have sinned a thousand times, but who incomprehensibly has never failed to be faithful to him and his people."[28]

The history of God with Israel gives shape to the character of Creator God and is fulfilled in the figure of the Messiah. In its covenantal direction, thought brought about and structured by Gen. 2:4b–7 already pushes forward, already engrosses the reader in achievement of that relation in which God and creation exist, over against all threats to the contrary. The hole opened in human understanding is quickly and concretely filled, which is to say, the proper identity of God and creature are coordinately established in the Christ.

Concerning God, "in the dogmatic tradition," Schmid writes, "the doctrine of creation belongs to the doctrine of God, and God—at least in the Christian tradition—cannot be spoken of amidst disregard for the Second Article [of the Nicene Creed], thus the First Article in total, including the doctrine of creation, is to be understood fundamentally from the perspective of the Second Article."[29] Concerning the creature, "the man of whom the saga spoke," Barth writes, "is—in respect of the solution of the riddle of Israel and the fulfillment of its hope—this man Jesus. So near are we in this second creation history to the threshold of the history of the covenant and salvation that . . . we cannot interpret it . . . in any other way."[30]

"God" just is *God* as lord of the covenant, and in turn, humanity just is *humanity* in the corresponding relation of faithful subject to LORD God, both of which realities are livingly established in the Christ. It is in anticipation of this one, in this forward-looking direction, that the creation story of Gen. 2–3 finds its ultimate meaning.

In this respect, the text shifts from "the heavens and the earth" in 4a to "earth and heavens" in 4b. Whereas each formulation functions as a *merism*, a reference to a collective reality—here, the cosmos—by identifying signature parts, the second is more than merely stylistic inversion of the first. As Bill T. Arnold observes, in turning to "earth and heavens" the text deliberately invokes intimacy. "Although Gen. 2 is devoted to creation of 'the earth and the heavens' (v. 4b)," he writes, "its scope is nothing like the universal perspective of Gen. 1's 'the heavens and the earth' (1:1). The interests here are much more narrowly focused: creation of the human (vv. 4b–7), the garden as his home (vv. 8–17), creation of the animals, and lastly, the woman as an appropriate partner for the man (vv. 18–25)."[31]

In Gen. 2:4b–3:24, there is no work or life of God conducted without regard to the tender care of the creature in creation. The event of "God" is a *personal* event; God exists and is known only in exercise of creaturely care. Likewise, the creation exists as realm of this care and the creature as its object. Verses 5–6 treat of the first, and v. 7 of the second.

The world exists as servant to God in God's dealings with the human, as the landscape along which horizon authentic human existence extends. It has no other identity. Verses 5 and 6 set the stage for v. 7. As we will see, the defining service of the world for the sake of divine dealings with humankind does not diminish its quality of being or justify its neglect by humankind. Quite the opposite, in that it is the realm of God's self-determinative, creative work, care for the world is essential: there is no sphere of creaturely realization outside of it, so the human can only come to exist as God desires insofar as the world exists as God intends. The creation is the performative realm of the covenant.

In commenting on v. 5, Terrence Fretheim notes the anticipatory nature of the world relative to humans: "the earth remains in a pre-creation state, not only because God has not yet done something, but also because no human beings are active."[32] Creation awaits its full reality at the nexus of divine and human agency. It awaits God's sending rain "not . . . simply as a phenomenon of nature [but as] a source of blessing to man from God."[33] And it awaits humanity's responsive stewardship. Both creation's dis-ordering and destruction (its lapse into cosmic nothingness) and its ordering and realization (its productivity and refinement) are tied to realization of the human in its affirmative response to God (cf. Rom. 8:18–27). The hope of the world is tied to the hope of humanity. Fretheim acknowledges that "verse 5 startles the reader due to the parallel it draws between the rain and human labor."[34] That the human should play so profound a part as *essential* correlate to God's part in creation is indeed unexpected and shocking, particularly in light of the larger cultural context, wherein the ground's produce (fertility and wares) is the provenance of the gods and the human is little more than their footman.[35]

But that disruption just is the point. Gen. 2:5 meets the reader in her ancient near-eastern world picture and invokes an alternative; it depicts such a lord as to rule not in capricious aloofness but covenantal charity. It reveals a God who gives to the creature such a share in life as to enable it a determinative role in the discharge and shaping of creation (its own and its environment). Gen. 2:5 arrestingly describes "creation" in the terms of responsiveness specific to human agency. That is its *essence*, if we may: to become again the ground of humanity's obedience to the Creator.

The creation is at once the result and instrument of the creature; consequent upon *and with* her. Awaiting the creature, creation is relegated to potency, not actuality. It holds the ingredients of life by virtue of God's command and presence—a "mist" in v. 6 (or better reflective of the verse's Mesopotamian setting, a *spring*, אֵד) rose up and watered the ground—but only the ingredients. Creation cannot actualize its intended self. "The change [from pre-creation to creation] gives responsibility to the human being, not simply for maintenance and preservation, but for intra-creational development, bringing the world along toward its fullest possible potential."[36] The crescendo of these opening verses sounds with the creation of humankind in v. 7. According to Gordon Wenham: "the focus on man and his relationship to the land in vv. 5–6 is but a prelude to man's (אָדָם) creation from the land (אֲדָמָה)."[37]

"Forming" is the operative verb in v. 7. God acts as *potter* (יָצַר). "This image reveals a God who focuses closely on the object to be created and takes painstaking care to shape each one into something useful and beautiful."[38] God's work in creating is not as conjuror but as sculptor artistically giving shape to a dynamic, eventful reality. Once more, creation is a holistic work in which what is made comes to responsive self-completion to the delight of its Maker. "Disorder" is not a general description of that which appears disproportionate; "chaos" does not refer abstractly to all that seems confusing. These words rather refer, much more tangibly, to whatever contradicts the definite way of covenantal communion, joyful co-encounter. They refer to whatever interrupts the covenantal unity between God and creation. As Potter, God's work of creation involves, ipso facto, filial interface between the Maker and made, or creation does not happen *at all*.

It is not that God first makes things, which possess being in themselves, and which God later coaxes into relation, but which, failing the coaxing, nonetheless stand alone. Rather, in creating, God first establishes a basic relation of mutual deference in which things take distinctive form. The human only takes to itself idiosyncratic existence as it realizes itself to be the object of divine favor. It confirms itself only as it determines to stand in a state of thankful acknowledgement mediated by time, that is, by con-sequential action in the realm of nature, vertically in the form of prayer, horizontally in the forms of service and love to other creatures and the world.

The human finds herself in a relationship of intimacy to the Creator, as pot to potter, such that she exists as medium of God's favor among creation. Although she has no being except through creation, she is to be distinguished from creation in this respect (and this alone): she is called forth among creation to call back or answer creation's Maker—this, on her own behalf and on behalf of creation. (Sin, as we will see, bursts on to the stage of creation right when and where she fails to answer the LORD's call.)

The human is not merely a נֶפֶשׁ חַיָּה ("living being"). The animals are also that (Gen. 1:20, 24, 30; 2:19). She is rather the delicate work of the craftsman's hands in *face-to-face* receipt of his breath. She is of the *dust* (עָפָר), yet she is also of divine animation, *the breath of life* (נִשְׁמַת הַיִּים). She is of the ground. But she is also, and more, the ground's realization:

> Here in Genesis, the image simultaneously expresses both the glory and the insignificance of man. Man occupies a special place in the hierarchy of Creation and enjoys a unique relationship with God by virtue of his being the work of God's own hands and being directly animated by God's own breath. At the same time, he is but dust taken from the earth, mere clay in the hands of the divine Potter, who exercises absolute mastery over His Creation.[39]

EXEGETICAL SUMMARY

Gen. 2:4b–7 initiates a movement in perception according to which the reader discovers himself in relation to God and creation. This movement starts by negation of whatever knowledge the creature presumes to possess concerning God and creation; the text presents "God" as *primus* to *secunda* and "creation" as *secunda* to *primus*. By their descriptive refusal of metaphysical or arch-substantialist qualities vis-a-vis "God" and their persistent association of creation with God, the biblical stories depict reality as at once the result and focus of sovereign charity. It is as consequential production, the seeded and cultivated produce of a farmer or the delicately crafted pot of a potter. These chapters situate the reader in a covenantal history, identifying the reader's humanity with the messianic history in which God and creation exist.

The biblical witness locates the human in existential interdependence to which he does not bitterly acquiesce but which he cheerily, indeed gratefully, confirms. This is to treat the biblical text as having a constructive and not merely expressive spirit; to suggest that its testimony is to a revelatory object and not, at least not primarily, to the collective experience of religious subjects. The Bible structures a kind of perception—a *faith*, as we described it in introduction—and does not merely give voice to intuitive sensibility. To explore this important distinction, we will turn for the remainder of this chapter to Schleiermacher and Barth.

I affirm Schleiermacher's account of absolute dependency as it describes creation in its determinative relation to God, manifested in the Christ. But following Barth's corrective critique, I translate that modality more clearly into an event of knowing and doing, relocating it from *religion* to *revelation*. The creative power of God is the Spirit of the Word, the compelling pull of the proclaimed text, not the anthropological category of religious intuition. The Spirit is not the text, but the pull of the text in the event of its hearing. The Spirit situates the text's recipient before the Creator as *secunda* before *primus* and compels responsive action, a "yes" to this situation. By the Spirit of the Word, the human affirms his place and readily takes part in the broader creation's realization, consciously giving himself to its cultivation, contributing his life to this stage in its cycle of life. In this event of the Spirit, creation (verb and noun) continues.

SCHLEIERMACHER AND THE FEELING OF ABSOLUTE DEPENDENCE UPON GOD

Schleiermacher carefully situated the theological enterprise within the life and concerns of the church. He understood theology to express the Christian community's self-conscious and painstakingly represented the arc of Christian teaching from within that consciousness. He did not consider theological reflection, as modernity might otherwise oblige, to be an act of synthetically gathering religious knowledge (however much, for Schleiermacher, constructive engagement with the community's self-consciousness entailed analytical interaction with broader philosophical and religious claims). "The present work [*The Christian Faith*] entirely disclaims the task of establishing on a foundation of general principles a Doctrine of God, or an Anthropology or Eschatology either, which should be used in the Christian Church though it did not really originate there."[40] Christian thought and speech of God, humanity, and the destiny of creation cannot be grounded in "general principles"—philosophical or ethical maxims derived extrinsically from communal Christian experience—which exercise a prejudicial effect on that thought and speech. That is the case even if those principles otherwise reinforce classical Christian teaching. Christian thought and speech are just that insofar as they take their shape and content from the special experience of faith in Christ.

Theology takes its origin from within that consciousness, which differentiates a community of Christ-followers as such—the shared consciousness of discipleship.[41] Schleiermacher therefore initiates the dogmatic task by describing the lived orientation that defines the church's existence as such and forms the basis of its self-expression or theology.[42]

Schleiermacher characterizes the experiential center of Christian faith as a kind of deep intuition or *feeling* (*Gefühl*). "The piety which forms the basis of all ecclesiastical communions is, considered purely in itself, neither a Knowing nor a Doing, but a modification of Feeling, or of immediate self-consciousness."[43] The church comes to exist not through consensus confession of dogmatic precepts or through distinctive activity but through common experience of a specific kind of self-awareness.[44]

Crucially, Schleiermacher assesses the relationship between the categories of feeling, knowing, and doing. "Feeling is the [category] to which piety belongs," but that does not mean "that piety is excluded from all connexion with Knowing and Doing."[45] The connection owes to the fact that "immediate self-consciousness is always the mediating link in the transition between moments in which Knowing predominates and those in which Doing predominates."[46]

There are times in a people's self-consciousness when identity is located more in confession than morality, and vice versa, or when common confession leads to concrete moral action and vice versa. But in each case, what connects the one to the other, or forms the point of transition between them, is an immediate, pre-reflective sense of *propriety*—that these actions appropriately express these beliefs and vice versa. There is a third modality at work in human consciousness, which transcends the more commonly acknowledged modalities of knowing and doing, and which, although not as commonly recognized, proves more basic than both knowing and doing.

The pre-reflective, third modality, which connects knowing and doing, is adjectively described as *pious* feeling. "It will fall to piety to stimulate Knowing and Doing, and every moment in which piety has a predominant place will contain within itself one or both of these in germ."[47] The Christian community is founded in immediate awareness of total dependence upon God. This awareness cannot be refined in thought or action, but constantly gives rise to both thought and action, and relates them. Distinctly Christian thought and speech (theology) derive from the feeling of absolute dependence, but their reflective output does not, indeed cannot constitute that feeling (sensitivity to dependence that is genuinely absolute is, as we will see, necessarily inarticulate).

The embeddedness of knowing and doing in feeling does not imply reciprocity. "Our proposition is opposing the assertions from other quarters that piety is a Knowing, or a Doing, or both, or a state made up of Feeling, Knowing, and Doing."[48] Piety strictly belongs to feeling and *not* to knowing or doing.

Piety cannot be both stimulus and product; it is piety that gives rise and shape to knowledge and action, not the other way around. Moreover, Schleiermacher reasons that if piety consisted of knowledge, then it would refer either to the content of Christian dogmatics or to the certainty with which one holds that content to be true. But if either was so, then "the most perfect master of Christian Dogmatics" or "he who thinks the religious propositions most clearly and completely" would be "the most pious Christian," and for patently clear reasons, "no one will admit this to be the case."[49]

Similarly, piety should not be confused with doing, because "not only the most admirable but also the most abominable, not only the most useful but also the most inane and meaningless things, are done as pious and out of piety."[50] A moral act clearly cannot be considered pious just on the basis of its composition or outcome; the good deed itself does not make for piety, for the action can be performed to shortsighted ends or unforeseen consequences. Even motive is not enough, for "underlying every motive there is a certain determination of self-consciousness."[51] An action is only "pious" if that prior determination of consciousness, which gives rise to motive, can be so-named.

So, piety is in essence feeling, which prompts and forms thought and action, but is not to be confused with or conflated into thought and action: "piety in its diverse expressions remains essentially a state of Feeling. This state is subsequently caught up into the region of thinking, but only in so far as each religious man is at the same time inclined towards thinking and exercised therein; and only in the same way and according to the same measure does this inner piety emerge in living movement and representative action."[52] The religious orientation upon which the community of Christian faith is grounded is an "inner" condition, which is "caught up into" knowing, "inclined towards" thinking, and "emerges" in "representative action," but cannot be objectified in any class or instance of knowing or acting. It is, again, *immediate* intuition.[53]

The immediacy of pious feeling allows Schleiermacher to sidestep the epistemic sweep of Kantianism by introducing an alternative to sense-derived cognition, on the one hand, and the dictates of practical morality, on the other. Here, we have neither knowing nor doing, but pre-sentiment, a consciousness of self from out of which action upon self and others takes shape, but which action is not the essence of the religious self, indeed cannot causatively alter the religious self, and so cannot be critiqued as if it represented the religious self. The attempt to introduce a category of existence materially precedent to knowledge and action is thus of apologetic value: it affords a ground on which to defend the Christian faith against its moral missteps.[54] And it fits with the edgy impulse of Schleiermacher's intellectual context (broadly, the era of Romanticism) to overcome the sterile restrictions of the Age of Reason.[55] The church is always more than its dogma and moral action; Christian faith is founded upon a transcendent modality, a condition beyond the reductionisms of sensate existence.[56]

Along these lines, for Schleiermacher, the essence of Christian faith is not the *product* of exegesis and proclamation, however distinct such knowing and doing might be by virtue of their content. Indeed, the work, *The Christian Faith*, contains little exegesis. Richard R. Niebuhr explains that "the exegetical approach to theological exposition is conspicuously absent" from Schleiermacher's dogmatics because "the conceptual framework of the religious consciousness . . . is something quite other than a simple Bible-determined structure. It has become historically differentiated."[57] The Bible gives expression to the God-consciousness of its authors. It does not give rise to that consciousness.

Piety does not result from the Bible's reading and hearing, but the other way around. Scripture is a form (really, forms) of knowing and doing that derive from an historically differentiated religious feeling.[58] It is, so Niebuhr, "the original translation of the Christian consciousness into public language."[59] More fully: "just as those disciples of the first generation . . . understood the words of their Master only because they had already been chosen by him and drawn into his sphere, so the disciples who are at a remove of eighteen centuries likewise are enabled to understand not alone out of the words themselves but out of the life that is mediated through them."[60]

Paradoxically, the enfleshed Word draws each generation of disciples into his life *extra verba*; it is experience of Christ's (mystically compelling) favor, his summons in the form of interpersonal consonance, which causes them to express confessionally the life of communion with him.[61] The words of Scripture express a pre-reflective feeling of dependence actualized by living encounter with Jesus, but cannot give that feeling rise. The somewhat-undefined "spiritual" mediation of Christ's consciousness to the community supersedes biblical testimony to Christ.

Now we begin to perceive both the opportunity and challenge of Schleiermacher's program. The opportunity lies in translating his mystical communication of Christ's consciousness into a pneumatocentric framework, that is, giving equally fulsome articulation of the way that creaturely transformation into the image of Christ takes place by the event of the Spirit of the Word or the reading and hearing of Scripture. (I intend here only to point in the direction of such articulation and make a gainful start at it.) The challenge is that this translation requires a more radical translation of underlying conceptual structures: out of *religious consciousness* into *actualistic revelation*, and correlatively, out of *feeling* into *knowing* and *doing*. We will have to show that determination of consciousness is consequent upon prophetic and apostolic testimony, not the other way around.

Anything less than a radical translation of this sort leaves us wondering at the nature of the mediator between Christ and the community—perhaps the most oft-made criticism of Schleiermacher. It may be nothing more than an assimilative potency of an aspirational psyche, a soul-ish inclination to communal identity beyond objective description and healthy critique. The feeling of dependence, for instance, may underwrite the will of a pernicious *Volk*, as Barth and others later contended. We will return to Barth's concerns in due course.

Schleiermacher renders problematic the character of, and relation between, religion and revelation by locating piety in the former and turning the latter into its outward manifestation. It would be preferable to recognize the marriage of the life-forming power of God's covenantal communion with humanity in the Christ to its witness, so that Christian religion takes the shape of answer to objective existence (a "subject-determining objectivity" rather than an object-determining subjectivity, as I wrote in my previous book).[62]

The life of the church is a consequence of the creative potency of the text and thus, at least by intention, a reflection of it. The church's historical action is very much subject to critique, a far more damning critique, in fact, than that of modern culture: it is subject to the judgment of conformity to the text. It will require, as such, regular repentance.

Niebuhr describes Schleiermacher's preference for a religion-centric account of Christian faith rather than a revelation-centric account in a way that helps us to frame the alternative:

> [For Schleiermacher], theology issues out of the life-matrix of religion . . . The datum [that Schleiermacher's theology] scrutinized was neither the religious phenomenon abstracted from its total subjective meaning nor the subject isolated from his natural and social world, but it was rather the psychical content of awareness that fills the self in and through the nexus of its existence-relationships and that thereupon reduplicates itself and symbolizes itself in these very relationships. . . . This kind of empiricism appeared to Schleiermacher to be the only alternative to the establishment in the church of a gnosis-Christianity, a faith based on privileged intellectual powers or arcane information and hence requiring a "priesthood of speculation."[63]

For Schleiermacher, theology describes "the psychical content of awareness that fills the self in and through the nexus of its existence-relationships." It seems a stretch to characterize such undertaking as "empirical," as Niebuhr does, for it is not certain that a peculiar psychical content, while experiential, in fact constitutes an observable phenomenon. To the extent that it does so, it is self-evident that this phenomenon's abundant subjectivity (as an expression of self-awareness, particularly one grounded in the insubstantiality of a "nexus of existence-relationships") would enjoin limitless description, rendering theology not so much empirical as solipsistic. Be that as it may, Schleiermacher worried that any other center of theology resulted naturally in a tyranny of knowledge; that if God-talk were located in comprehension of any other datum than experiential religion, then it would become the privilege of an intellectual class, the provenance of the best-informed. My contention is that this is *not* the only possibility.

Another possibility is to construe thought and speech of God as an actualistic, secondary event dependent upon the primary event of its object. The event of God gives rise to accounting of "God"; this, even as God only exists in the accounting. There is an interdependency between theology and its content, structured according to a defined relation: the content is primary and the activity of its accounting, secondary, which relation is given in the content. "God" *exists in* this relationality, *as primus* to *secunda*. Such God-talk resists Schleiermacher's feared tyranny of knowledge because it constantly reaffirms the absoluteness of the theologian's dependence: her every word turns contingently on the God-event.

A theology grounded in revelation turns entirely on a Revealer. We might describe it as a sense of Revealedness (so, again, Barth), which opens in thought and speech (knowing and doing) a hole , positioning the theologian as perpetual learner and rehearser. A theology grounded in revelation demands the obedience and humility of faith.[64]

Returning again to Schleiermacher: the essence of that faith which constitutes the Christian church and forms the basis of theological reflection is *feeling*, specifically, "the consciousness of being absolutely dependent, or, which is the same thing, of being in relation with God."[65] To describe what is meant by the feeling of absolute dependence, Schleiermacher engages in some fairly intricate speculation and deduction. It is worth following his thought closely at this point, technically challenging as it can be, since this material prefaces his broader theological project, and it initiates our attempt to translate salient features of it from religion into revelation.

Schleiermacher begins with a couple of propositions to which "assent can be unconditionally demanded."[66] It is self-evident, he contends, that "in every self-consciousness there are two elements, which we might call respectively a self-caused element . . . and a non-self-caused element . . . or a Being and a Having-by-some-means-come-to-be."[67] In apprehension of self, one is automatically conscious of existing thusly and potentially, self-possessed and open to determination. Contained within the very consciousness of selfhood is the intuitive understanding that one is constituted both in self-rule and subjection, sovereignty and reception, voluntary movement and sub-voluntary input.

Schleiermacher construes these coordinated determinations as the associated feelings of *dependence* and *freedom*: "the common element in all those determinations of self-consciousness which predominantly express a receptivity affected from some outside quarter is the *feeling of Dependence*. On the other hand, the common element in all those determinations which predominantly express movement and activity is the *feeling of Freedom*."[68]

Both determinations are constantly operative in the course of quotidian experience. Even banal objects present occasion for feelings of both freedom and dependence. The desk on which I write is an object of utility to me, subjected to use as and when I choose. But it also presents a kind of delimitation to my consciousness, and not only in regards to shared space. Its properties of solidity, mass, and texture exercise regulative input. They co-structure consciousness not only of my own such qualities by comparison but also what is possible for me in a world of these qualities. They set edges even to my pre-reflective sense of potentiality: what kind of impediment and potential solidity of this order and density presents, and the same of mass, and of texture.

This codetermination happens not only with respect to individual objects, but "also when we think of the total 'outside' as one."[69] The totality of that which is external to us can also be conceived as co-constitutive of our self-consciousness. The world is at once the realm of my free activity and the means of that activity. My self-awareness as free agent takes shape according to the agencies represented about me: how my kinesis has been structured by their properties (gravity, drag, energy) and how I might act "with," or "against," or "around" them; in other words, how I can only be "me" as I act in the world and how the world has made "me" (by inter-action).

Whether with regard to desk or world, then, the feeling of freedom entails the feeling of dependence and can never be without it, that is, can never be "absolute" itself: "if the feeling of freedom expresses a forth-going activity, this activity must have an object which has been somehow given to us, and this could not have taken place without an influence of the object upon our receptivity. Therefore in every such case there is involved a feeling of dependence which goes along with the feeling of freedom, and thus limits it."[70] We do not have an intuition of unlimited freedom relative to an object or the world. Sovereignty and sub-voluntary receptivity are intuitively wedded in us, because no object presents itself to us as having been derived entirely from us. Objects about us and the world at large both present themselves as enjoining existence with us.

The inherent relativity (non-absoluteness) of freedom is also the case with respect to voluntary movement directed internally (e.g., the exertion to control emotions). "The totality of our free inward movements, considered as a unity, cannot be represented as a feeling of absolute freedom, because our whole existence does not present itself to our consciousness as having proceeded from our own spontaneous activity."[71] Just as absolute freedom in relation to an external object would presuppose our total derivation of the object—that is, a total absence of receptivity, which again is never the case—so also would absolute freedom in relation to our internal states require our complete generation of them, which is also never the case. Sentiments or attitudes are also reactions to environmental stimuli beyond our initiating or controlling.

We thus receive both the entities about us and the conditions within us as in some measure having been given to us, and so experience only limited freedom. Once more, "the contrary could only be possible if the object altogether came into existence through our activity, which is never the case absolutely, but only relatively."[72]

But what of the feeling of dependence? Schleiermacher shows that this determination of consciousness is for the most part limited and not absolute. *Absolute* dependence "cannot in any wise arise from the influence of an object which has in some way to be *given* to us; for upon such an object there would always be a counter-influence, and even a voluntary renunciation of this would always involve a feeling of freedom."[73] Receptivity is never pure so long as it is in relation to a thing or condition that presents itself to us, like desk, world, or inward state, because such things always presuppose the possibility of our acting upon them in some kind of willful discharge. Schleiermacher cleverly reasons that even restraining oneself in the exercise of restraint—say, refusing to hold back the rush of passion—assumes a voluntary foregoing of personal determination.

Just as the feeling of freedom can only be absolute in the total absence of the feeling of dependence, so also the feeling of dependence can only be absolute in the total absence of the feeling of freedom. Yet this, too, cannot be the case so long as we are dealing with discrete objects in us or about us. For, such objects always jog the impulse to act upon them, or to resist that impulse, both of which amount to a presupposition of freedom.

Since each moment of our existence is comprised of myriad given objects, "a feeling of absolute dependence, strictly speaking, cannot exist in a single moment as such."[74] A moment in time is always comprised of our self-consciousness among objects in the world, the world itself, and our inward states, but relative to these, again, we experience a spontaneous sense of counter-action or of restraint, and so a limited dependence. Anything on which we might be *absolutely* dependent cannot be coterminous with space-time.

It is only with regard to the sum total, *ex-temporaneous* nature of our freedom per se—the fact that we might and do act voluntarily *at all*—that we experience a feeling of *unqualified* dependence: "the self-consciousness which accompanies all of our activity . . . and negatives absolute freedom, is itself precisely a consciousness of absolute dependence; for it is the consciousness that the whole of our spontaneous activity comes from a source outside of us in just the same sense in which anything towards which we should have a feeling of absolute freedom must have proceeded entirely from ourselves."[75] Accompanying every moment of voluntary agency is awareness that the very essence of that agency is *entirely unchosen*; we experience the causal origins of our free action just to be there (and not as something presented to us upon which we might freely/reciprocally act). This constitutes an *absolute* feeling of dependence, in that it entails the total absence of voluntary structure. We cannot voluntarily influence the fact of our voluntariness, so to speak. Just as the feeling of perfect freedom could only be realized in an object which constitution derives absolutely from ourselves (in the complete absence of a sense of dependence), so also the feeling of utter dependence is realized in a self whose willful constitution is absolutely unwilled (in the complete absence of a sense of [responsible] freedom).[76]

How might we call this absolute Giving that endows us with the relative agency whereby we exist in the world? In that it is identified in and by a consciousness of unqualified non-self-giving, always taking place within our existence yet beyond each *moment* thereof, it can only be a kind of comprehensive Source or All defying reflective objectification. This, for Schleiermacher, is "God." "The *Whence* of our receptive and active existence as implied in this self-consciousness, is to be designated by the word 'God' . . . this is for us the really original signification of that word."[77]

"God" is the implied correlate to our innate sense of utter dependence, which cannot be objectified other than as "the-total-whence-of-human-exi stence-as-such." For again, if God could be otherwise objectified, then God would amount to another object in the world, or the world itself, or our internal states of will, toward which we act in at least relative freedom and, thus, on which we exercise at least some measure of existential determination (which would undermine a feeling of absolute dependence and imply a corollary measure of self-willing-into-willful-existence).

Yet we *are* conscious of ourselves as absolutely dependent, and so it is appropriate to posit a focal point of this consciousness that is not of the same class as other objects: "God signifies for us simply that which is the co-determinant in this feeling and to which we trace our being in such a state; and any further content of the idea must be evolved out of this fundamental import assigned to it. . . . To feel oneself absolutely dependent and to be conscious of being in relation with God are one and the same thing."[78] God comes to consciousness in and with the self-consciousness that defines genuine religion. "In whatever measure this actually takes place during the course of a personality through time, in just that measure do we ascribe piety to the individual."[79]

So far, the opening stanza in Schleiermacher's account of *The Christian Faith*. That "piety," which distinguishes Christian faith and forms the basis of its distinctive thought and speech (theology), is the feeling of absolute dependence upon God. The person may be considered pious in proportion to his or her having this feeling. "God" is the name of the feeling's object, its co-determinant, or again, the whence of discretely human agency.

In important ways, this conclusion clearly correlates with that drawn exegetically from Gen. 2:4b–7 earlier and forecasted in the Introduction. God is the creature's codetermination. The God-ness of "God" is discovered, and more, reiteratively established in the creature's existential experience of absolute dependence. God is God in a necessary priority to the creature. God is God in existing as *that on which* all things depend.

But we must add a critical qualification. The freedom of God on which the creature's absolute dependence hangs requires that "God" be *utterly* self-determining, so much "God" as to be open to creaturely determining. The totality of creaturely dependence requires, as we have seen, a corresponding totality to God's freedom. But Schleiermacher offers a diluted order of divine freedom. Schleiermacher argues that the creature cannot entertain a feeling of freedom toward its Whence without reducing its sense of dependence (we will discuss this more below), but this claim must be qualified, for restriction of the creature's ability to exercise a determinative influence on "God" entails restriction of God's freedom, in that it supposes that God cannot be God *responsively*, but only a-temporally, in a kind of abstract originate-ness. A more fulsome divine freedom requires opportunity for the creature to exercise secondary, derived determination also on God without God forfeiting God's standing as *primus*.

For God to be "God," *on Schleiermacher's terms* of an absolutely *free grounding*, God must *confront* the creature right when and where God opens God's self to the creature; the creature must immediately affirm its dependence, for in any experience in which such affirmation is absent, even if only because it awaits the transition from feeling to knowing, God is not God, *primus*. The creature must act freely toward God in her experience of dependence, *at once* consenting to the relation of *primus* to *secunda* in which she finds herself to have existence, or God is not God. This intuitive response can only happen as part of a comprehensive event of revelation, an event which embraces knowing and doing from the beginning.

Only in revealedness does the creature experience an order of freedom that transcends the temporal/a-temporal dichotomy, a freedom that takes the form of willed temporality (a *primus* who exists "moment-by-moment" in relation to *secunda*). In the feeling of religion, as we have seen, there can only be the relative freedom of the temporal or the absolute freedom of the a-temporal. But absolute freedom must be excused from this logic of the excluded middle; the divine must be allowed its right of temporality. God must at once be both ground and means of the creature, the Creator who wills to exist, and does not cease to be Creator by existing, in the creature's covenantal affirmation.

What has to happen for theology to make internally consistent and constructive use of Schleiermacher is that it must translate everything Schleiermacher wishes to say about feeling into the specific knowing and doing of Christian witness. How can we gainfully begin to do this?

First, we gain some clarity by way of critical assessment: it is an overreach to contend that space-time objectivity *necessarily* precludes consciousness of absolute dependence. For, in a consciousness much more thoroughly informed by physical science (and less by deductive dictates of speculative philosophy), this mutual exclusion dissolves: we discover objects (e.g., recently, the Higgs Boson) in relation to which we have *no* intuition of freedom. The objects are of such a determinative quality (as, again, the mass-endowing particle whereby there is *any* matter and energy, the fundamental constituents of entity) that all agency can only be *recognized* as entirely dependent upon them.[80]

This is not to say that we are scientifically obliged to make the move, which Schleiermacher rightly refused to make, and conflate our consciousness of dependency on God into dependency on world (crudely, that we identify the Higgs Boson as the "whence" of our being or the "God particle"). No, it is possible to contend for species of absoluteness, classifying the god-species as "not-world," like Schleiermacher does, even though dependency on God has to be experienced in the same way as world-dependency. Even better would be to identify the complexity of God as object of our dependence. I argue that in revelation God so assumes into God's life the fabric of creation that the whence of all existence is a coordinate, eternal/temporal reality. God takes on time as absolute Lord of time. The sense of our dependence on world and God can thus be the same, absolute, yet admitting free response.

As Niebuhr rightly observes—and besides unpacking that last claim, we transition with this to the second part of our answer—the significance of Schleiermacher's *Gefühl* lies not only in giving expression to the creature's radical, ontological *contingency*, but also in establishing its genuine relationality. In absolute dependency, the self exists as agent-in-relation-to-another:

> We would be mistaken in interpreting Schleiermacher, were we to conclude that he has anything more than a descriptive distinction in mind here [between immediate self-consciousness and that mediated by world and society] and that he intends to indicate a nucleus of the self shut up in an inviolable privacy. . . . Such feeling always manifests itself in association with relations to society and the world. . . . His intention . . . is to point to the fundamental state of consciousness that expresses the basic unity of the self's existence within which the dialectic of a particular life with other lives occurs.[81]

There is no real distinction for Schleiermacher between the immediate feeling of dependence on God and the mediated feeling of dependence on the world, only a logical one. The significance of affirming factual continuity between states of dependency in human consciousness is to affirm the unity of the self—a divided consciousness being a form of psychological deficiency. The human exists in relation to "God" as *whence* of its being and at once exists interdependently in the cosmos, what we might call the *occasion* of its being. But consciousness of the one cannot be strictly differentiated from the other, as the quality of feeling in each case (dependency) is identical, differentiated only by its degree (for Schleiermacher, absolute versus relative).

Schleiermacher is to be applauded for affirming the unity of human consciousness with regard to dependence upon God and world. He is also to be commended for not so isolating "feeling" as to cloister piety away in mysticism; the absoluteness of her dependence pushes the human beyond the world even as her interdependence always locates her in it. Nonetheless, we do better to differentiate our sense of dependence between God and world not according to the degrees of "relative" versus "absolute," but according to the *objects* of absoluteness. There are temporal objects on which we absolutely depend, not because they exercise genuinely absolute freedom, but because they are co-constitutive of creaturely existence. And there is the eternal/temporal Object on whom all things depend precisely because of the (genuine) absoluteness of his freedom.

Revelation dialectically relates self to self,[82] as new to old *adam*: in the Christ figure, it places a Thou before an I, which the I recognizes as its own life, but to which it assents and does not command. The life before it once more comes to it, and in this coming, yet once more turns the I beyond itself, inviting it to move freely into the way of this Thou. The communion of Christian faith is once more founded upon the living movement of Christ in knowing and doing. It is founded upon the Spirit of the Word.

CONCLUSION: BARTH'S CRITIQUE OF SCHLEIERMACHER

Barth wondered whether we might justifiably read Schleiermacher as a pneumatocentric theologian. He recognized that "Schleiermacher, in principle, enters into the course of Trinitarian theological thinking together with the Reformers."[83] That may seem like a strange affirmation in view of the infamous criticism that Schleiermacher's theology lacks Trinitarian conviction, and indeed, that in something of an explicit contrast to Schleiermacher (who treats the dogma at the end of *The Christian Faith*), Barth front loaded the doctrine of the Trinity in his *Church Dogmatics*. But Barth simply means, for Schleiermacher no less than Luther and Calvin, that "Trinitarian thinking compels theology . . . to be completely in earnest about the thought of God in at least two places: first, at the point where it is a question of God's action in regard to man, and, secondly, at the point where it is a question of man's action in regard to God. It is aware of God as the Word of the Father which is spoken to man and as the Spirit of the Father and the Word which enables man to hear the Word."[84]

Theology is *Trinitarian* when it is concerned with God not in the abstract or, again, the metaphysical, but in concrete historical engagement with humanity and humanity in its free response to God. It thinks and speaks of no other God than the one who deals and exists with humanity in Word and Spirit. The Reformers thought and spoke within a Trinitarian frame of reference, and as we have seen, so does Schleiermacher.

But whereas Luther and Calvin thought in a definite order from the Word of the Father to the Spirit of the Father and the Word, to put it as Barth just did, and so from the action of God in regard to humanity to the action of humanity in regard to God, "Schleiermacher reversed the order of this thought. What interests him is the question of man's action in regard to God."[85]

This focus is not, in itself, problematic. "What Schleiermacher constructed by means of his theology of awareness . . . *could* be the pure theology of the Holy Spirit; the teaching of man brought face to face with God by God, of man granted grace by grace."[86] Such a theology would have to understand the human as constituted agentially by an absolute source, as Schleiermacher does, but it would have to describe the subject's experience of dependence as consequent and not precedent. It would have to recognize that the feeling of dependence on God is *itself* an act of God—that the human exists "with God by God." It is critical, in other words, that "spirit" is not cypher for transcendent self-awareness but connotes some kind of confrontation with the self (at least initially).

Can Schleiermacher's thought be understood as a "pure theology of the Holy Spirit"? Barth answers by considering the two basic "motifs" around which Schleiermacher's theology orbits: humanity and God (in the order that Schleiermacher treats them), or again more fully, humanity in its relation to God and God in God's relation to humanity.[87] He concludes that Schleiermacher's attempt to do justice to the second, to *God*, is "an unmistakable source of embarrassment" and something that Schleiermacher "finds particularly strenuous."[88]

The Reformers construed the relationship between God and humanity in the dialectical, Trinitarian terms of *relation* and *distinction*. There is an inherent relation between the Incarnation of the Word and the giving of the Spirit, and yet Personal differentiation (Word and Spirit cannot be collapsed into each other), which tension reflexively characterizes the relation and difference between God and humanity. Schleiermacher did not follow the Reformers in this theo-logic:

> Why is it so difficult for him to acknowledge and ensure the validity of this second motif [God in God's relation to humanity]? Because apparently it did not escape him that the first and the second motifs were, in the Reformed theology at all events, related to each other in such a way, and were opposed to each other in such strict distinction, as the Incarnation of the Word and the pouring out of the Holy Spirit are. . . . Schleiermacher could not acquiesce in this opposition, because it was not his intention at all strictly to characterize these two moments as revelation, nor to protect them from being confused with a mode of human cognition.[89]

For Schleiermacher's thought to be characterized as sharing the Trinitarian impulse of Luther and Calvin, it would have to do justice to the deity of God *in opposition to* human being precisely when and where God stands in self-determinative relation with human being. Precisely in the coordinated event of Word and Spirit, or in Schleiermacher's order, Spirit and Word, the transcendence or precedence of God in God's relation to humanity must be made real and authenticated. But for this to happen, Schleiermacher would have to understand the first motif, humanity in its action relative to God, as something God-sparked, -energized, and -directed, that is, inspired, in such a way that the second motif of God in God's relation to humanity takes the form of an address, revelation that it can hear but not invent or contrive. But as we noted above, Schleiermacher centers faith and its reflective expression on religion as a kind of psychical modality (in Niebuhr's terms), not on revelation as external confrontation.

From Barth's perspective, such religio-centrism inevitably collapses the second motif of God in relation to humanity into a form of human self-awareness:

> Schleiermacher presents as the theme of theology, as seen from the anthropocentric point of view, not the outpouring of the Holy Spirit—this might in itself have been possible—but religious consciousness as such. Faith understood in this way, not as God's revelation, but as man's experience, allowed, nay demanded, that the second objective moment should be understood accordingly, i.e., not presupposing a strict opposition to the first, and not as a correlate to the concept of the Holy Spirit, as understood in the Trinitarian sense, but as a correlate to this human experience.[90]

Schleiermacher thus allows for two options with regard to the fulfillment of God's covenantal relation in the Christ. "*Either* Schleiermacher's view of the matter allows and demands that we should substitute Christ in the very place where he was speaking of God. This would then decide the fact that 'Christ' is not to be understood as an objective quantity, but only as this factor which also determines feeling itself."[91] Piety might take Christ as its point of focus when speaking of God, since there is no distinction between humanity in its relation to God and God in God's relation to humanity; Christ is, after all the *deus homo*, God-Human. But because Schleiermacher does not permit a distinction between the human in relation to God and God in relation to the human, there could be no order to the Word-flesh relation, either,[92] and no way of objectively distinguishing Christ from pious feeling. The God-Human relation that constitutes his existence would be determined according to the same regulative convictions of religious consciousness generally. "In speaking of him we are speaking immediately of our feeling itself."[93]

Still, Christ would be "divine" in whatever sense the Whence of human existence is divine. Humanity is absolutely dependent on him in the same way that it is absolutely dependent on God. That is one way Schleiermacher could have proceeded with regard to the fulfillment of covenantal existence in the Word made flesh:

> *Or* on the other hand Schleiermacher's view allows and demands that we should at all events understand Christ as an objective quantity, and thus distinguish him from pious feeling as such. . . . This, however, directly implies that he is part of the world, i.e., that he is of the quintessence of all that in relation to which we have relative freedom, and upon which, therefore, we are only relatively dependent. This is to deny the only thing which, according to Schleiermacher's way of thinking, could be his Godhead.[94]

The object of Christian faith might be an historical figure. But that conclusion comes at a price: it introduces an interval between Christ and God, in that humanity can only be *relatively* dependent upon the former, yet is *absolutely* dependent upon the latter. Famously, "Schleiermacher did not opt for the first, but for the second of these possibilities. . . . He was bound to renounce the idea of the Deity of Christ or, to put it differently, to understand the Deity of Christ as the incomparable climax and decisive stimulator within the composite life of humanity."[95] Christ can be understood as possessing a perfect God-consciousness, which allows for the closest possible union with God and stimulates humanity to such union, but which is *not* the same as oneness with the absolute source or all.

Barth therefore concludes that Schleiermacher's theology is anthropocentric and not properly pneumatocentric, in spite of its potential to be the latter. It does not achieve the Trinitarian dialectic necessary to be an authentic theology of the Holy Spirit, wherein the event of the Spirit and the Word of God are seen in their decisive opposition even as they stand in relation. *"The Word is not so assured here in its independence in respect to faith as should be the case if this theology of faith were a true theology of the Holy Spirit.* In a proper theology of the Holy Spirit there could be no question of dissolving the Word. Here, quite seriously, there is a question of such dissolution."[96]

Barth's conclusions closely parallel those drawn above and also augment and focus them a bit. If we are to translate Schleiermacher's insights into a truly pneumatocentric theology, then we must do justice to the Trinitarian opposition between Spirit and Word even in their relation. In this regard, we must think dialectically of the relationship between humanity and God—that God is not humanity right when and where "God" exists and is known in the terms of human agency.

God is *known*: theology may well start with humanity in relation to God, but this relation must be construed as part of the event of divine *revelation* and not pre-reflective *religion*. *God* is constituted extrinsically from humanity precisely when and where God exists as one with humanity. God is *God* in a knowledge event over which the human bears no control even though it is an entirely human event, an action taking place entirely through a quintessentially human organ. This can be insofar as the content of the knowledge event immediately engenders its own acceptance, as the sovereignty constitutive of God is enacted in it. The knowledge event must be comprehensive. It must be an activity robust enough to include *concurrence*.[97] Willed covenantal participation is not secondary to perception, but integral to it. Revelation involves its own existential affirmation, what Barth called "revealedness."[98] Immediately engendering this affirmation is the life and work of the Spirit of the Word.

I have argued in this chapter that this Trinitarian operation is married to the operation of the biblical text. It is in the preaching and hearing of Israel's redemptive history culminating in the person and work of the Christ that the comprehensive knowledge event takes place in which humanity stands in constitutive relation to God and vice versa, that God stands *as God* in and with humanity. In this regard, constructively, I have argued for a more thoroughly actualistic account of the self-defining action of God in the work of creation than that provided by the otherwise-gainful efforts of Schleiermacher. "God" exists and is known as the human is drawn into a specific relationship: existentially *secunda* to *primus*, utterly dependent and not autonomous, summoned to covenantal constitution. This dynamic, noetic/practical encounter between the subject of the text and its audience happens as an event that is eventuated by the spirit of the text itself, or as it were, the Spirit of the text's subject.

The Spirit of biblical "God" is, again, the divine capacity for otherness in which the creature finds its ground of existence; the Spirit of God is not a partitioned component of metaphysical deity but the self-defining means of authentic, covenantal existence. The Spirit becomes again the Creator or Giver of Life in the event that an other seizes as a gift, or gratefully acknowledges, its constitutive mutuality—as the human *consciously* accepts and enacts its dependence, or in Schleiermacher's terms, experiences pious self-awareness.

In this regard, pneumatocentric theology does not simply supply philosophical background for the existential event of the Spirit in creation but describes at least some of its physical, emotional, and social dimensions. It signals the many factual ways that the creature only exists within networks of dependence.

For instance, it is not just that, operating at the most obvious level, to remove O_2 from the environment is to remove an essential element of earthly human life. It is rather, a little more complexly, that living among O_2 and a series of other gases comprising the environment gives shape to human consciousness as a breath-animal among other breath-animals. Pneumatocentric theology points to breath function as a way of highlighting the absoluteness of humanity's dependence; at no point is humanity independently constituted, but from the first, at the level of its cells and metabolism, humanity manifests environmental integration. So also at the level of its perception of objects and sense of free agency among them; these, too, take structure in and through a matrix of atmospheric gases[99] and acquaintance with motion and drag in the same (theirs and the objects about them).

Things are much more complex, of course. The human ingests oxygen from other sources (food) and metabolizes it along with carbon and hydrogen to give it sense of energy and potential. Years of performing this operation trillions and trillions of times contribute to an overall self-awareness; our sense of agential potency is thoroughly entwined with integrated cellular activity both as it is given us genetically and influenced environmentally, both as it simply "happens" to us and as, in its recurrent happening, we alter its makeup—by, for example, various dietary habits, like overindulgent introduction of sugars. We in turn characterize these dietary habits as, rudimentarily, "healthy" and "unhealthy," which public act of characterization feeds back on our self-awareness and causes us either to retreat into it or to act constructively upon it. We have feelings of "dependency" and "freedom" not only with respect to interior and exterior objects, then, but also with regard to our metabolic selves. But obviously enough, these "feelings" are nothing more than acts of self-*perception*, co-occurring *in* and *extra se*.

Human self-consciousness is further shaped by resistance against a particular gravitational force, maintenance of a specific temperature from within a continuum of tolerable temperatures (outside of which vitality breaks down), intake of sounds within a certain auditory range, detection of objects across a particular light spectrum, stimulation of the olfactory nerve, proportionally, which co-stimulates taste receptors. Sequence and extension also have to be considered. The human is a time-space creature. Her particular motion on this particular planet in its particular orbit among the vast sea of planets and galaxies in the expanding cosmos sets a cadence, a rhythm and tempo to her living. She finds herself in a motion that she cannot set, in which she can only participate—grow, learn, shift, refine, decline, fade, vanish. She, of course, reflexively sets standards of measurement to that cadence (second, minute, hour, etc.), but these are, from a cosmic perspective, arbitrary, relative to and assuming her being-here, living at this motion. Still, they are relevant to her consciousness as units that set her life within a more or less allotted span.

Her corporeality participates in the construction of her time. The human has a kind of motion on earth in the Milky Way in this universe that, at least under extant conditions, is not the cheetah's or the sloth's or the golly-womp's. There is no sense of *self* that is not found with, or that mystically transcends, the structuring effect of being a time-space, embodied, molecularly constructed entity.

This is all to say: Schleiermacher was correct that the human is constituted in the primal experience of absolute dependence on God, but that dependence cannot be authentically absolute unless the act of consciousness itself evinces dependence, unless human self-awareness takes the character of a knowing-and-doing event, unless the human constantly perceives the reality of her very perception in relation to a larger reality and acts accordingly. In the event of such living consciousness, God comes to be again who "God" is: the promise of each instant and its source, the Lord of life and its Giver.

NOTES

1. I am grateful to Brooks Schramm and Herb Spomer, both retired professors of Old Testament at the Lutheran Theological Seminary at Gettysburg (now United Lutheran Seminary), for hours of patient consultation on translation and exegesis of the Hebrew text of Gen. 2:4–3:24. Besides their expertise and the aid of commentaries, my rendering draws upon Everett Fox, *The Five Books of Moses: Genesis, Exodus, Leviticus, Numbers, Deuteronomy: A New Translation with Introductions, Commentary and Notes*, The Schocken Bible vol. 1 (New York: Schocken, 1995).

As a systematic theologian and not a scholar of the Hebrew language, I have endeavored in translation only to vary from standard English versions where doing so is warranted by the text in concert with what I understand to be its underlying trajectory of meaning. My translation readily correlates with commonly available modern Bible translations. Where necessary, I have input the Hebrew text myself, but wherever possible I have made use of the excellent script available through Logos: *Biblia Hebraica Stuttgartensia with Werkgroep Informatica, Vrije Universiteit Morphology*, Logos Bible Software (2006).

2. The biblical text thinks from within the conceptual structures and speaks from within the literary devices of the Ancient Near East. Whatever scriptural inspiration entails, it has nothing to do with elevating the biblical authors to a perceptual peak whereby they describe scientific intricacies of the created world. Neither does the text offer any evidence that, although the authors themselves failed to understand the facts of biochemical life in an expansive cosmos, God furtively sowed this information into their writings so that the modern reader, at last attuned to such important matters, might decipher scientific messages on the biblical pages as if cracking a secret code.

The Bible has nothing to do with a Big Bang, an expanding or collapsing universe, parallel universes, bosons, quarks, leptons, atoms, molecules, deoxyribonucleic acid, cell structures, histone methylation, or for that matter, a spherical earth in a heliocentric galaxy. It is not that such discoveries are necessarily at odds with biblical revelation, or that Scripture cannot speak to them, but that what the Bible may say about such things it says from within a series of messages that were composed, comprehensibly, to ancient Hebrews living among ancient Babylonians, Assyrians,

Hittites, and Egyptians. Paradoxically, what the text has to say about a spherical earth orbiting the sun, it says in the terms of a flat earth covered by a dome and positioned above an underworld, altogether orbited by the sun.

The issue is hermeneutical. The plenary sense of the Bible, while reaching beyond the historical sense, is framed by the historical sense. The history of God with Israel, relayed on *its* foreign, distant terms, gives structure to all of God's history with humanity, God's covenantal time with us and for us. We do not, then, discover hydrogen bonding of double helix base pairs in the creation of "inmost parts" and the human's "knitting together" in Ps. 139:13. Yet we can appeal to the fragility of our genetic makeup and complexity of our evolutionary heritage as illustration of the biblical truth that our lives are transient and interdependent.

3. The biblical account proceeds in a manner consistent with other creation narratives. So, for example, Richard J. Clifford, S. J.: "that the gods created the world was simply taken for granted throughout the ancient Near East"; Clifford, *Creation Accounts in the Ancient Near East and in the Bible*, CBQMS 26 (Washington, DC: The Catholic Biblical Association of America, 1994), 1. This common taking of the divine factor for granted certainly admits at least a degree of comparison between creation narratives. But commonalities should not be overstated. There is a good bit of uniqueness to the Bible's reserve in characterizing the divine, particularly in view of the gods' origins and motives for acting in, say, Gilgamesh. Moreover, the compound event that I am trying to describe considers knowledge of God not as disinterested affirmation of the deity, but as the specific content and object of faith.

4. Schmid, "Schöpfung als Thema der Theologie," in *Schöpfung*, ed. Konrad Schmid, Themen der Theologie 4 (Tübingen: Mohr Siebeck, 2012), 5.

5. Schmid here reflects the fact (so, for example, Claus Westermann, *Genesis 1–11: A Continental Commentary*, trans. John J. Scullion [1966/1974; Minneapolis: Fortress, 1994]) that in view of the redacted form of Genesis, chapters 2–3 stand in intimate connection with chapters 4–11 and the emergence of vocation, culture, and society.

6. This is a daring claim, which has to be made lest the existential authority by which God is God, or again, the determinative encounter in which God wills to have existence and the human comes to find its existence, is located somewhere else. We have to guard against bibliolatry, yes, but we have to guard even more judiciously against latent idolatry.

7. At no point does Scripture engage in abstract speculation about supra-historical qualities of the divine. It rather surfaces divine qualities—some of which transform temporality—in and through the use of historical categories. To say, for instance, that God is "eternal," the text contends that God is "the God of Abraham, the God of Isaac, and the God of Jacob," and that "Jesus Christ is the same yesterday, today, and forever" (Ex. 3:16; Heb. 13:8). It thereby structures the meaning of "eternal" after the historically-conditioned rubric of ancestry.

In turn, the Bible identifies the object of God's life-act at the level of *generation*. The levels of *individual* and *species* are subordinate in Scripture, especially in the book of Genesis, to that of generation. An identifiable people takes rise in continuity and discontinuity with ancestors. The life and witness of forebears becomes a determinative factor in their living, even as their life and witness will likewise become a factor for their offspring. Thus Ps. 102:18, "let this be written for *a future generation*, that a people *not yet created* may praise the LORD" (NIV; italics added). I hope one day to further explore creation as dynamic generation (regeneration) within the doctrine of redemption. For now, eternal life includes just this historical sensibility: awareness of earlier and later peoples per se and the formative inheritance of their witness.

8. Biblical and theological studies witness a long history of debate about the content and centrality of "covenant" as an organizing motif vis-a-vis the Old and New Testaments. It is not my purpose to argue for a side in that debate. As I contend for the determinative character of God's covenantal history, certain positions (e.g., regarding the relationship between the "old" and "new" covenants) will be cast in a more or less favorable, and others in a more or less critical light. I assume, minimally, that "covenant" refers to *God's redemptive dealing with humankind fulfilled in Jesus of Nazareth*, and secondly with particular epochs of divine-human engagement (the covenants of Adam, Noah, Abraham, Moses, and David). Such secondary covenants are only individual manifestations of a single, divine intention for creation (finding formulaic expression in the reciprocal language and logic of "I will be their God/ they will be my people"). For fuller presentation of a similar line of thinking, see Rendtorff, *The Canonical Hebrew Bible*, 432–46; idem, *The Covenant Formula: An Exegetical and Theological Investigation*, Old Testament Studies, trans. Margaret Kohl (Edinburgh: T & T Clark, 1998).

9. Bernhardt, "בָּרָא III Meaning," in *Theological Dictionary of the Old Testament*, ed. G. Johannes Botterweck and Helmer Ringgren, trans. John T. Willis (Grand Rapids: Eerdmans, 1974), 2:246. Bernhardt's observation reflects the fact that in every OT use of בָּרָא, God is the explicit or implicit subject. A certain easy confidence in the otherness of "God," then, influences the meaning of בָּרָא: incongruity with human activity accrues to the term. Whether that incongruity is aptly characterized by *creation out of nothing*, however, is not clear from the text.

10. This is especially the case when we observe that the objects of בָּרָא in Isa. 45:7 are darkness and evil!

11. Bernhardt, TDOT "בָּרָא III Meaning," 2:246.

12. This intentional parallelism need not indicate manuscript continuity between a story that ends in 2:4a and one that begins in 2:4b, or perhaps one that ends in 2:3 and a second that begins in 2:4b. Gen. 2:4a seems to have been constructed as an editorial transition in parallel with 2:4b, added by a redactor drawing upon a poetical pattern in order to sew two accounts together. To be precise, the verse is structured in chiastic parallelism:

> "These are the generations of
> the heavens and the earth
> in the day when they were *created*
> when the LORD God *made*
> earth and heavens."

As for the purpose of the verse's construction, Bill T. Arnold summarizes the standard conclusion that Gen. 1–3 "preserve early traditions that once served as part of Israel's sweeping national epic," and that "the purpose of 2:4a was to tie the new priestly account of creation [1:1–2:3] to the older account of 2:4b-3:24, which presumably by that time wielded impressive authority"; *Genesis*, The New Cambridge Bible Commentary (Cambridge: Cambridge University Press, 2009), 54–55. This suggests that the origin of 2:4a owes either to the (later) author of 1:1–2:3, or to a (yet later) editor of both. For a helpful discussion of this matter, see Mark S. Smith, *The Priestly Vision of Genesis 1* (Minneapolis: Fortress, 2010), 118–38, see esp. pp. 129–38.

Regardless, with respect to its *meaning*, it is best to treat the verse as we have it, that is, as a poetic unity. The same is true in a broader sense with regard to Genesis as a whole. So Robert Alter: "the edited version of Genesis—the so-called redacted text—which has come down to us, though not without certain limited contradictions and disparate elements, has powerful coherence as a literary work, and . . . this coherence is above all what we need to address as readers"; *Genesis: Translation and Commentary* (New York: Norton, 1996), xlii.

The text exhibits canonical coherence, which points us as readers to plenary meanings. (On this, I endorse the logic of Brevard S. Childs' canonical study of the Bible; see *Introduction to the Old Testament as Scripture* [Minneapolis: Fortress, 1979]). Indeed, from within the canon itself we identify verbal continuities among different texts, which direct our attention to broader thematic elements than those addressed in any one account (e.g., continuities between the construction of heaven and earth in Genesis 1 and that of the temple in Ex. 39–40; see Smith, op. cit. 178–79). Covenant, creation, sin, redemption—these grand themes are introduced and developed at the level of individual verses, chapters, and books, but find their fuller sense in treatment across the arc of the biblical narrative. Informed Bible reading involves locating meaning first within the narrow, historical and linguistic context of individual pericopae, but not stopping there, moving on to place that narrow meaning within the framework of the grander canonical presentation.

With respect to Gen. 1–3, we may first exegete 2:4–3:24 as a distinct account that probably predates 1:1–2:3, then consider each in relation to the other, taking the former to function as the rational foundation or explanatory backdrop of the latter (or considered from the reverse angle, as Smith has it [op. cit. pp. 129–38], seeing the composition of the latter as "commentary" on the former). The covenant is the *ground* of the creation. We may eventually work in the opposite direction (in a forthcoming second volume), from 1:1–2:3 to 2:4–3:24, understanding creation to be the *performative realm* of the covenant.

13. Not only canonically, but also grammatically: the latter part of the verse employs a temporal-adverbial construct (בְּיוֹם עֲשׂוֹת יְהוָה אֱלֹהִים), which connotes a kind of action *in media res* ("*in the day/course of* making" or *when* the LORD God made") that echoes the temporal-adverbial construct בְּרֵאשִׁית בָּרָא אֱלֹהִים "*when* God created" of Gen. 1:1 (taking בְּרֵאשִׁית to be in the construct state).

14. John Walton has made a compelling case that considered from within the framework of Ancient Near Eastern thought, the biblical creation accounts present a "functional" sculpting and forming rather than a "material" bringing into existence. See Walton, *Ancient Near Eastern Thought and the Old Testament: Introducing the*

Conceptual World of the Hebrew Bible (Grand Rapids: Baker, 2006), 165–99; see esp. pp. 181–99. They describe not the making of light, water, and creatures from out of nothing, but the fashioning of time, weather, and fecundity (days 1–3 of Genesis 1) and their respective functionaries (days 4–6). As with Sumerian, Akkadian, Hittite, and Egyptian accounts, they depict the shaping or causing of cosmic order over against chaos:

> *Chaos* is the opposite of *cosmos*, which refers to the ordered whole. . . . The precosmic condition was not lacking in that which was material, it was lacking in order and differentiation. Thus the accounts regularly begin with a precosmic, unordered, nonfunctional world. Creation then takes place by giving things order, function, and purpose, which is synonymous with giving them existence. Once established, the order that exists in the cosmos is constantly threatened with being undone. As a result creation is not restricted to a one-time event. Whether the jeopardy derives from the cosmic waters, from what we would term "natural" occurrences, from supernatural beings, from human behavior, or simply from the darkness of each night, the gods are responsible for reestablishing order day by day and moment by moment. (ibid., 184–86)

For Walton, the biblical creation accounts ultimately aim to depict the construction of God's cosmic temple (represented by Eden in Genesis 2), that is, the conditions by which God makes himself to be present among humankind. In this, the authors of Scripture both reflect the presumptions of their broader thought world and seek to correct them; *reflect* in that their God is also known only from within his dealings with creation, yet *correct* in that unlike other gods, he remains the differentiated cause of those dealings and is never conflated into them (as, for instance, Shamash the Assyrian sun god elides into the movement and function of the sun itself). We might say that for the authors of Scripture, God is God-with-*us*, but always *God*-with-us.

15. There is a logical case to make for "creation out of nothing" as properly divine action. If "God" is to connote *absolute* sovereignty, then "creation" must refer to a *contingent* condition, something entirely distinct even protologically from God. Moreover, if God alone is eternal, and God creates *everything*, so that nothing "preexists" with God, then whatever is caused to exist externally to God must come from no-thing, that is, from whatever is extrinsic to the only eternal Something (nothing).

But this is, once more, a logical exercise. It is not a textual claim (although, both Ps. 148 and Prov. 8:22–31 do indicate a comprehensiveness to God's creative act; apart from God, specifically in concrete precedence, no thing has existence.) And we must be precise in our use of the language of *creatio ex nihilo*. It must not be taken to indicate an "out of which," a raw material even if that is a-materiality, but rather must mean something like *creatio ab deo*. God is that by which creation comes, not as raw material, but means and *ratio*. From that self-sufficiency which makes God the Giver of Life, God constitutes and sustains an other.

About a year after composing the previous paragraph, I was gratified to discover, while researching material for a later chapter, that Augustine also wrestled with language to express the "from which" of creation in relation to God. Matthew Drever demonstrates that Augustine differentiates between use of the propositions "de" and "ex"/"ab" in order to distinguish between the senses of *procession from* and *causation by*, respectively. Summarizing Augustine's work in his anti-Manichean writing, *De*

Natura Boni, Drever writes, "that which proceeds from God (*de*) shares a substantial relation to God (i.e., it is God), while that which God creates (*ex/ab*) shares a causal but not a substantial relation to God"; Drever, "Redeeming Creation: *Creatio ex nihilo* and the *Imago Dei* in Augustine," *IJST* 15:2 (2013), 142–43.

16. Clifford identifies multiple systems for classifying accounts of creation in the ancient Near East (e.g., according to *structure* or *action*). Such systems have yielded a variety of ways in which the creative work of the gods might be depicted: as ordering chaos, giving birth, active separation and forming/sculpting, among others; see Clifford, *Creation Accounts*, 1. The biblical authors and redactors are evidently aware of such accounts and feel freedom to allude to them without compulsion to endorse any of them.

17. Obviously, the *scope* of God's making "the heavens and earth" or ordered cosmos is unique, and so, too, the power implied in fashioning this particular object. It connotes such a power and authority as can constitute and sustain existence. But *how* God constitutes and sustains existence, that is, what quality is exercised in this coordinated activity, and the nature of the activity—how it is that by divine constitution the ingredients of non-divine life take shape and become just that—on such matters the text is silent.

18. To get a sense of the range of meanings at work vis-a-vis "creation" in the OT, see for starters the list of "Objects of the Verb *Bārā*'" identified by Walton, *Genesis 1 as Ancient Cosmology* (Winona Lake, IN: Eisenbrauns, 2011), 129. It merits noting, further, that the Septuagint provides no direction concerning the identification of a particular quality, which would distinguish a given kind of creative work as divine. For, it employs an almost dizzying array of terms to render בָּרָא and its cognates, depending upon context—so, for example, for בָּרָא: ποιέω ("to do" or "make"), κτίζω ("to create"), ἄρχομαι ("to begin"), δείξω ("to make known"), κατασκευάζω ("to build"), γίνομαι ("to become"); see G. Johannes Botterweck, "בָּרָא II.3 *LXX*," TDOT 2:245–46.

19. Westermann summarizes the matter exactly (*The Genesis Accounts of Creation*, trans. Norman E. Wagner, Facet Books Biblical Series 7 [Philadelphia: Fortress, 1964], 26):

> The narrator is not concerned with reporting the fact of creation—knowledge of which he can presuppose; rather, he would assert something special about that fact. . . . [This] is what concerns the narrator: God's activity and that which it encompasses, existence and the story of man. . . . He took this idea [the common ancient near eastern motif of God forming humankind out of clay] and handed it on with the object of indicating in this way the *mystery* of man's creation. For precisely this quite primitive presentation of man's creation forces the reader who no longer shares this view to conclude that we do *not* know how God created man.

20. There is an epistemological ordering in the text determinative of the existence of God and creation. We are given a this-then-that, a first, which being first presupposes a second, but which as first is self-sustaining in a way that is not true of the second (which cannot *be* apart from the first). Above and before anything else, the content of the term "God" is supplied in this dialectical ordinal-ing.

21. Outside of Gen. 2–3, the combination occurs in only one other verse in the Pentateuch (Ex. 9:30), and four other passages in the entire OT (2 Sam. 7:25; 1 Chron. 17:16–17; 2 Chron. 6:41–42; Ps. 84:8[9]).

22. Sarna, *Genesis*, The JPS Torah Commentary (Philadelphia: The Jewish Publication Society, 1989), 17. Sarna's modesty befits the reality that from a source-critical standpoint, rationale for the unique, concentrated use of the doublet in Gen. 2–3 eludes consensus.

23. Ibid. Terence Fretheim is similarly modest: "in linking the names Yahweh and Elohim in 2:4–25, the writer may have intended to identify Israel's special name for God with the creator of the world;" see Fretheim, *The Book of Genesis: Introduction, Commentary, and Reflections,* The New Interpreter's Bible vol. 1 (Abingdon: Nashville, 1994), 349.

24. Cuthbert A. Simpson is typical; see *The Book of Genesis*, The Interpreter's Bible vol. 1 (Nashville: Abingdon, 1952), 465, 492. "The two stories cannot come from the same hand. The first is basically from P, the second from J²" (p. 465; the superscripted number "2" reflects the eventual division of J into multiple sources). The literature on this shift is abundant. For a helpful orientation, see Westermann, *Genesis 1–11*; Gordon J. Wenham, *Genesis 1–15*, Word Biblical Commentary vol. 1 (Waco, TX: Word, 1987); Smith, *The Priestly Vision of Genesis 1.*

Since Julius Wellhausen's paradigmatic formulation of the modern Documentary Hypothesis (*Die Composition des Hexateuchs und der historischen Bücher des Alten Testaments* [3 editions 1876–1899; Berlin: De Gruyter, 2012], and *Prolegomena zur Geschichte Israels* [6 editions 1878–1927; Berlin: De Gruyter, 2001], ET: *Prolegomena to the History of Israel*, Scholars Press Reprints and Translations, trans. J. Sutherland Black and Allan Menzies, [Atlanta: Scholars Press, 1994]), the tendency has been to break down the composition of Genesis as follows: about half from Yahwist source tradition, a third from Elohist, and a sixth from Priestly (see Wenham, *Genesis 1–15*, xxvi and *passim*). Deriving from J (10th/9th c. BC), Gen. 2:4b–3:24 is considered the older narrative, whereas being from P (6th/5th c.), Gen. 1:1–2:3 is younger. (Although scholars before Wellhausen generally considered J to be later than P; see Douglas A Knight, "Forward," in Wellhausen, *Prolegomena* (ET), v-xvi; Wenham, *Genesis 1–15*, xxxvii–xlvi, esp. xxxviii; for a brief discussion of more contemporary figures who see evidence that "the [canonically] second creation story presupposes the priestly account," see also Smith, op. cit., p. 267 n. 2).

Several factors are cited to demarcate the accounts. These include the loftier and more transcendent character of the God of Genesis 1 relative to Gen. 2–3 (reflecting a later commitment to monotheism), the unusual concentration of YHWH in Gen. 2–3 (as the personal name of Israel's God over against the gods of other nations), and the typically priestly usage of תּוֹלְדֹת ("generations," or "story" or "account") in 2:4a, suggestive either of priestly authorship or a later editorial effort to link the traditions.

The last century and-a-half of OT scholarship has seen various emendations and criticisms of the Documentary Hypothesis, especially Wellhausen's formulation of it. One of the most notable among the critics has been Umberto Cassuto; see *The Documentary Hypothesis and the Composition of the Pentateuch*, trans.

Israel Abrahams (Jerusalem: Shalem, 2008); *A Commentary on the Book of Genesis Part One: From Adam to Noah*, trans. Israel Abrahams (Jerusalem: The Hebrew University Press, 1961/1989). Yet the hypothesis continues to be advocated in some form by most scholars of the Hebrew Bible. Utilizing a series of case studies from Genesis, Exodus, and Numbers to demonstrate how the sources can be differentiated and how they fit together, Joel S. Baden contends that "the Documentary Hypothesis remains the best explanation for the composition of the Pentateuch"; *The Composition of the Pentateuch: Renewing the Documentary Hypothesis*, The Anchor Yale Bible Reference Library (New Haven: Yale University Press, 2012), 33.

Debate begun decades ago by Gerhard von Rad and Martin Noth concerning stages of source tradition, including the dating and formation of Jahwist material, goes on today; see Thomas B. Dozeman and Konrad Schmid, *A Farewell to the Yahwist? The Composition of the Pentateuch in Recent European Interpretation*, SBL Symposium 34 (Atlanta: Society of Biblical Literature, 2006). For our purposes, it is sufficient to affirm that Gen. 1:1–2:3 and 2:4–3:24 are distinct creation narratives and to align with the majority view vis-a-vis dating. Doing so allows us to begin our exegesis with the latter, understanding it to predate the former and thus to treat it as explanatory background to the former.

25. Delitzsch, *A New Commentary on Genesis* vol. 1, trans. Sophia Taylor, Clark's Foreign Theological Library vol. 36 (Edinburgh: T & T Clark, 1888), 114.

26. CD III.1, 234.

27. Twentieth-century biblical scholarship argued over the relationship between doctrines of creation and redemption. Representative are the views of Gerhard von Rad and H. H. Schmid. For brief, translated, and edited summaries, see von Rad, "The Theological Problem of the Old Testament Doctrine of Creation (1936)," in *Creation in the Old Testament*, ed. Bernhard W. Anderson, Issues in Religion and Theology 6 (London: SPCK, and Philadelphia: Fortress, 1984), 53–64; Schmid, "Creation, Righteousness, and Salvation: 'Creation Theology' as the Broad Horizon of Biblical Theology (1973)," in ibid, 102–17.

Von Rad contended that:

> In genuinely Yahwistic belief the doctrine of creation never attained to the stature of a relevant, independent doctrine. [It is] invariably related, and indeed subordinated, to soteriological considerations. This is not to say, however, that it is necessarily of later origin. Evidently a doctrine of creation was known in Canaan in extremely early times, and played a large part in the cultus in the pre-Israelite period through mythical representations of the struggle against primeval chaos. Yahwistic faith early absorbed these elements, but because of the exclusive commitment of Israel's faith to historical salvation, the doctrine of creation was never able to attain to independent existence in its own right. (62–63)

By "commitment . . . to historical salvation," von Rad is referring to Israel's self-consciousness as God's elect people, that is, a sense of historical identity inexorably linked to divine action: they were only this people insofar as they were the object of God's favor (this, again, particularly for the Yahwist). As such, Israel's consciousness of creation cannot be expressed except as the realm of God's redemptive activity; the doctrine of creation has no independent significance. "Either it remained [for Yahwistic faith] a cosmic foil against which soteriological pronouncements stood out the more effectively, or it was wholly incorporated into the complex of soteriological thought" (63).

Schmid faulted von Rad for helping to establish "the broad *communis opinio* [of modern scholars] . . . that a theology of creation does indeed belong to Christian theology but that it must be accorded a secondary position to christology or soteriology" (102). Against the consensus view, Schmid made three observations about the ancient Near Eastern background to Israel's doctrine of creation. One, creation faith "did not deal . . . with the origin of the world, [but rather] . . . with the present world and the natural environment of humanity now" (103); two, annual reconstitution of created order (in the *Chaoskampf*) "is just as much the order of the state" (104)—that is, in, for example, Mesopotamian accounts, repulsion of the enemy of order in the world applies just as much to the maintenance of political stability; and that means, three, that "legal order belongs to the order of creation" (104), which is to say, "in the whole ancient Near East, including Israel, an offense in the legal realm obviously has effects in the realm of nature (drought, famine). . . . Law, nature, and politics are only aspects of one comprehensive order of creation" (105).

Schmid argued that Israel's concepts of salvation and righteousness were shaped by this ancient Near Eastern background. They cannot be narrowly construed to refer to a merely forensic condition, but must be understood to involve achievement of a particular world order. In short, "for extensive and major literary contexts of the OT creation-faith in the broad sense is not simply a 'foil'; rather, this faith centrally determines their content" (108). For Schmid, the doctrine of creation is not subordinate to the doctrine salvation, but superordinate; the doctrine of "salvation" finds its content in the doctrine of creation.

Final adjudication of this debate is beyond the scope of this project. It would entail, in any case, thorough exegetical engagement not only with the Genesis creation accounts, but also with those found in the wisdom literature (particularly Job and the Psalms [8, 74, 89, 93, and esp. 104], and deutero-Isaiah, as well as texts that closely interweave God's covenantal faithfulness and creation (Genesis 6, Exodus 15). It is enough to observe the close correlation between creation and redemption, and, while appreciating Schmid's corrective, to incline to the view of von Rad: Israel's self-consciousness as God's elect definitively stamped especially the Jahwist's narrative of creation. This narrative naturally reflected (thematically and even to a degree linguistically) other narratives of the ancient Near East, but found distinctive form by way of existential encounter with the concretely covenant-God. It may be too strong to say that the doctrine of creation remained a "cosmic foil" for soteriological concerns, but it is not too strong to say that creation was "incorporated into the complex of soteriological thought."

28. CD IIII.1, 234.

29. Schmid, "Schöpfung," 2; ". . . dadurch der erste Artikel insgesamt, die Schöpfungslehre miteingeschlossen, grundsätzlich vom zweiten Artikel her zu verstehen."

30. CD III.1, 239. The Creator God exists and is known only as *abba*, loving Father to the Son; the created-human exists and is known only as ἀγαπητός υἱός μου, beloved Son of [the Father].

58

Chapter 1

31. Arnold, *Genesis*, 55. Alter characterizes the transition to Genesis 2 similarly: "In this more vividly anthropomorphic account, God, now called *YHWH 'Elohim* instead of *'Elohim* as in the first version, does not summon things into being from a lofty distance through the mere agency of divine speech, but works as a craftsman, fashioning (*yatsar* instead of *bar'a*, "create"), blowing life breath into nostrils, building a woman from a rib"; *Genesis*, 7. Perhaps most instructive for our purposes is Sarna's construal of the shift:

> While God the Creator was the primary subject of the previous chapter, the focus of attention now shifts to humankind. This change in perspective and emphasis is signaled by the inversion of the regular sequence, "heaven and earth" in the opening sentence. The almost unique expression, "earth and heaven" suggests pride of place for terrestrial affairs. *Information about the physical world is offered only to provide essential background for the understanding of the narrative, which seeks to explain the nature of man and the human condition.* (*Genesis*, 16, italics added)

32. Fretheim, *The Book of Genesis*, 349.

33. Sarna, *Genesis*, 17.

34. Fretheim, *The Book of Genesis*, 349.

35. In the Ancient Near East, creaturely work is in scullion service to the gods. That is the aim, so to speak, of humanity's having been made; it is *not* to realize a share in the divine work of making. Creation supplies food and enjoyment for the gods, which the human offers, hence the close correlation between depictions of creation and the temple. In commenting on minor Akkadian cosmogonies, Clifford summarizes, "the temple is important in creation because there the gods receive the services and goods for which they created the human race. It is, as it were, the concrete expression of the finality of the creation. There were deposited the food offerings to satisfy their hunger and there the ceremonies giving them honor took place"; *Creation Accounts*, 61.

36. Fretheim, *The Book of Genesis*, 349. As Wenham concludes, "without man to irrigate the land, the spring was useless" (Wenham, *Genesis 1–15*, 59).

37. Wehnham, *Genesis 1-15*, 59. Wenham notes that the wordplay is just that; there is no explicit etymological connection between אָדָם and אֲדָמָה. In this respect, we are warned against thinking that humanity is merely shaped dust (or in more modern terms, merely this particular molecular substrate and collection of biochemical processes), or conversely, that the ground is merely unshaped flesh. Each is true enough in the abstract. Nevertheless, as we will see, with the giving of the breath of life *directly* from God (for in this, humanity is also not merely an animal, which indirectly receives the breath of life), a distinction is introduced between humanity and creation. This distinction holds even in view of the fact that humanity comes from the earth and returns to it (3:19). "Man is more than a God-shaped piece of earth. He has within him the gift of life that was given by God himself"; (ibid., 60).

38. Fretheim, *The Book of Genesis*, 349.

39. Sarna, *Genesis*, 17. It strikes me as somewhat flatfooted the way that many modern commentators, unlike Sarna, are content merely to observe continuity between the fashioning of humankind from dust or, perhaps, *clay* in Gen. 2:7 and the

same in other ancient near-eastern writings (e.g., the Epic of Gilgamesh and Enuma Elis), as if here we have little more than the Hebrew version of a recognized myth. It is not to be doubted that the biblical author is drawing upon a common figure. However, it is plain—and there can be even less doubt that this is how the rest of the Bible reads the story—that in the hands of the Genesis redactor this familiar tale uniquely accentuates the sovereign determinacy of God on the one hand and responsible activity of the creature on the other. See for starters Job 10:9; 34:14–15; Ps. 90:3; 104:29; Isa. 29:16/Rom. 9:20–21. The central point of each of these verses, which are connected by vocabulary and motif to Gen. 2:7 (together with 2:17 and 3:19), is to emphasize the sovereign will and wisdom of the LORD as the conditions by which humankind may live before God.

40. Schleiermacher, *The Christian Faith*, 3.

41. In this regard, Barth's suggestion that he practiced properly "church" dogmatics over against the likes of Schleiermacher is not entirely fair. Schleiermacher's method can be construed as anticipating Barth's precisely for its ecclesial focus. The main point of difference, as I see it, is that Barth sought to adjudicate the accuracy, stability, and effectiveness of the church's witness according to its conformity to exegetical study of the Bible and the historical content (though not necessarily philosophical substructure) of classical dogma, whereas Schleiermacher adjudicated such things according to their ability to express the feeling of absolute dependence, according to which he also adjudicated classical Christian teaching.

42. Schleiermacher opens the *Glaubenslehre* by considering the church from within three spheres of discourse: ethics, philosophy of religion, and apologetics (see ibid., 5–31, 31–52, and 52–76, respectively). Ethics "principally" supplies the basis or essence of the church, "since in every case the 'Church' is a society which originates only through free human action and can only through such continue to exist" (ibid., 3). After describing the nature of the human agency upon which the church is established, Schleiermacher considers this agency in relation to other religions (philosophy of religion) and articulates its peculiar *redemptive* center (apologetics).

43. Ibid., 5.

44. The German, *Gefühl*, can be translated as "feeling" or "intuition" or "sense." In whichever case, the concept is of a penetrating awareness, which transcends reasoned knowledge (*Vernunft* in either of Kant's "pure" or "pure-practical" forms) and behavior or action (including responsive action or morality).

45. Ibid., 8.

46. Ibid., 8–9.

47. Ibid., 9.

48. Ibid.

49. Ibid., 9–10.

50. Ibid., 10.

51. Ibid.

52. Ibid., 11.

53. Again, however, this does not entail total severing of pious feeling from action, as if Christian religion could be externally apathetic and inert. On the contrary, Schleiermacher has every expectation that Christianity *necessarily* involves work

in behalf of the Gospel (it is just that, critically, this work derives from a prior self-consciousness and not the other way around). Barth argues that, in fact, *ethics* forms the teleological rationale of Schleiermacher's dogmatics; see *Protestant Theology in the Nineteenth Century: Its Background and History* (Valley Forge: Judson, 1976), 434–39, here 434–35:

> By birth and upbringing in its innermost sanctuary his theology is cultural theology: in religion itself which is the true object of his theology, it is the exaltation of life in the most comprehensive sense, the exaltation, unfolding, transfiguration, ennobling of the individual and social human life which is at stake. Civilization as the triumph of the spirit over nature is the most peculiar work of Christianity, just as the quality of being Christian is for its own part the crown of a thoroughly civilized consciousness.

Schleiermacher was compelled not only to defend the Christian faith in the midst of nineteenth-century western culture, but more, to understand Christianity as contributing decisively to the achievement of that culture (especially its Prussian form). "He did not only advocate modern civilization, but proclaimed and demanded it" (ibid., 435). Barth acknowledges that this emphasis is not as obvious in Schleiermacher's two most famous writings, *Speeches on Religion* and *The Christian Faith*, but is decisive elsewhere (in his sermons and writings on ethics).

54. Of course, critics then may charge that by de-historicizing Christianity Schleiermacher surreptitiously scours its misdeeds as nonessential to piety. Keith W. Clements contends that although Schleiermacher's thought entails the upside of securing a place for religion over against the modern critique of its past, it was not Schleiermacher's sole purpose to "rescue" religion in this way. The momentary association of feeling with knowing and doing discussed above indicates for Clements that Schleiermacher had a broader, more constructive agenda, namely, to introduce a robust theological anthropology into the restrictive, critical spirit of his age; see Clements, "Introduction," in idem., ed., *Friedrich Schleiermacher: Pioneer of Modern Theology*, The Making of Modern Theology: Nineteenth- and Twentieth-Century Texts (Minneapolis: Fortress, 1991), 36–37.

55. For a helpful overview of the way that Schleiermacher was shaped by and gave expression to defining features of Romanticism, see ibid., 7–65; on "Schleiermacher in His Context," see pp. 7–34 (esp. pp. 10–20).

56. To a degree, Schleiermacher recognizes the "input dynamic," so to speak, of sensate influence on human self-consciousness—see the discussion of freedom and dependence below. He allows reciprocity in the awareness of *relative* dependence, or that which we encounter among objects in space-time.

However, genuine *christliche Frömmigkeit* (Christian piety), entails *das schlechthinniges Abhängigkeitsgefühl* (the feeling of *absolute* dependence). For this, there can be no receipt through sensate cognition, no "givenness" to the object, as givenness to the object (God) implies a measure of freedom by the subject in relation to it, which vitiates the degree of dependence upon it.

The question is whether the appropriate non-givenness of God necessitates transcendence of space-time, that is, sensate transcendence, or whether this crucial aspect of *absolute* dependence can be secured, perhaps even better secured, by spatial-temporal objectivity. That is, might it be the case that cognition entirely brought forth, sustained, and oriented around a *particular* history, by a figure the uniqueness of whose time orients all time, so that the testimony to him exercises such a determinative summons and liberation, such a profound command and permission, as to engender a dependency yet more absolute than that of Schleiermacher's *Gefühl*?

Obviously enough, this would entail a broadened epistemology. It would suppose that the absoluteness of dependency on God can be grounded in a discrete, space-time object, this even as the object only exists in space/time by way of testimony (so that the testimony to the object takes on the all-determinative quality of the object).

Or conversely, it supposes that a kind of objectivity exists, which does not as such entail a reflexive consciousness of freedom, which is to say, that freedom is not given in the nature of objectivity per se. It supposes that such an objectivity exists as can negate every sense of freedom, as can engender a complete sense of dependency—an absolute freedom of *this* object. It strikes me that the *uniqueness* of the Christ event can engender just this coordinate sense in the human subject, for as it is perceived to rely on no precedent, as the flesh assumed is not given but created in the assumption, so the object (Incarnate One) enjoys absolute freedom and not relative freedom precisely in his space-time existence. This is actualistic epistemology: a moment-by-moment re-cognition of the moment-by-moment authority of God in the assumption of flesh.

Because it is the act of God in this event to set aside freedom, to assume not only flesh but also guilt of sin, thus to become bound by death, the objectivity of the event at once engenders a secondary freedom. The observing subject whose freedom is immediately negated by the non-precedence of the event finds a derivative freedom to respond to it, an ability given in it to say "yes" to it.

57. Niebuhr, *Schleiermacher on Christ and Religion: A New Introduction* (New York: Charles Scribner's Sons, 1964), 149–50.

58. Barth notes that Scripture is of lesser significance in Schleiermacher's account of the Christian faith than the pious feeling: "for Schleiermacher proclaiming God means proclaiming one's own piety, that is why for him preaching consists essentially of self-imparting by the preacher. And since what is to be proclaimed here is indeed a determination, but a determination of feeling, Schleiermacher gives to the Word, and with the Word, to intellectual truth, only a position of secondary importance"; (*Protestant Theology*, 454).

59. Niebuhr, *Schleiermacher on Christ and Religion*, 151.

60. Ibid., 150.

61. See ibid., 46, fn. 55: "it is clear that Schleiermacher does not believe that human words have the power to create the relationship to Christ but rather he believes that the relationship is established by Christ himself or by the Spirit of Christ. But preaching is still the means by which Christianity spreads and is nourished, according to Schleiermacher, who was a preacher all of his life."

62. Rather than sidestepping Kant, it would have been preferable for Schleiermacher to confront Kantian epistemology directly. Rather than turning to an alternative locus from which the creature reaches outward to the Creator, he ought to have moved in

the reverse, from the moment-by-moment activity of the Creator to the consequent, moment-by-moment realization of the creature. That is, Schleiermacher should have conceded that human knowing is a conjunctive happening of external influence and internal projection and allowed God to accommodate himself to this happening—but *as God*, as one who is *not* susceptible to this mode of our existence precisely when and where he makes himself susceptible to it.

63. Niebuhr, *Schleiermacher on Christ and Religion*, 139, 143.

64. I endorse Kevin Hector's reading of Schleiermacher along pneumatocentric lines. See Hector, "The Mediation of Christ's Normative Spirit: A Constructive Reading of Schleiermacher's Pneumatology," *Modern Theology* 24:1 (January 2008), 1–22. Hector demonstrates that redemption is central to Schleiermacher's program (or that, in the terms being used in this book, new creation is logically precedent to creation). Schleiermacher only wishes to speak of God and humanity in terms of the new-making work of God in Christ. The question, then, is how this new making actually transpires in the here and now, or, how redemption amounts to factual new life. Hector shows that, for Schleiermacher, there is an instructive parallel between the disciples at first and second hand: the disciples take on the life of Christ (or take part in his authentic humanity) as they take on his *judgments*. As they rightly "bind and loose" sin (Matt. 18:18), not by compulsion, but spontaneously, freely, they can meaningfully be said to enjoy new life. The same is true for us today. As Christ's normative judgments are passed along in the community formed by Christ's disciples, they become ours; or, we actually participate in that community, the church, insofar as we come to share in the disciples' normative judgments. The Spirit of Christ, then, just is this spirit of normative, communal judgment rooted in apostolic discernment:

> The Holy Spirit mediates the new humanity to us through the church's socially mediated norms. . . . Schleiermacher makes sense of the Spirit's work by talking about Christ's normative judgments becoming our own as we learn them from those whose judgments have been recognized as going on in the same way as his, and as we in turn are recognized as going on in the same way. "Going on in the same way" as Christ is a matter of *knowing* how to judge whether a certain belief or action counts as following him, and the Holy Spirit is the normative Spirit according to which such judgments are *learned and assessed*. (pp. 9–10; italics added)

Hector elaborates constructively on this notion of the Spirit as the condition of communal recognition in his book, *Theology without Metaphysics: God, Language and the Spirit of Recognition*, Issues in Theology 8 (Cambridge: Cambridge University Press, 2011).

The only emendation I would make to Hector's insightful proposal is that the disciples' normative judgments—their content and authority—are not located in the community per se, but in the scriptures upon which the community is constantly founded and brought to life. The new life of faith is always, dialectically, extrinsically-grounded even as it is existentially apprehended. The community, in turn, projects that vision forward in its distinctive living, that is, in its proclamation of the testimony of the prophets and apostles.

The reason for this is obvious: we disciples always bind and loose sin *as sinners*. That is true even as we come by the Spirit to enjoy Christ's redemption, or take part in his new life here and now. The community must constantly affirm the "not yet" of its "already" redeemed life; it must constantly, *in existential dependency*, recognize the *extrinsic* basis of its authentic self.

65. Schleiermacher, *The Christian Faith*, 12.

66. Ibid., 13.

67. Ibid.

68. Ibid., 13–14

69. Ibid., 15.

70. Ibid., 15–16.

71. Ibid., 16.

72. Ibid.

73. Ibid., 16

74. Ibid.

75. Ibid.

76. But again, for us to experience this feeling of utter dependence, we have to experience that we do indeed have freedom, that it has in fact been found to be essential to us: "but without any feeling of freedom a feeling of absolute dependence would not be possible"; ibid. We have to intuit that we *can* act for us to intuit that we cannot be otherwise than *such* actors.

77. Ibid.

78. Ibid., 17.

79. Ibid., 18.

80. This is a somewhat ironic critique given Schleiermacher's overall appreciation of the sciences; see for starters, Schleiermacher, "The Second Letter," in *On the Glaubenslehre: Two Letters to Dr. Lücke*, trans. James Duke and Francis Fiorenza, American Academy of Religion Texts and Translations Series 3 (Chico, CA: Scholars, 1981), 64–67. The issue, it seems, is not that Schleiermacher's self-consciousness was uninformed by science (or at least by the factual effectiveness of the empirical method), but that it was *insufficiently* so-informed relative to ours. Our self-consciousness obliges a judgment of inadequacy vis-a-vis the greater role of speculative philosophy in constructing meaning in his era insofar as, per Schleiermacher's own terms, it is historically mediated, just as Schleiermacher's historically mediated self-consciousness obliged him to find so much fault in earlier formulations. It is of the essence of our history to be so-disposed . And this judgment cannot be dismissed as the untoward result of sensuous-consciousness muting God-consciousness, for as Schleiermacher rightly noted, there is nothing latent in empirical investigation as such that should oppose it to Christian truth, more roundly, that should oppose a consciousness empirically informed to one attuned to its Whence.

81. Niebuhr, S*chleiermacher on Christ and Religion*, 122.

82. In understanding the human as self before self, I am more sympathetic to Johann Gottlieb Fichte than Schleiermacher was; see Fichte, *The Vocation of Man*, trans. Peter Preuss (Indianapolis: Hackett, 1987). Fichte, regrettably, subordinates knowledge to faith, but he helpfully recognizes that faith validates knowledge, and in this action, ever summons the human forward: "every knowledge presupposes something still higher as its foundation, and this ascent has no end. It is faith, this voluntary

acquiescence in the view which naturally presents itself to us because only on this view can we fulfill our vocation; it is that which first gives approval to knowledge and raises to certainty and conviction what without it could be mere deception. Faith is no knowledge, but a decision of the will to recognize the validity of knowledge" (p. 71).

83. Barth, *Protestant Theology*, 458.

84. Ibid., 458–59.

85. Ibid., 459.

86. Ibid., 460.

87. See ibid., 457 passim.

88. Ibid., 460.

89. Ibid., 462.

90. Barth, *Protestant Theology*, 463.

91. Ibid., 467.

92. This bit of reasoning anticipates an important feature of Barth's dogmatic work as it matures: the possibility of a *logos asarkos*, a Word without flesh existing in eternity prior to a *logos ensarkos*, an enfleshed Word. In early writings like the one referenced here, Barth might have appealed to a *logos asarkos* as a way of protecting the opposition between God in relation to humanity and humanity in relation to God (against Schleiermacher). But by the later volumes of the *Church Dogmatics* Barth explicitly rejected the doctrine of a *logos asarkos* (see CD IV.1, p. 52). That is because he learned to maintain the objectivity of God in the *actualism* of God's self-revelation (God elects such an existence in relation to the creature moment-by-moment) rather than in metaphysical speculation. No one has more assiduously demonstrated this train of development in Barth's thought than Bruce McCormack. See for starters, McCormack, *Karl Barth's Critically Realistic, Dialectical Theology: Its Genesis and Development 1909–1936* (Oxford: Oxford University Press, 1995). McCormack locates the decisive shift happening with the development of Barth's unique doctrine of election (see CD II.2). Barth argues that the primary referent of election is not humanity (groups of saved and damned), but God in God's self: God elects to be for humanity and not against it. Thus, with regard to Schleiermacher, Barth could continue to argue for a distinction between humanity in relation to God and God in relation to humanity, not by appeal to a metaphysical construct, but by appeal to divine will. God maintains within God's self-determination God's priority to the creature in the very event that God has existence with (and only with) the creature.

93. Barth, *Protestant Theology*, 468.

94. Ibid.

95. Ibid.

96. Barth, *Protestant Theology*, 471; italics in original. Barth notes that "in some depth of his mind Schleiermacher must have intended otherwise" than to make human religious consciousness the theme of theology (ibid., 472), and so to lose the otherness of God in the depths of the human psyche.

97. I am attempting to make productive use of salient features of Schleiermacher's thought while sharing with Barth (and others) critical reservations about an

anthropocentric tendency latent in that thought, which I correct, also with Barth, by appealing to a more deliberately dialectical kind of theology. There may, however, be a way of reading Schleiermacher as less anthropocentric and more christocentric, and so muting the degree of critique in my presentation.

Hector stresses the actualism underwriting Schleiermacher's Christology; see "Actualism and Incarnation: The High Christology of Friedrich Schleiermacher," *IJST* 8:3 (July 2006), 307–22. As we have seen, God is, for Schleiermacher, pure activity; "God" can never become for us an object without entailing a measure of counterinfluence (relative freedom), in which case, we would not be *absolutely* dependent on him, and he would not be *God*. Christ Jesus, pace Barth, was fully God and historically particular insofar as "at every moment of his life, [he] perfectly apprehended God's pure activity, and perfectly reproduced it" (311). God is God in giving life to the other, existing as generative love; Christ is God in that he incarnates that life-giving love.

Indeed, it is of the very action that makes God of God constantly to be uniting deity and humanity in Christ: "the union of divine and human is new every moment . . . not because Christ is not fully divine, but because this is precisely the way a human can *be* fully united with divinity-as-pure-act" (313). God exists in the continual act of uniting himself to another, which he does in Christ, thus Christ is at once the product and reproducer of the divine life-act.

Christ perfectly receives God's work and perfectly instantiates it. His own work reproduces the love of God in others. This takes place as they are made to share his perfect God-consciousness. Christ "acts upon us, in such a way that *his* activity becomes *our* activity" (318). Christ makes us to be purely receptive of God and to reproduce his work in the world. This "acting upon" takes the form of Christ's Spirit, that is, the common spirit of the community founded upon Christ (319).

Such a reading *may* allow us more readily to connect with Schleiermacher to the extent that it objectifies (in Christ) what appears to be a universal human potentiality, and in this, more thoroughly differentiates between Christ and humanity, clarifying the relation of God to humanity and humanity to God, or, the distinction and relation between Word and Spirit. My only reservations continue to be that, one, this account trades upon a diluted construal of sin (still making redemption into a progress of maturing in Christ rather than confrontation by Christ and transformation into his way of life). And two, the making-present of Christ by his Spirit in the form of the communal spirit still tends in an anthropocentric direction by relativizing the significance of the witness of the prophets and apostles as the ongoing ground of the community.

It will not due for Barth apologists simply to regurgitate Barth's witty quips against Schleiermacher, since doing so obscures their common interests. And it will not due for Schleiermacher apologists simply to point out that "Schleiermacher was not dim-witted" and that "we can learn from his theology" (321) as a means of skipping over Barth's criticisms. Of course Schleiermacher wasn't muttonheaded. But if we must resort to this kind of base argumentation, then we have to note that Barth wasn't dopey, either. Theology that would learn from the one must constructively engage the other.

98. See CD I.1 §8.

99. The astrophysicist reminds us that we launch the James Webb telescope into orbit not in order to get closer to the heavenlies, but to get powerful perceptual apparatuses beyond the "fishbowl" distortion of earth's atmosphere.

Chapter 2

The Human and Creation

וַיִּטַּ֞ע יְהוָ֧ה אֱלֹהִ֛ים גַּן־בְּעֵ֖דֶן מִקֶּ֑דֶם וַיָּ֣שֶׂם שָׁ֔ם אֶת־הָֽאָדָ֖ם אֲשֶׁ֥ר יָצָֽר׃
וַיַּצְמַ֞ח יְהוָ֤ה אֱלֹהִים֙ מִן־הָ֣אֲדָמָ֔ה כָּל־עֵ֛ץ נֶחְמָ֥ד לְמַרְאֶ֖ה וְט֣וֹב לְמַאֲכָ֑ל וְעֵ֤ץ הַֽחַיִּים֙ בְּת֣וֹךְ הַגָּ֔ן וְעֵ֕ץ הַדַּ֖עַת ט֥וֹב וָרָֽע׃
וְנָהָר֙ יֹצֵ֣א מֵעֵ֔דֶן לְהַשְׁק֖וֹת אֶת־הַגָּ֑ן וּמִשָּׁם֙ יִפָּרֵ֔ד וְהָיָ֖ה לְאַרְבָּעָ֥ה רָאשִֽׁים׃
שֵׁ֥ם הָֽאֶחָ֖ד פִּישׁ֑וֹן ה֣וּא הַסֹּבֵ֗ב אֵ֚ת כָּל־אֶ֣רֶץ הַֽחֲוִילָ֔ה אֲשֶׁר־שָׁ֖ם הַזָּהָֽב׃
וּֽזֲהַ֛ב הָאָ֥רֶץ הַהִ֖וא ט֑וֹב שָׁ֥ם הַבְּדֹ֖לַח וְאֶ֥בֶן הַשֹּֽׁהַם׃
וְשֵֽׁם־הַנָּהָ֥ר הַשֵּׁנִ֖י גִּיח֑וֹן ה֣וּא הַסּוֹבֵ֔ב אֵ֖ת כָּל־אֶ֥רֶץ כּֽוּשׁ׃
וְשֵׁ֨ם הַנָּהָ֤ר הַשְּׁלִישִׁי֙ חִדֶּ֔קֶל ה֥וּא הַֽהֹלֵ֖ךְ קִדְמַ֣ת אַשּׁ֑וּר וְהַנָּהָ֥ר הָֽרְבִיעִ֖י ה֥וּא פְרָֽת׃
וַיִּקַּ֛ח יְהוָ֥ה אֱלֹהִ֖ים אֶת־הָֽאָדָ֑ם וַיַּנִּחֵ֣הוּ בְגַן־עֵ֔דֶן לְעָבְדָ֖הּ וּלְשָׁמְרָֽהּ׃
וַיְצַו֙ יְהוָ֣ה אֱלֹהִ֔ים עַל־הָֽאָדָ֖ם לֵאמֹ֑ר מִכֹּ֥ל עֵֽץ־הַגָּ֖ן אָכֹ֥ל תֹּאכֵֽל׃
וּמֵעֵ֗ץ הַדַּ֙עַת֙ ט֣וֹב וָרָ֔ע לֹ֥א תֹאכַ֖ל מִמֶּ֑נּוּ כִּ֗י בְּי֛וֹם אֲכָלְךָ֥ מִמֶּ֖נּוּ מ֥וֹת תָּמֽוּת׃

The LORD God planted a garden in Eden, to the east, and he put there the human that he had formed.

And the LORD God caused to sprout from the ground every tree that was pleasing in appearance and good for food, with a tree of life in the middle of the garden, and a tree of the knowledge of good and evil.

A river flowing from Eden watered the garden; from there it was separated and became four headwaters.

The name of the first was Pishon; it wound through the whole land of Havilah, where there was gold.

The gold of that land was good; bdellium was there, and onyx stone.

The name of the second river was Gihon; it wound through the whole land of Cush.

The name of the third river was Tigris; it ran along the east side of Assyria. And the fourth river was Euphrates.

The LORD God took the human and settled him in the garden of Eden to work it and to keep it.

And the LORD God commanded the human, saying, "You surely may
eat from every tree in the garden,
but as for the tree of the knowledge of good and evil, you may not
eat from it, for in the day you eat from it, you surely will die." (Gen.
2:8–17).

Elizabeth Johnson attaches an aesthetic quality to nature's evolutionary
interdependence:

[Darwin's] is a deeply ecological vision of nature. It entails a network of intricate interdependencies and mutual relations expressed in competition or profitable cooperation. Over time, each being's structure becomes related, in the most
essential yet often hidden manner, to that of all other organic beings with which
it competes for food, or on which it preys, or from which it has to escape, or near
which it has to reproduce, or with which it cooperates. . . . The natural world's
beauty is due to the mutual interactions of species in the struggle for life.[1]

As we observed at the end of chapter one, the forces of nature decisively
shape creaturely existence, including the force of evolutionary adaptation.
The story of freestanding individuals over against the world and other creatures is a fable. We are as we become, and are forced to become, within the
struggle for life.

That predation, for instance, should be characterized as contributing to
"beauty" remains controversial. Squarely facing the bloody and vicious
brutalities of "the mutual interactions of species" invites alternative description—bestial, pitiless, hideous. The struggle for life appears less attractive
from the perspective of the prey. Or is it that the very living of life is only as
participant in a web that obliges sacrifice, that the very existence of all lives
happens for the sake of others (so that death, even violent, might contribute
to a total good)—is it that such thorough, finely-grained mutuality evokes a
more sublime order of beauty? Does Eden depict creation *absent* evolutionary
interdependence or creation as *fulfillment* of such interdependence?

We have already established that the creature finds herself in an effected
harmony, and in contributing to it. Life emerges out of relationship for the
sake of relationship. As Larry Rasmussen puts it, "Covenantal bonds—
between God and Earth, between God and humankind, between humans and
one another and the rest of life—establish, order, and sustain creation as we
know it. The way of covenant, for better and worse, is the way things *are*."[2]
Humanity's covenantal constitution between God and world confers upon
it the elective potential to be self-determinatively for the world; to bear the
will of God to the world for the sake of the world. Creation's harmony recurs
in continuing creaturely affirmation, as the human is moved to recognize

("know," in Schleiermacher's language) her dependence and to act ("do") in behalf of the world.

This chapter and the next explore the dynamic, life-giving circumstance of humanity's volitional self-determination in behalf of creation. In this, they look forward, not backward, to Eden. Schleiermacher's close correlation between "creation" and "preservation" points to this direction: creation entails the ongoing quality of *becoming*. And Pope Francis supplies a practical framework within which to locate the ethical consequences of creation's vibrant interdependence. But first, some observations on the spiritual aims of the biblical text.

EXEGESIS OF GEN. 2:8–17

"The LORD God planted a garden in Eden, to the east." The mythopoeic quality of the creation account, present but under-toned in 2:4b–7, now takes over. The account shifts away from humdrum shrubbery and turns to a mysterious garden in a mythical land out of which flows a mighty river watering, among other things, a tree of life and a tree of enigmatic knowledge, which river divides into geographically evasive headwaters (other than the familiar Tigris and Euphrates), which seem to encircle the then-known world.

Such description tempts imagination of a halcyon paradise. The Septuagint inclines this direction. It renders גַּן־בְּעֵדֶן ("garden in Eden"), παράδεισος ἐν Εδεμ ("paradise in Eden"), highlighting the rhapsodic, almost other-worldly character of the garden, and suggesting a time-past free of sin, suffering, and mortality. But this is a wrong turn. Westermann notes the existence of a Persian loan word, פַּרְדֵּס ("paradise"), that made its way into the OT (Neh. 2:8, Eccl. 2:5, Song of Songs 4:13), associations with which may have exercised undue influence on later interpretation of Genesis 2. "As a loan word [פַּרְדֵּס] is impressed with distinct associations, such as we attach to the word paradise. But this is not the meaning in [Gen.] 2:8. It is rather a fertile, beautiful and well-watered garden with trees."[3]

Eden is not Elysium.[4] It is a depiction of vigorous, vibrant existence; life in harmony with its source. It is a depiction of fertility, lushness, effortless abundance. Eden is humanity's intended home. The name does not refer to an isolable location but sketches a scene of ultimate vitality. Eden cannot be found by a cleverly led expedition or in any sense discovered "under," "over," or "within" the world. The garden depicts a *state of existence* that God wishes *for the whole of the world*. It is a *way of being* promised to creation and into which creation is summoned. Conjuring an ancient temple scene with its images of abundant life, the account invites the reader to perceive and desire, in fact to seek a characteristic harmony between God

and the world. Uninterrupted fertility and lushness are found "here," in this
covenantal union.

"Garden in Eden" designates a fictive geography, then, but in order to
engender a factual hope. Eden connotes a "there and then" only to frame a
manifestly existential "here and now." It situates the reader in a definite perception of what might be, and so initiates a distinct turn from what is. This
movement is imbedded in the account's rhetorical style, as Barth writes:

> It is of the very essence of such passages that while they are concrete in their men-
> tion of places they are only semi-concrete; that while they are geographical, their
> geography is indefinite and unpredictable. . . . It is palpable that in these passages
> we have to do with a genuine consideration of real events, persons and things,
> but only with a consideration and therefore not with a historical review but with
> constructions which do not have their origin in observation but in imagination.[5]

Gen. 2–3 offers a kind of narrative that by its structure and thematic content
enlarges perception to encompass new possibilities. These chapters stir up
not contemplation of cartography and archaeology, but, through their peculiar
geography and landscape, of imagination of alternative existence. "In Eden"
(בְּעֵדֶן) and "to the east" (מִקֶּדֶם) point to place but with a deliberate abstruseness
so as evoke a sense of exploration, to move the reader into a state of eager
prospect.

Again, not a fantasized pleasure: we may summarily agree with the bulk
of modern interpreters concerning עֵדֶן that though meaning "luxury, dainty,
delight,"[6] *Eden* functions as a proper name. Similarly, although מִקֶּדֶם can
mean "from before," which is to say "ancient time, aforetime,"[7] in Gen. 2:8,
it simply means *eastward*. Pointing to the east gestures toward light's origin.
In an ancient view, it symbolizes divine illumination (revelation). Together
with the fecundity of the garden, which "was a sign of God's presence in and
blessing on Eden," the total description is "symbolic of a place where God
dwells"[8]

That is the central point: Gen. 2:8ff translates the constitutive unity of
humanity with God established in 2:4b–7 into the symbolism of *place*. They
decisively locate the human "there." We note that the human is not created
in Eden but יְהוָה אֱלֹהִים וַיָּשֶׂם שָׁם אֶת־הָאָדָם ("and the LORD God put the human
there"). The human is *brought to* its intended existence, drawn into fuller life
than simply animated dust. We cannot assume that the human is fully the
creature that the Creator willed strictly by virtue of the gift of breath. The
creature is more dynamically constructed than that; her being is in actual living before God and thus a dwelling-into.

The creature is not a thing unto itself, which may or may not subsequently
enter into relation with its Maker and surroundings, but which, whether doing

so or not, remains fully and completely this self-composed entity. On the contrary, the creature *only* realizes its creatureliness in coming once more to harmonious relation; her "ontology," if we may appropriate an ancient and potentially misleading category, is in this determinative movement. Or more strongly, the creature only exists *as* a particular *relation*. Any state of existence that falls short of covenantal mutuality is nonexistence.

The creature is made for covenant—such an entity to exist only as the integrated unity of divine breath, earthen dust, and existential interdependence—among creation before Creator:

> [Humanity's] creation does not begin in the Garden but is completed in it. His creation commences by reason of the fact that elsewhere, in a place not indicated, he is formed from dust and quickened by the divine breath. And it is continued in the fact that when this has taken place he is put by God in the Garden and brought to rest there—the rest of his normal existence in relationship to his Creator and to the earth as the creaturely sphere.[9]

Barth rightly observes that *adam* comes to be what he is, he inhabits his authenticity, in the eastward harmony of Creator and creation. Thus, the "there" of Eden is the anticipative condition of the creature's genuineness; that his being should be authenticated in the event that he has life in God's presence for the sake of the world. In each instant, by coming to know and to enact this liminal state—by confessing utter dependence upon God and participating with God in bringing life to the ground—creation takes life.

The second creation account cultivates a sense of longing and expectation standing in constructive pull with a sense of privation. The privation is not the loss of a once-held possession. Rather, it is a paradoxical sense of not yet inhabiting creation's natural state. The garden *is* creation's right state of existence, but as such, even though it is entirely recognizable and desirable, it remains unrealized. Humanity fails to enjoy it because of the exercise of a certain fallibility, a certain covenant-shattering instinct to self-actuation and self-regard, which we will discuss in due course. (We will see in two chapters that this fallibility is not yet "sin," but it is the ground of sin.)[10]

For now, the Edenic creation account situates humankind relative to its homeland. The garden in Eden designates a species-future. It indicates a dwelling in God's rest and only as thus, a *residence*. All other dwelling is a temporary *sojourn*, as a stranger in a foreign land. It is only in Eden that the human qua human in-habits; only there that the conventional shape of her existence takes place. The there-ness and then-ness, in other words, of the biblical saga, the not-yet-ness of Eden, constructs a here and now particularized by eschatological tension. Eden's beckoning structures a "today" characterized by promise.

It "belongs to [humanity's] creation that God prepares for him this pleasure garden—which is supremely delightful because it is God's Garden, but also delightful because it is a normal dwelling-place appropriate to him—and that God brings him to this part of the earth to fulfill his determination for the whole earth and therefore really to live."[11] Authentic human existence is characterized by the condition of delight that comes by standing openly before God and by responsibly stewarding creation. By moving the reader Eden-ward, or, in structuring a present *after* a definite harmonious future and so according to a concrete longing, the account places the reader in a twofold temporality; it makes her to live con-temporarily with the world as it is and as it will be, in constant expectation of its transformation.

The text identifies the human as a being of the world by describing the world's material constitution in the same language as that of the human. Not only does God bring forth the *adam* "from the *adamah*" (מִן־הָאֲדָמָה), but God does the same with every tree. Because of a shared ground of origination, there can be no difference between the fate of the human and of other lives "from the earth." All are of the same promise. It has always been an aberrant faith that has ascribed to humanity qualitative specialness concerning its redemption relative to the world. The world eagerly awaits its redemption along with the human's (Romans 8).

The human does manifest the creation's shared dependency in a unique way, however, which makes it to become a coordinate means of creation's hope (in which effected becoming, again, humanity is achieved). The human receives a share in God's knowledge and thus made to take a part in the divine intention for creation. The human lives into her promise only as she gains this perspective.

A tree of the knowledge of good and evil becomes comprehensible as a symbol of that knowledge whereby humanity enacts its constitutive relation. Its significance is not in supplying an object lesson in general obedience but rather in occasioning a concrete order of existence. Sarna compellingly concludes that עֵץ הַדַּעַת טוֹב וָרָע ("[the] tree of the knowledge of good and evil") functions as a merism. We are "to understand 'good and bad' as undifferentiated parts of a totality."[12] The tree represents God's comprehensive knowledge and is thus forbidden as a thing that the human per se might possess. This understanding need not preclude others, which focus on the particularly moral character of heavenly wisdom; that differentiation between good and evil resides finally in divine (not creaturely) determination. Humanity is established in the obedience that trusts God and waits expectantly on God's promise.

The self-knowledge whereby humanity is achieved is more, therefore, than mere content. It involves also dispositional acceptance of her station as *secunda*. That this is so is confirmed by the fact that when, against God's command, the human eats of the tree and her knowledge is expanded she still does not become the *means* of her own achievement. New knowledge does not automatically confer new ability. In fact, with acquisition of this knowledge, the human more fully experiences her *inability*. No doubt to the great surprise of the ancient reader, acquiring the knowledge of good and evil does not confer the privilege of *theosis*.

Humanity's realization in dependence on God, over against becoming god, is given in acceptance of the divine prohibition, but not in remaining ignorant of a given sum of knowledge content. As we will discuss, God creates the human to enjoy the expansion of knowledge, to learn without preset stops. The tree of the knowledge of good and evil is closely connected to the "tree of the life" (עֵץ הַחַיִּים), because the obverse of accepting the divine limit is not staying ill-informed, but receiving the divine permission. The two function together in the same existential moment. "The prohibition," Bonhoeffer comments, "means nothing other than this: Adam, you are who you are because of me, your Creator; so now be what you are. You re a free creature, so now be that."[13] Appointment of divine limit does not inhibit humanity's free agency or the fullness of its potential as creature, but the opposite: it is the means of human vitality. The human may freely receive the gift of life and the growth, including growth in understanding, that it entails.

As we come to vv. 16–17, we arrive at the linchpin that holds the second creation myth together: the command and permission of God. "Command inheres as an integral part of the created order," Fretheim writes. "To be truly a creature entails limits; to honor limits becomes necessary if the creation will develop as God intends."[14] A certain relational order is essential to the creature's, and by extension, to creation's achievement; limitations are written into the fabric of createdness. *"The human being's limit is at the center of human existence,"* concludes Bonhoeffer, "not on the margin."[15]

The truth that humanity achieves authenticity in affirming the goodness of limit (that accepting the command not to eat of the tree of the knowledge of good already affirms the good) correlates with the overarching metaphor of sculpting, which as we have seen informs the Yahwist's account—that the divine act of creation rightly entails the establishment of contours and edges. Constitutive relation, which is to say, the quality of mutual interface according to which thing-ness is given rise, involves the positing of "this-not-that." Or, the very construct of possibility—how this might become that, or become other than that—supposes the underlying actuality of posited limits.

In a threefold sense, the divine decree that something shall be (not only with respect to an object but also any state of things) is a *binding* Word. The creative command is binding in the sense that it definitively refuses the alternative, namely, nothingness. It is, begging indulgence of a clunky double-negative, establishment that nothing shall not be. Thus, second, the decree is binding also of God. God commits God's self as if by law to the continuance of non-nothing (as we discussed under theses 7–9 in introduction).

It is binding, third, in the sense that it establishes the boundary conditions of *creaturely* existence. The divine decree binds createdness to spatial-temporality; the human qua human instantiates space–time agency, enacts a history. The human only has existence historically, as an entity with and among entities for a generation. Standing "before" and "after" others in sensate navigation—taking in and giving off light, sound, motion, and setting one another in place via discourse—gives shape to, creates, distinctive existence (a more or less coherent series of events that establish a lifespan).

The opposite of limitation is not infinity, but un-creation, nothing. Or, the alternative to space–time is not a timeless cosmos, but nothing, unlimitedness. Unlimitedness is not the antithesis of nothing, but its equivalent. To create is to measure and fathom, to negate or bind, to set limits to chaotic disorder (Genesis 1). To be Creator is to exist in active refusal of un-limit and non-being. It is constantly to uphold the divine existence precisely *as* self-limiting limit-setter.

"Eternity" does not describe the divine condition as abstracted *Gegenstand* to nothing. For God to be "eternal" is perpetually to will and enact a self-establishing decision: to live by refusal of the prospect of nonexistence, this with reference to "God," first, and to another that is not God, second (as the decision made only with reference to God would likewise remove all limit by equating "God" with sheer "existence"). For God to be eternal means always to have existence in *ad extra* motion. For God to be eternal is to create.

For the creature, we can conceptualize how life takes rise through limitation in a variety of ways.[16] Modern physics has shown that world-existence is not comprised of things naturally at rest, which are subsequently set into motion, so that (thinking theologically) any cosmic telos would take the shape of return, after development through motion, to a natural, albeit higher, restful state. Things are just the opposite. And we should note that, in commending this historic shift in scientific perspective, we here part company with much of the classical theological tradition, including our dear friend, Augustine, with whom we will otherwise have occasion to interact favorably.

Things are most naturally in motion, and to achieve classifiable existence, they must manifest some sort of reiterative interaction—bonds and rules of engagement or "natural laws" whereby they sometimes attract, other times repel, sometimes fuse, other times fissure, sometimes amplify, other times moderate, but always with tightly interconnected consequences. Thing-ness emerges as relation constructs possibility. Atoms form molecules; molecules give rise to cells; cells give rise to organs; organs give rise to corpus; corpus interacts productively with corpora. Things never come to *be* in themselves, but their self-hood is achieved as associative event; they obtain existence as *outcome* only in simultaneous, participative *contribution*.

Language operation also demonstrates the pregnancy of limit. Enwording is an act of territory-marking; a setting out of this concept and not that. It is a *practice* no less so than any physical action; one grows also into her concept-making and -expressing. Territorial boundaries become more precise and defined and can be made less-so. Language operation involves co-structuring, constructing. Not merely intake and description of human interaction, language also confers meaning, value, and direction upon creaturely existence. It frames what came before, what is, and what can be by description and evaluation. It structures reality at a meeting between what has been and what might be, and so becomes a force, a determinative factor in life.

As the human engages the spiral of linguistic reception and performance, he finds and cultivates the ability to introduce false limits, or, as the case may be, to posit in speech false description and misleading evaluation (such as the falsehood of unlimited existence), and this, as we will later see, seeds his destruction. Through language the human can construct and desire an entirely artificial existence, pursue it, and in a way, he also may achieve it. He surely will die. Once again, Bonhoeffer: "losing *the limit* Adam has lost *creatureliness*. Adam as limitless or boundless [Der grenzenlose Adam] can no longer be addressed with regard to Adam's creatureliness."[17]

Verses 16 and 17 foreshadow this consequence. They present parallel intensive constructions (an infinitive absolute followed by an imperfect verb in repetition): מוֹת תָּמוּת . . . אָכֹל תֹּאכֵל, "to eat you eat . . . to die you die," or as above, "you surely may eat . . . you surely will die."[18] This parallel intensification has the effect of creating a kind of bookend, not between "you surely may eat" (of all the trees) and "you surely may not eat" (of the tree of the knowledge of good and evil) as we might expect (the latter prohibition is a simple Qal imperfect—לֹא תֹאכַל). That is, we do not have a balanced contrast between divine permission and command. We rather have a statement of the consequence of using the divine permission to violate the divine command.

The biblical deity's intent, as a rule against that of other ancient near-eastern deities, is to situate the human in such a condition as to invite fulfillment of his distinctive creatureliness. God is such a God as to orient the human toward Eden and move him there. In the act of such placement, God freely supplies for the human, quite before and apart from any supplication by the human, the means of his fulfillment. Not only this: in freely supplying human need, God makes the human to delight in that supply, which is to say, God predestines him to be at home in the garden. The human is made to use God's permission to obey God's command.

In this, the tree of life does not contain magical vegetation, nor does it present a symbol of life attained by physical or spiritual discipline. On the contrary, however trees of life functioned more broadly in ancient near-eastern religious practice,[19] the Edenic foliage is a symbol of the free gift of God, intended for equally free receipt by God's creature. The freedom of the human to receive it correlates, as noted, with obedience; the human who at once accepts the goodness of his limit before God, in creation, accepts the potential latent in it. The human may reach for the tree of life precisely as he does not reach for the other tree. It is of the essence of the divine permission that humankind might evermore fully and richly confirm its *placement* in Eden. But again, he might not thus live; he might die. In fact, he surely will die insofar as he does not thus live.

SCHLEIERMACHER AND HUMANITY'S LIMINAL EXISTENCE

As God settles the human in the garden, he inclines and empowers her לְעָבְדָהּ וּלְשָׁמְרָהּ, "to work it and to keep it." She lives in this responsive co-action, working at the permission of God.[20] Her cooperation by grace actualizes her liminal existence: by accepting the divine permission she enacts both her utter dependence upon the Creator (along with creation) *and* her concurrent union with the Creator, her being a partner alongside the Creator (in behalf of creation). Schleiermacher reaches a handful of conclusions as he considers the twin doctrines of creation and preservation, which enhance understanding of the human in this in-between condition.

Schleiermacher treats the doctrine of creation at the outset of his discussion of dogmatics proper; it is the "first section" in the "first part of the system of doctrine," which follows his famous discussion of method in the introduction to the *Glaubenslehre* discussed previously. He notes the traditional, twofold formulation of creation proper and preservation: expression of the primal relation "that the world exists only in absolute dependence upon God, is divided in Church doctrine into the two propositions—that the world was created by God, and that God sustains the world."[21] But as in other areas, the principle of absolute dependence obliges Schleiermacher to revise the traditional formulation.

He first modulates the usual distinction between creation proper and preservation. For Schleiermacher, "there is no sufficient reason for retaining this division."[22] Schleiermacher reasons that differentiating between the divine activity in generating the world and in sustaining it implies that God moves between activity and rest (from making the world to managing it, if you like). This amounts to a "God" *dependent* upon patterns of creaturely sequence. Cessation of God's creative activity further suggests that the world at large initially took its determination from God but subsequently became self-determining with regard to its individuals (as the system of nature once established by God produced its own outcomes in the stead of God's life-producing influence), which destroys the feeling of *absolute* dependence. And conversely, moving from preservation to creation, alternation in divine activity would suggest that at least some parts of the world originated outside of God's life-giving influence, that although the whole world is now sustained by God, the elements comprising any present circumstance might have been conditioned by some other preexisting causation, which also would destroy the feeling of *absolute* dependence:

> If we think of the creation of the world as a single divine act and including the whole system of nature, then this conception may be a complete expression of the feeling of absolute dependence, so long as we do not conceive of that act as having ceased, and consequently imagine on the one side, in God, an alternation of activity and rest relatively to the world, and on the other side, in the world, an alternation between a determination of the whole through God and a determination of all single individuals through each other. In the same way if we regard Preservation as a continuous divine activity exerted on the whole course of the world, covering the first beginning no less than each subsequent state, then this is a complete expression of the self-consciousness in question, provided we do not think the origin of the world is conditioned by something else before and after that activity. For otherwise, in every situation only some elements would be dependent on the divine activity, while the rest, though ever so small a part, would be conditioned by what had previously existed.[23]

If we are rightly to express the world's dependency on God, which piety demands, then God must remain "the sole Determinant"[24] throughout a unified doctrine of creation and preservation.[25] Not only the world as a whole, but also its individual parts in their respective continuance must find determination in some fashion through God, and that determination must not cease or "alternate." That does not mean that God exercises *direct* influence on creation in each instant or that in creating God occasions all things *simultaneously*. God's life-giving activity can remain uninterrupted and without alternation and still entail sequential or successive creative acts. We must quote Schleiermacher once more at some length:

> With our increased knowledge of the world, we may indeed conceive the heavenly bodies and all the life developing upon them as particular things which have not all necessarily come into existence simultaneously; yet their successive origination must obviously be also conceived as the active continuance of formative forces which must be resident in finite existence. And thus however far our consciousness extends, we find nothing the origin of which cannot be

brought under the concept of Preservation. . . . In the same way, if we regard individual things as created, and follow this a step further, we find that the preservation of these same things is equivalent to that alternation of changes and movements in which their being perdures. But as these always form more or less coherent series, there is always something new implied either in the beginning of each series of activities or in the effects produced by a subject—something which was not formerly contained in that particular thing. This is, therefore, a new beginning and can be regarded as a creation.[26]

Heavenly bodies can be brought into existence through powerful cosmic forces yet today. Their successive origination, and whatever (alien!) life develops on them, remains a part of God's original work of creation *through* "the active continuance of formative forces which must be resident in finite existence." However it may be conceived (power, gift, germination, energy transfer), or scientifically encountered (the formation of elements in the collapse of stars, the emergence of planets through clumping gas and dust), the creative agency by which things begin is not exhausted in and by their beginning but endures throughout their existence. Thus, creation can be thought of as a kind of preservation or reiterative enactment of life's source resident in discrete things.

Coming at it from the other angle, a thing is preserved, or endures as such, through development and adaptation, alternation of coherent series of changes and movements. It is hard to know all that Schleiermacher might have in mind by such series, but minimally, for instance, we observe that offspring are of the same qualities as their forebears, but are genuinely new beings, in that their existence manifests possibilities that were not there in earlier generations (characteristics like height, agility, intellectual range). Thus, preservation can be thought of as events of becoming, or creation.

Schleiermacher's treatment of creation-preservation as an integrated whole thus entails a highly dynamic characterization of the God–world relation. The world exists as consequence of God's continuing determination and ever-manifests God's creative agency. And God exists in the act of sourcing and upholding the interconnected productivity of the world. This dynamism is, in my judgment, highly commendable; it helpfully expresses the existential correlation between redemption and creation to which Israel's history bears witness. The world exists not only as *outcome* but also as continuing *manifestation* of generosity, of bidding newness. The being of the world—the essence of space-time—is as grace, opportunity-making regardless of merit, indeed in the face of every force that would deny opportunity and take life; it is as covenantal love.

However, as I have indicated, even though Schleiermacher situates his reflections exclusively within the life of the church, he is not so much concerned about the biblical witness. He does not correlate the re-creative force resident in the world with the action of the text, its Spirit; he does not connect the transformative power of creation within a definitive faith-event, but with a general religious feeling of dependence. Neither, in this regard, does he connect the doctrine of preservation (and with it, creation) to the Person of Christ, God's assumption of creation—that God has existence in relating God's self to creation in a productive, mutually determinative way.[27]

This leaves a powerful vein of thought untapped. Schleiermacher might have described the coming into being of the world and its enduring readiness for newness by appealing to a more-clearly "Christo-morphic"[28] structure. He might have described the world's perseverant generosity after the manner of God's own, that is, God's moment-by-moment, self-determinative activity of setting God's self in relation to a definite people by the action of Word and Spirit. This would have added a good deal of concrete, referential substance to Schleiermacher's account of creation-preservation.

Had Schleiermacher availed himself of this option, he happily would have been forced to reconsider his absolute distinction between divine and temporal existence (the way that he ties the absoluteness of the experience of dependence to the abstract absoluteness of ontological contrast between God and time). By connecting the interrelatedness of creation-preservation to the new-making work of God *in Word and Spirit*, Schleiermacher would have had to conclude that God's self-determination entails willed limitation. God assigns God's self a being-with-time, a "being-as" Lord over time within each instant of time, a being in becoming (after which the world has its existence). Schleiermacher could have taken this Christo/Pneumatological direction.

But instead, he explicitly refuses any notion of divine limitation and reinforces the distinction between God and time: "if . . . we think of God the Creator in any way as limited, and thus in His activity resembling that which should be absolutely dependent on Him, then the feeling expressing this dependence . . . could not be true (since equality and dependence neutralize each other)."[29] Of course, this reasoning does not follow as simply and directly as Schleiermacher suggests. Van Harvey states the problem exactly:

> It doesn't follow . . . from the fact that we are absolutely dependent on God, that God is absolutely independent from us. Yet Schleiermacher affirms that statement over and over again, and he says it, it seems to me, in direct violation of the limits he sets himself in terms of his own method, namely, that we will say nothing about God that is not actually given in the feeling of absolute dependence. That God is absolutely independent is not given in the feeling of absolute dependence. All that is given in the feeling of absolute dependence is

that I am absolutely dependent. . . . God may be receptive to my existence, in some sense dependent, so to speak, on me.[30]

Schleiermacher's conclusion derives from propositional polarity—the abstract opposition between *ideas* (or semantic ranges) of "dependence" and "equality"—not from the actual content of pious feeling. Nothing in the feeling of absolute dependence requires the absolute independence of its Whence; only a secondary inference in the realm of *knowledge* could require that, but appealing to such reasoned inference contradicts Schleiermacher's very method.

"God may be receptive to my existence," as Harvey writes, and still be the One on whom I am absolutely (and not only relatively) dependent. We covered this ground well enough in chapter 1, but it bears mentioning again in this context as a way of at least signaling how we might translate Schleiermacher's religion-centric theo-logic in to a more deliberately revelation-centric pneumato-logic. "God" could receive a *name* from the creature, from the creature's timebound linguistic faculty, and not cease to be God; God could be YHWH, the intimate companion of the creature in the history of redemption and still be Creator. In fact, God could be Creator just as God *is* with the creature in the history of redemption—*as* Giver of Life.[31]

But again, Schleiermacher instead reinforces the God/time polarity, now, ironically, by rejecting the classical distinction between matter and form: "from Hilary and Anselm we can see how easily, behind the denial of matter, may lie the idea of the pre-existence of form . . . [but] if there are two divine activities which, like preparation and creation, can be conceived of only in a definite time-sequence, then God is no longer outside all contact with time."[32] Ancient and medieval theologians of the West argued that material things do not preexist, but only immaterial things do; *forms* of material reality were present in the mind of God before they were made. They argued in this way in order to remove any mutability or possibility of change from "God"; ever-decaying matter does not inhabit the realm of God's preexistence. In this, they more or less thought within the defining constructs of Neoplatonic metaphysics. In God's *immutable* reality (mind) are preexistent archetypes of changeable matter. Schleiermacher reasons that such a distinction already implies change in God, a stage of preparation *followed by* a stage of creation: "as the two terms of the antithesis, matter and form, are not in the same relation to God, He is drawn away from an attitude of neutrality to the antithesis and placed in some degree under it."[33]

Schleiermacher thus revises the traditional understanding of form and matter to deny preexistence to *both*. "It cannot be said of the original creation that it was created by the activity of foreknowledge prior to its actual existence."[34] In this regard, as Augustine also observed,[35] there can be no time "before" the world, "since a time before the world could only have referred to God, and He would then be placed in time."[36] The very conception of before-ness already supposes time and cannot be predicated of God vis-a-vis the world without making "God" subject to a characteristic of the world and thus compromising piety.

Indeed, although he does not think that the feeling of dependence would be destroyed if God created the world "in time," which is to say, if God generated the idea of time itself and the forces and objects of material reality in this construct, that feeling would be "endangered" by such a teaching. "In so far as the idea of a creation in time must be related to that of a beginning of divine activity *ad extra* or a beginning of divine sovereignty . . . God would be brought within the region of change and subjected to time."[37] In order to steer clear of any conceptual territory where "beginning" applies to God and "the antithesis between Him and finite things would be lessened,"[38] Schleiermacher concludes that we must think of creation taking place eternally. This conclusion is not, as I suggest, problematic, but Schleiermacher does make problematic concessions in getting to it.

Schleiermacher could have accepted the classical differentiation between form and matter as a simple way of reinforcing the ontic distinction he wishes to maintain between God and time (in order to preserve his abstractly postulated absoluteness of creaturely dependence). That was, after all, part of the point of the classical differentiation in the first place! Or, even better, since Schleiermacher rightly saw the inherent weakness in the classical position (it supposes the sequence against which it wishes to protect God's eternity), he could have rejected the position and with it the God–time distinction. Instead, Schleiermacher took the middle ground: he discarded the classical position but retained the God-time distinction.

At least, in this, he attempted to transfer the logic of the distinction out of traditional metaphysics; rather than stages of unchangeable preparation (ideal forms) and changeable creation (matter), Schleiermacher argues, again, for eternal creation. But his own logic remains largely metaphysical (in the sense of abstracting "God" from the physical): he retains Neoplatonic commitment to immutability/mutability along the less coherent register of divine atemporality/creaturely temporality; this, as we have seen, because it seems dictated to him by the conceptual opposition of "dependence" versus "equality."

Schleiermacher might have explored the possibility that God self-determinatively takes up time; that eternally, in the coordinated realities of Son and Spirit, God assumes sequence. The *eternality* of "God" would then be understood as the constancy of the assumptive act: there is no "time" in which God is not willing time to God's self for the sake of generation. Because history itself originates in the assumption, we would have in this formulation a thoroughgoing absoluteness of creation's dependence. Time itself would be utterly reliant upon the continuance of the primal act of divine self-election.[39]

The aim in registering these critiques is to highlight the actualism present but untapped in Schleiermacher's close association of creation and preservation, as a way of further translating his thinking into revelation-centric, Pneumatological terms. Moment-by-moment, creation receives and manifests the power to take part in its own happening, as God makes God's life in the happening of creation's newness by Word and Spirit. Schleiermacher offers resources toward such conclusions, even as he fails to reach them himself.

Before we leave Schleiermacher for a bit, it is worth returning to the relation he posits between the experience of interdependence in the world and the feeling of absolute dependence on God, specifically within his discussion of world-preservation. The integration of the two invites practical exploration of the ways that the human might actualize her dependence on God and concomitant partnership with God.

Schleiermacher writes that "the religious self-consciousness, by means of which we place all that affects or influences us in absolute dependence on God, coincides entirely with the view that all such things are conditioned and determined by the interdependence of Nature."[40] He acknowledges that "we find the opposite idea to this very widely spread,"[41] namely, that the feeling of absolute dependence upon God and the perception of nature's interdependence do not coincide, but stand in opposition. It may seem that the more that we can account for the world's endurance through nature's interconnections, the less that we are even aware of God, let alone that we should accord the world's endurance absolutely to him. It would rather seem that the world endures by virtue of intricate, self-sustaining lifecycles.

Schleiermacher concedes that such inverse proportionality does obtain but contends that it is so only at the entry level. Nothing "prevents the one activity, after having satisfied itself, from stimulating and passing over into the other."[42] Rigorous scientific observation of nature's interconnection need not impede pious self-consciousness in the end. Quite the contrary, such observation over time can "stimulate" and "pass over" into a potent feeling of dependence upon God. How so?

"The reason why [great natural phenomena can] so readily arouse religious feeling lies . . . in the immensity of their operations both in the promotion and destruction of human life and works of skill, and thus in the awakening of the consciousness of the limitation of our activity by universal forces."[43] The more that we come to appreciate the life-giving and life-taking cycles of nature, the more vulnerable we find ourselves within nature. Observation of nature can eventually stimulate a consciousness of self as not independently sustainable, even better, perhaps, than a consciousness that remains uninformed by natural observation. (The piety of the studiously unscientific may prove artificial, or at least shallow.)

This is a tenuous argument from the standpoint of modern atheism and its criticisms of natural theology (e.g., Freud), but we may pass over those considerations for the time being. Schleiermacher's case looks stronger when we focus on the stress he lays on humanity's place within nature. As an observer of creation's mutual conditioning and reliance, the human does not stand outside creation, but finds herself taking part in it, mutually conditioned in and through it. The nature-watching human, as we have noted, only comes to be through nature's processes; her environment and her participation in a biochemical web precondition her development. She therefore enjoys only a *relative* sense of freedom and dependence. This relative dependence, or finding oneself to participate in the world's interdependence, can stir up a consciousness of *absolute* dependence on the world's Maker and Preserver insofar as the latter brings the former to completion. "The feeling of absolute dependence can be aroused through stimulations of our sensuous self-consciousness. For that feeling is most complete when we identify ourselves in our self-consciousness with the whole world and feel ourselves in the same way as not less dependent [than the world]."[44]

Observation of the world can stimulate piety insofar as in observing nature we come to see ourselves as part of the nature-system, and so to manifest, in feeling, its sum-total-non-independence as finite, if the reader will excuse the inelegance of that expression:

> This identification can only succeed in so far as in thought we unite everything that in appearance is scattered and isolated, and by means of this unifying association conceive of everything as one. For the most complete and universal interdependence of nature is posited in this "All-One" of finite being, and if we also feel ourselves to be absolutely dependent, then there will be a complete coincidence of the two ideas—namely, the unqualified conviction that everything is grounded and established in the universality of the nature-system, and the inner certainty of the absolute dependence of all finite being on God.[45]

To the degree that all entities, which might otherwise be considered isolated and unrelated, are thought as one, as arising and existing in connection with each other, sensory observation of creaturely interdependence and the feeling of absolute dependence on God, while intrinsically distinct, can be mutually reinforcing. As awareness of its mutual conditioning grows in comprehensiveness, humanity's false consciousness of independence is undermined, until this feeling finally coalesces into a consciousness of *absolute* dependency.

Once more with reference to our discussion in chapter 1, Schleiermacher contends that a feeling of relative dependence must be differentiated from the feeling of absolute dependence, as it always derives from finite objects or from finite self-reference, and so always entails a counter-consciousness of freedom. Still, it does not have to be *opposed* to the feeling of absolute dependence. It remains a feeling of *dependence* however much it might bring a feeling of freedom in tow. Relative dependence leads to absolute dependence, not away from it.

In the event that the human discovers her non-independence in the world, she at once may discover her shared dependence with the world on God. Or, consciousness of oneness with the world may stimulate consciousness of God and vice versa. "If we conceive both tendencies as fully developed in a given man, then each would with perfect ease call forth the other, so that every thought, as part of the whole world-conception, would become in him the purest religious feeling, and every pious feeling, as evoked by a part of the world, would become a complete world-conception."[46] This is a pivotal conclusion. In the first place, Schleiermacher here reunites thought and feeling in a productive synthesis. By "productive," I mean that each modality feeds the other to create an upward spiral alike to that which I am advocating: perception of interdependence feeds religious self-awareness and vice versa.

The shortcoming of this synthesis, which I will simply reiterate, is that Schleiermacher's thinking is rendered unnecessarily cumbersome by the prior division of feeling and knowing. It would be more efficient for Schleiermacher, rather than to formulate a synthesis of thought with feeling, to expand the one to encompass the other in a more holistic category of *perception*. The human becomes conscious of God as the history of God with humankind given in the biblical text generates consciousness of her need, of her *movement* by God into Eden.

In the second place, again on the upside, the connection between consciousness of interdependence and consciousness of absolute dependence (whether expressed as Schleiermacher's synthesis or in my preferred form of a more robust perception) informs a right view of divine activity. There can be no strict difference between the effectiveness of the operations of the whole world-system and the influence of God's work of preservation: "Divine preservation, as the absolute dependence of all events and changes on God, and natural causation, as the complete determination of all events by the universal-nexus, are one and the same thing simply from different points of view, the one being neither separated from the other nor limited by it."[47]

In that knowledge of God is mediated existentially, in fulsome creaturely perception of absolute dependence, account of divine action can only be given in the terms of world action. The frame of reference within which the creature encounters God, or better, within which she is confronted by God, is the same as that within which she encounters herself in the world. The apparatus of her knowing the one, indeed as *primus*, is the same as that of her knowing the second, indeed as *secunda*.

She does not enjoy any other knowing apparatus, any other means of accounting for God, the world, and their relation than her historically conditioned one. To be sure, her creaturely organ of perception is in need of transformation, as we will more fully discuss in treating *sin*. But even made new, it is still a *creaturely* organ. Its structures are given rise and tuned by the forces and operations of the world within which she evolves. Even her knowledge of God is mediated accordingly; the work of God's Spirit does not elevate creaturely comprehension beyond its nature, but so radically shapes its nature in the action of revelation ("revealedness") as to make "God," "creation," and their relation existentially meaningful—understandable and actionably relevant.

In sum, for Schleiermacher, experiential realization of creation's interdependence becomes the condition of the creature's consciousness of absolute dependence, in which consciousness the creature comes authentically to exist. In the vernacular of piety, "determination of all events by the universal-nexus" is the same as "divine preservation, as the absolute dependence of all events and changes on God." I commend this insight as a way of making the creature's actualistic existence between God and the world practical and applicable. The creature lives into the promise of its existence with God, Eden-ward, as he embraces his interdependence in creation, that is, as he acknowledges this condition as good and right (even, as we will discuss, "beautiful") and gives himself to it by giving his vitality in behalf of creation.

In his encyclical, *Laudato si'*, Pope Francis highlights the interrelation of the earth's environment and human activity and supplies a framework for making such application. After briefly interacting with Francis, we will finish this chapter by assessing some ethical implications of creation's fundamental interdependence.

EXCURSUS: PRACTICAL APPLICATIONS OF BIOCHEMICAL INTERDEPENDENCE

Issued May 2015, the papal encyclical, *Laudato si'*, takes the shape of prophetic call to action against the human causes of climate change.[48] Chapter 1 describes a dark ecological scene. It cites such well-documented data points as pollution and waste (multiplication of environmental toxins through industry and through simple trash), water poverty and unsafe water quality (lack of fresh drinking water especially in poorer regions and countries, and sicknesses like dysentery and cholera that accompany it), and loss of biodiversity (e.g., loss of coral reefs through warming oceans and destruction of forest habitat, as well as the breakdown of ecosystems dependent upon lifeforms in that habitat, including algae, microorganism, and insects).[49] Chapter 2 presents a distinctly Christian account of the environmental condition. The Genesis creation stories "suggest that human life is grounded in three fundamental and closely intertwined relationships: with God, with our neighbor and with the earth itself. According to the Bible, these three vital relationships have been broken, both outwardly and within us. This rupture is sin."[50] The ecological scene has been darkened not by accident but by a concrete failure with regard to the covenantal work of the human, or as we have been saying in this chapter, the failure of the human to actualize its liminal existence in cooperative care for creation.

Chapter 3 digs into the ground of this failure, "the human roots of the ecological crisis."[51] These include misplaced trust in technology (focusing on improvements that have come through technology while lacking reflective critique of its harms, like the consequences of unchecked carbon emissions), immoral pursuit of relations of power (confusing mastery over nature with progress—enhanced ability to extract energy resources does not equate to energy advancement), globalization of the "technocratic paradigm" (spreading the myth of the exalted subject who conceitedly manipulates the external world—because the human *can* engineer the means to uproot forests, it *ought* to do so), and "misguided anthropocentrism" (the modern assumption that humanity is at the center of creation and that promotion of humanity's well-being is the ultimate purpose of creation, at whatever cost to creation). Against the disposition toward covenantal unity with the world and purposive action for the world, humanity exhibits tendencies toward self-differentiation from the world, to the detriment of the world.

Chapters 4–6 summon the reader toward alternative ideals. They articulate a principle of common goods over goods apportioned strictly according to competitive success (and with this, commitment to intergenerational justice);[52] call for international dialogue and political transparency;[53] connect lifestyle changes to theological doctrines of sacramental participation and trinitarian interrelation (caring for the environment is not a moral extra, but a constitutional necessity for a human that is drawn into the eternal mutuality of Father, Son, and Spirit);[54] and pertinently for this book, commend "educating for the covenant between humanity and the environment."[55]

Scope does not permit full adjudication of these alternatives (and I do harbor reservations about some of their details), but by way of overarching assessment in light of this chapter's central thesis that humanity exists authentically in purposive motion Eden-ward, they frame a helpful start to that movement. We will talk more about them below, particularly the ethic of shared goods versus goods apportioned through competition and educating for the human/world covenant. Suffice it to say that humanity lives into its promise as it reiterates within its sphere of action the grace of its Creator in such ways as buffeting the consequences of resource-scarcity produced by competition (through just distribution); inviting responsible cooperation and consensus and resisting the politics of sovereignty and privilege (we recognize that no nation rightfully holds title to creation's resources); making lifestyle choices to recycle and reduce carbon footprints and contribute to clean water projects, learning to encounter the redemptive presence of God in the healing of the world; and learning to understand the ecological consequences of consumerism and consumption, to perceive the connection between the flourishing of the world and the endurance of human life in the world.

Francis argues that it is not only to the world's benefit but also to the human's for the human to embrace its connection to the world and to take its unique part in acting for the world. Humanity exists in a relatively stable range of environmental conditions. Change those conditions and the human is threatened not only homeostatic-ally but also with regard to its sustenance. "The melting in polar ice caps and in high altitude plains can lead to the dangerous release of methane gas, while the decomposition of frozen organic material can further increase the emission of carbon dioxide. . . . Carbon dioxide pollution increases the acidification of the oceans and compromises the marine food chain"[56] The human is climate-ly rooted. Our existence depends on the maintenance of certain food sources that require a particular range of temperatures and weather patterns, wet and dry cycles, disease and pest resistance. The human compromises her existence when she over-plants, over-fishes, and over-hunts, and when she contributes to the alteration of climate conditions whereby planting, fishing, and hunting are rendered ineffective.

The species will first feel this threat at its margins, among those most reliant on the consistency of the earth's life cycles. "Many of the poor live in areas particularly affected by phenomena related to warming, and their means of subsistence are largely dependent on natural reserves and ecosystem services such as agriculture, fishing and forestry."[57] Among those immediately reliant upon productive oceans and fertile soil, humanity's attempt to extract itself from the environment will be grimly acute (as, for example, lack of resources not only results in lack of sustenance but also mass migration and refugee conditions).

Threats to supply cause shifts in demand and elevated prices, which further exacerbate inequalities. As global fish yields reduce, prices rise and consumers turn to other food sources. Local fishing may survive, but reduction in trade cannot sustain all the local fishermen. In an integrated world economy, workers in developing nations where products remain in demand often still find themselves without income virtually overnight because demand has fluctuated elsewhere, and lacking institutional support structures of developed nations, they can be thrust into poverty. The COVID-19 pandemic of 2020 demonstrated how global crisis first impacts the poor when demand reduces. Garment workers in Bangladesh experienced mass unemployment due to decreased demand in the West: by early April, because of just a few weeks of reduction in consumption in Europe and the United States, "more than a million Bangladeshi garment workers—80% of whom are women—have already been laid off or sent home without pay after orders were cancelled or suspended," reported Pan Pylas.[58]

For Francis, caring for the environment is simply part of affirming our existence within a larger creaturely family. "As part of the universe, called into being by one Father, all of us are linked by unseen bonds and together form a kind of universal family, a sublime communion."[59] This affirmation takes place not only spatially, in cultivating empathy for siblings across the globe as they suffer the consequences of climate change but also temporally, as humankind confirms the commonness of its ancestry; that it is an offspring of the same germinal parent as all earthly life.

Biologist Neil Shubin observes that "inside our bodies are connections to a menagerie of other creatures."[60] Genetically, developmentally, and anatomically, human bodies share characteristic features with other forms of life. Shubin documents this common corporeal heritage by comparing, among other things, hands, teeth, and bodily dimensionality among a variety of species[61] and by tracing its ancestry to ancient, predecessor creatures.[62]

Concerning hands, for example, Shubin not only shows a basic continuity in bone structure between the human arm, wrist, and hand and that of a lizard, as well as the wing of a bird (observation of this continuity dates to Richard Owen in the nineteenth century) but also, he shows how this compositional pattern is incipient in ancient species of fish.[63] It began to evolve from a more rudimentary fin formation to the humerus, ulna/radius, carpals/metacarpals/phalanges formation that we know, as fish began to respond to the survival pressure to function out of water. This transitional fish:

> Was capable of doing push-ups. . . . The elbow was capable of bending like ours, and the wrist was able to bend to make the fish's "palm" lie flat against the ground. . . . Why would a fish ever want to do a push-up. . . ? Fins capable of supporting the body would have been very helpful indeed for a fish that needed to maneuver in [mudflats and stream banks]. . . . But why live in these environments at all? What possessed fish to get out of the water or live in the margins? Think of this: virtually every fish swimming in these 375-million-year-old streams was a predator of some kind. . . . It is no exaggeration to say that this was a fish-eat-fish world. The strategies to succeed in this setting were pretty obvious: get big, get armor, or get out of the water. It looks as if our distant ancestors avoided the fight.[64]

Anatomical similarities between modern humans and very old fish fossils are only part of the story. Genetically and developmentally, the human hand exhibits likeness to appendages of other species, for example, the wing of a chicken. The "zone of polarizing activity" is a patch of tissue that regulates arrangement and size of "digits" in the human hand and in a chicken's wing, and this zone is controlled in each creature by versions of the same gene.[65] The same sort of malfunctioning in the gene causes the same sort of malformations in hand and wing (number and size of digits, for instance). The human shares with other creatures not only eventual structures but also underlying instruction for the emergence of those structures.

Summarizing Shubin's conclusions, ethicist Larry Rasmussen writes, "*to be* is t*o be different*, yes, but from the same recycled stuff. The same genes, the same parts, turn up again and again from species to species. . . . The modern world's sense of the human is a shrunken one, given what we know about our evolutionary journey."[66] Modern consciousness of the self as extracted from its world, existing as an entity unto itself against all others, is sinfully mistaken. "We do not regard ourselves *internally* related to as kin to the rest of a shared and indispensable community that also lives embedded in the Earth and cosmos. This constricted and alienated sense of ourselves is the species counterpart of the self-absorption [which Luther dubbed] the heart-turned-in-upon-itself."[67]

Francis identifies one source of corrective education in the appreciation of beauty. "By learning to see and appreciate beauty, we learn to reject self-interested pragmatism."[68] This is a rich insight, with which we may reconnect to the observations made at the start of this chapter and round out our brief excursus.

There are two ways in which perception and acknowledgement of beauty inclines consciousness away from the artifice of self-construction and -perpetuation. One is that it affirms inherent value in the other. It accords a moral standing to a thing for its own sake. We will return to this point in conclusion.

The second way that learning to appreciate beauty exercises a corrective influence on our self-consciousness is that it enhances a sense of imbeddedness in the created order. The human recognizes proportionality or fit within her environment. As Elizabeth Johnson observed, evolution enforces symbiosis across a number of continuums[69]: predator to prey; parasitic feeding to cooperative growth; passive interaction to active separation. And they operate not only on the biological but also social and psychological plains. Natural selection is neither more nor less than a relentless, aggregate pressure toward situated existence, a pushing of each species into bio-social association with other species in an environment. Natural selection is a continual process of hewing among species within a context. It contributes to the limit-setting by which life emerges.

Paradoxically, it is in open-eyed affirmation of its wholesale interdependence among all of creation that the human at once confirms her uniqueness. "Do the facts of our ancient history mean that humans are not special or unique among living creatures," Shubin asks? "Of course not. In fact, knowing something about the deep origins of humanity only adds to the remarkable fact of our existence."[70] As humanity's deep and interconnected history becomes a shaping factor in its self-consciousness, as it knows itself in the terms of such radical interdependence, humanity comes to appreciate its distinctiveness: the human comes to see itself as that creature which *can* appreciate beauty.

The human comes to see herself as part of a dependent world-system and at the same time as that creature who might perceive the integration of that system and work toward its efficiency and productivity. The human might affirm her place between God and the world by giving herself to the will of God for the world—by embracing the gift-character of life (its non-givenness), or the generosity of creation, in acting with generosity of Spirit toward creation. By turning away from exploitative practices that, in the end, also compromise the human, by rather turning to practices of sustainability in fishing, farming, and mining, of reducing pollutants in air and water, of counteracting the causes of ice melt and drought and sea-level rise—that is, by taking on *redemptive* practices—the human takes part in God's *creative* work. She actualizes a capacity for newness revealed in God's redemptive history, according to which the world also has its existence. The human participates in the Spirit of God as she invokes the Spirit to once more animate the world.

CONCLUSION: ETHICAL CONSIDERATIONS

A horizon opens up before the human; in the terms of our exegetical work above, he finds himself being set into a place that he could not otherwise inhabit; he sees himself as existing *inter aetates*, or more exactly, *inter saeculum et aetatem*. As he appreciates the non-given, non-self-possessing character of creaturely life, its ephemerality and recycled impermanence, as he becomes unsettled and dislocated from his unsound abode of self-containment, the human suddenly grasps existence as a moving-into the next age. He enjoys life in the Spirit, when "Spirit" is understood not as incorporeality but as capacity for otherness, for new life that is yet one with the old, regeneration. This is what it means for the human to learn to appreciate the beauty of God's creation.

But here we cannot gloss over the complicating and controversial elements of our specifically *evolutionary* interdependence. In the first place, the human does not learn to appreciate beauty in abstraction from the objects of his perception, from that on which aesthetic understanding operates. The valuing action itself is evolutionarily sculpted. Appreciation of proportion or fit is not a secondhand action on existents in an existent's perception, but a determination of the existent in the very action of perceiving existents. In the evaluative act, the human situates himself in relation to that which he evaluates, and indeed, the measures by which he situates himself have already received a kind of fore-structuring by the environment within which the human is and will be situated. The situating is neither more nor less that the enacting, if also co-shaping, of these measures. In observing the circumstances of his production, the human also observes and confirms the limiting effects of his existence.

That the human should find the landscape before him, for instance, to be of a scope, color, and shape to inspire feelings of particular action (to garden it, or paint it, or play in it, or protect it) is given in the human's own sculpting by forces resident in that landscape— temperatures and gases and nutrients and corrosives and attractive properties. That he recognizes what to do among it is given by it; how he might be a creature for it is given in his being a creature of it.[71] Human acting is really only a form of creaturely participation, a taking-this-part (and not that) in moment-by-moment ascertainment of place, and moment-by-moment establishment of place in the act of ascertaining.

This means that evolutionary interdependence is both a fact and an invitation, an event of self-confirmation into which the human must recurrently live, and upon which, by his living, the human might exercise a degree of determination. The human not only perceives the symbiotic shape of evolutionary sculpting but also might contribute to it as he self-consciously accepts his life within it. He might, for instance, try to manipulate its selective pressures within a particular environment in order to enhance a species endangered there. This possibility of contributing something to the beauty of life, however, entails risk. It means that the human rightly ascertains the fit that he believes himself to perceive—not at all certain given the extraordinary timeframes and deep intricacies of evolutionary sculpting. It means that he appreciates the long strings of consequences that come from his manipulative work, not only for the targeted species, but for the many others whose heritages are entwined with it—even less certain given the manifold entanglements of such lives. And it means that his motivation is toward the result of life's preservation, that his work reiterates the creative will of God—least certain given the intricate tangle of motivations according to which human activity takes place. Later chapters return to these risks as we more thematically consider the matter of sin.

In the second place, evolution presents a paradox: interdependent emergence of life on one side and zero-sum competition for resources among lives on the other. The engine of evolution is, again, natural selection (crudely and a bit misleadingly, "survival of the fittest"), and it is driven by scarcity or inconsistent distribution of resources. Darwinism starts with the self-evident observation that all lives are birthed into competition for the things needed to survive. Evolution does not easily sync up with a form of "beauty" that prizes equitable distribution of nature's resources, for its theoretical substructure trades upon the opposite reality.

Our account of the beautiful must take into account evolution's zero-sum side. A few possibilities suggest themselves. One is utmost relativism: beauty is intrinsically perspectival, judged as such relative to the benefits enjoyed by very narrow interest groups (even species within species) at any given time over against other species. Winning life's competition is beautiful unto itself; the human considers beauty as a winning species and accords the same designation to those species which exist and, thus, also have won. In ethical terms, I would characterize this as *indefinitely contested consequentialism*. The opposite is a graded universalism: the beautiful encompasses extinct species because they, too, are part of creaturely harmony, which is always and everywhere perceived in the same way: the fit of lower forms of life is in their service to higher forms, even their existing for the sake of serving as objects of chase and as food, in fact, even their going-out-of-existence insofar as it promotes the flourishing of other species (if nothing else by removing one more competitor). This view nakedly assumes rank among species (not necessarily fixed, as higher and lower forms can change according to alterations in their environments), and we might call it *hierarchical deontology*.

Both of these have obvious shortcomings. A third prospect is a teleological ethic in which the beauty of creation is *not yet* although it is *already* signaled: the flourishing of all life through productive abundance and just (not necessarily equivalent) distribution of goods. This third way envisions a kind of evolution that is positive-sum, where the flourishing of one life does not by definition entail the selective taking of resources from or inbred martyrdom of another life. We would have to resist the latent temptation to arrogate to humanity the capacity to create this kind of beauty by itself, even as it works toward it, for as creatures evolved through zero-sum brutality our perspective will be deceptively self-serving. We would have to be confronted with an alternative perspective in each instant, and the translation to a positive-sum reality would have to be affected in us by another Spirit.

We might call this the ethic of *anticipative virtue*. As the human practices *self-willed* sacrificial love, she works toward (although does not finally achieve) the positive-sum reality of new creation, creation as God intends. She lives into her fitness, into Eden, in that she perceives and works toward the good of *shared* resources, and in this, the *promotion* of life through self-sacrifice rather than the trade of life. She slows the life-denying aspect of competition—although the force of competition is still very much resident in the world and still gives shape to its creatures, her included—as she reduces the horsepower (to continue our engine metaphor) of scarcity. Creatures learn to respond to the generosity of the world instead of its lack. In this giving of herself, life is given to another and, reciprocally, in the event of beauty's achievement, to her.

Because evolutionary competition still exists, death does also. Creaturely biochemistry returns itself, in the end, to the dust, and the evolved human lives into her fitness, ironically, as she learns to hold her life loosely, not simply consenting to her mortality, but finding peace and joy in the prospect of spending her life for the sake of another. This, too, is beautiful. Evolution's *inclinatio morti* reinforces humanity's utter dependence on the sacrificial love of God.

But we also cannot cynically accept a beauty that includes suffering and killing. Our consciousness can hardly be considered redeemed, can hardly be inclined Eden-ward, if it makes peace not just with mortality, but with the affliction and slaughter of predation. Perception of creaturely existence in the light of revelation, which is to say, as object of God's agency, entails a tension. It appreciates the beauty of the created order, itself a piece with that order, while it envisions and works toward a genuinely new creation. The paradox of the redeemed consciousness is that it locates creation's true identity in the dawn even as it can only construe tomorrow in the terms of today. Covenant-formed consciousness always perceives reality in the light of *promise*.

NOTES

1. Johnson, *Ask the Beasts: Darwin and the God of Love* (London: Bloomsbury, 2014), 54–55.

2. Rasmussen, *Earth Honoring Faith: Religious Ethics in a New Key* (Oxford: Oxford University Press, 2013), 17.

3. Westermann, *Genesis 1–11*, 210.

4. See also Sarna, *Genesis*, 18: "It is significant [in the light of Ancient Near Eastern parallels] that our Genesis account omits all mythological details, does not even employ the phrase, 'garden of God,' and places gold and jewels in a natural setting."

5. Barth, CD III.1, 252–3.

6. BDB (2000), 726.

7. BDB (2000), 869.

8. Wenham, *Genesis 1–15*, 61.

9. Barth, CD III.1, 251.

10. That Gen. 2–3 exhibit an intricate literary, thematic, and structural continuity is the wide consensus of modern biblical scholarship. The command and permission of

God, represented by the trees in the middle of the Garden, supply a focal point for this continuity. So, e.g., Westermann (*The Genesis Accounts of Creation*, 30): "this story is misunderstood when one severs these two chapters into one story about creation and another regarding the fall into sin, making separate epochs out of each—that is, an 'original state' before the fall and another afterwards."

11. Barth, CD III.1, 251.

12. Sarna, *Genesis*, 19.

13. Dietrich Bonhoeffer, *Creation and Fall: A Theological Exposition of Genesis 1–3*, trans. Martin Rüter and Ilse Tödt, ed. John W. de Gruchy, Dietrich Bonhoeffer Works 3 (Minneapolis: Fortress, 1997), 85.

14. Fretheim, *The Book of Genesis*, 351.

15. Bonhoeffer, *Creation and Fall*, 86; italics in original.

16. Even if it is the case, as many commentators contend, that the biblical account picks up the ancient near-eastern motif of human struggle against the gods, wherein the gods, concerned to protect against usurpation of their authority, issue self-guarding decrees, it seems that the biblical authors turn that motif on its head. Limitation is not protection against achievement of human potential in relation to YHWH-Elohim, but the means of it.

17. Bonhoeffer, *Creation and Fall*, 115.

18. For example, Wenham, *Genesis 1–15*, 44: "you may freely eat . . . you will certainly die." With regard to the latter, Wenham notes that the infinitive plus Qal construction is "characteristic of divine or royal threats in narrative and prophetic texts (e.g., 20:7, 1 Sam 14:39, 44; 22:16; 1 Kgs 2:37, 42; 2 Kgs 1:4, 6; Ezek 33:8, 14)"; ibid., 67.

19. As, for example, symbols of fertility, which might be ritually enjoined (tapping the power of life through the cult); see for starters Ex. 34:13; Judg. 6:25f; 1 Kgs 16:33; and esp. Josiah's reforms in 2 Kgs 23 on Asherah groves and Asherah worship.

20. Sandra L. Richter writes that "although there is no specific declaration of covenant making in Eden, we find the profile of *bĕrît* [covenant] throughout the narrative. I believe this is so because the concept of *bĕrît* as it was learned at Sinai so profoundly affected Israel's self-understanding that *bĕrît* was used to organize the earliest narratives of the Bible as well"; *The Epic of Eden: A Christian Entry into the Old Testament* (Downers Grove, IL: IVP Academic, 2008), 92. We can be even stronger: the concept of covenant as developed at Sinai so profoundly shapes the Israelite imagination that it is written into the fabric of the biblical creation myths. It forms a thematic thread running through and in fact unifying the entire canon. Richter is correct, therefore, that the epic of Eden conveys "God's Original Intent" for creation (92–118), and the New Jerusalem "God's Final Intent" (119–37), as the one initiates and the other consummates the covenant. But unfortunately, she takes this continuity to imply that God's saving work is *restorative* in nature, bringing creation *back to* Eden. "God has been leading humanity back to Eden by means of a sequence of steps, a series of rescues, a series of covenants" (130). On the contrary, Eden is not yet; its function in the narrative is not to conduct thought to a past state of being (its narrated pastness being strictly an imaginative placeholder), but existentially to pitch

the reader in a forward looking and forward moving trajectory. Our soteriological model ought not to be restoration, but transformation.

21. Schleiermacher, *The Christian Faith*, 142.

22. Ibid., 143.

23. Ibid., 147.

24. Ibid., 146.

25. For a handy overview of Schleiermacher's conviction that God is pure activity, see Hector, "Actualism and Incarnation," 210–12.

26. Ibid.

27. For something like this, see Robert W. Jenson, *Systematic Theology Volume 2: The Works of God* (Oxford: Oxford University Press, 1999), 3–52. I especially commend Jenson's treatment of the noetic distinction yet ontic continuity between creation and preservation (9), as well as his overall discussion of time (29–49), including his insight that "God takes time in his time for us. That is his act of creation" (35).

28. See Niebuhr, *Schleiermacher on Christ and Religion*, 210–14.

29. Schleiermacher, *The Christian Faith*, 152.

30. Harvey, cited by Gerhard Spiegler, "Theological Tensions in Schleiermacher's *Dialectic*: Response and Discussion," in *Schleiermacher as Contemporary*, ed. Robert W. Funk, Journal for Theology and the Church 7 (Herder and Herder, 1970), 29.

31. The problem is biblically obvious: "[Christ Jesus], who, though he was in the form of God, did not regard equality with God as something to be exploited, but emptied himself, taking the form of a slave, being born in human likeness" (Phil 2:6–7). Non-exploitation of the feeling of equality with God (or positively, actualization of the feeling of dependence) is continuously founded upon the event in which *God* makes a consequential sacrifice in order to stand in a relation of mutual determination with the world. "God" enacts such a freedom as not to be bound to abstracted incongruence, but to become Immanuel, Creator and Sustainer *of* creation *with* creation.

32. Schleiermacher, *The Christian Faith*, 153–54.

33. Ibid., 153.

34. Ibid., 154.

35. See Augustine, *Confessions*, The World's Classics, trans. Henry Chadwick (Oxford: Oxford University Press, 1992), XI.ix–xxxi.

36. Schleiermacher, *The Christian Faith*, 155.

37. Ibid.

38. Ibid. In spite of their shared resistance to relating God and time, Schleiermacher opposes Augustine in that he finds a residue of before-and-after logic with regards to the world's creation in Augustine's thinking. Augustine retained the view that the Incarnation took place as a genuinely new event in time. Yet he had to combat the Neoplatonic notion that such a teaching implies change in God (see Chadwick's observation in *Confessions* XI.x, n. 16). In broad terms, Augustine needed an account of creation in which God could effect a new state of things without introducing newness into God's life. Augustine found this by appeal to the divine will, which he associated with the divine substance: "a single act of the Divine Will is sufficient to account for the earlier non-existence and the later existence of the world"

(Schleiermacher, *The Christian Faith*, 155). In one inward motion, God prevents the world's self-origination and originates it.

Schleiermacher rejects this conclusion, reasoning that it implies a conceptual ability to the world to have come into existence absent the divine will, or independently of God, before God willed against its self-existence, which compromises Christian piety. For the feeling of dependence to be absolute, there could be no conceptual possibility of world self-existence, and that means world-origination cannot owe to God willing against world-non-origination, since this would imply that the world could exist *unless* God willed against it But Schleiermacher's logic simply does not compel agreement.

Does Schleiermacher really wish to counter-imply that the conceptual pattern of "unless God wills otherwise, then X" is a *deficient* form of *Christian* piety? Surely Augustine is on the stronger footing by suggesting that no possibility, even conceptual or hypothetical, including the hypothetical antecedent existence of the divine alternative (theoretical world self-existence), takes place apart from the singular will of God. (To run it through the torture rack of Schleiermacher's abstractions: antecedent world non-existence as a possibility—as such only insofar as God wills against the opposite, the possibility of antecedent world self-existence, and so "at once" wills absolute world dependence—is not improper but proper to Christian piety.)

39. Here I endorse the logic of both Robert Jenson and Bruce McCormack, who make a similar case vis-a-vis the ancient doctrine of *impassibility*. See Jenson, "Ipse Pater Non Est Impassibilis," in *Divine Impassibility and the Mystery of Human Suffering*, ed. James F. Keating and Thomas Joseph White (Grand Rapids: Eerdmans, 2009), 117–26; McCormick, "Divine Impassibility or Simply Divine Constancy? Implications of Karl Barth's Later Christology for Debates over Impassibility," in ibid., 150–86.

40. Ibid., 170.

41. Ibid., 171.

42. Ibid.

43. Ibid., 172.

44. Ibid., 173.

45. Ibid.

46. Ibid., 174.

47. Ibid., 174.

48. Francis restates a number of themes raised by eco-theologians beginning in the late twentieth century. For a helpful orientation, which anticipates many of the pope's claims and conclusions, see Norman Wirzba, *The Paradise of God: Renewing Religion in an Ecological Age* (Oxford: Oxford University Press, 2003). Pope Francis, *Laudato si'* (May 2015); http://w2.vatican.va/content/dam/francesco/pdf/enc yclicals/documents/papa-francesco_20150524_enciclica-laudato-si_en.pdf.

49. Ibid., 20–42.

50. Ibid., 66.

51. Ibid., 101–36.

52. Ibid., 147–62.

53. Ibid., 164–88.

54. Ibid., 203–8, 228–40.

55. Ibid., 209–15.

56. Ibid., 24.

57. Ibid., 24.

58. Pylas, "Half Billion More People Face Poverty Due to Virus—Report," Associated Press, April 9, 2020. https://apnews.com/b219627e31d87779e5253f9a07 2be4dc.

59. Francis, *Laudato si'*, 89.

60. Shubin, *Your Inner Fish: A Journey into the 3.5-Billion-Year History of the Human Body* (New York: Pantheon, 2008), 182.

61. See ibid., 44–59, 60–80, and 97–115, respectively.

62. Shubin's early expertise was in transitional water/land fossils, ca. 375-million years old; see ibid., 3–27.

63. Shubin, *Your Inner Fish*, 30–43.

64. Ibid., 39–41.

65. Ibid., 50–59.

66. Rasmussen, *Earth-Honoring Faith*, 18–19; italics in original.

67. Ibid., 20; italics in original.

68. Francis, *Laudato si'*, 215.

69. See also ibid., 68. Francis gives a similar account of the consequential interconnection among forms of life, using the language of "the delicate equilibria existing between the creatures of this world."

70. Shubin, *Your Inner Fish*, 43.

71. This action in perception of fit is, as we have said, co-constitutive. It is not mechanistic reaction, or the like, but construction. Human activity as a species takes place in a web of species activity, always mutating new threads into the fabric for the prospect of selection. Thus, we again encounter the importance of boundary-setting: perception of beauty entails a mixture of light and shadow, indeed life and death, as species engage species in new cycles of influence. Death cannot simplistically be equated with "ugliness" or "evil." Nevertheless, part of humanity's adjudication of beauty entails hopeful, in fact passionate investment in life over death. Christian theology does not rest satisfied with an indefinite "both-and" simply because evolutionary history implies this. It learns from the resurrection a higher-order beauty than that of evolutionary proportionality. It values not death per se, but the death of death in the Son's dying.

Accounting of creation within the orbit of Christian faith always involves the meeting, without confusing, of these two horizons. The horizon of resurrection confronts the horizon of evolutionary life and death. But it must also subsume that horizon; resurrection becomes a productive horizon of perception insofar as it frames the evolutionary horizon in *promise*. Over against life *and* death, the horizon of resurrection introduces into the horizon of evolution the prospect of life *through* death, until there is no more death, but only life.

The obvious ethical upshot of this is that the human ought to seek to conform her free agency to the promotion, rather than resign herself to the inevitable destruction, of life in its various forms. Her participation in the web of evolution ought at once to be anticipation of a *deeper* and *more lasting* beauty.

Chapter 3

The Human among Humans

וַיֹּאמֶר יְהֹוָה אֱלֹהִים לֹא־טוֹב הֱיוֹת הָאָדָם לְבַדּוֹ אֶעֱשֶׂה־לּוֹ עֵזֶר כְּנֶגְדּוֹ:
וַיִּצֶר יְהֹוָה אֱלֹהִים מִן־הָאֲדָמָה כָּל־חַיַּת הַשָּׂדֶה וְאֵת כָּל־עוֹף הַשָּׁמַיִם וַיָּבֵא אֶל־הָאָדָם
לִרְאוֹת מַה־יִּקְרָא־לוֹ וְכֹל אֲשֶׁר יִקְרָא־לוֹ הָאָדָם נֶפֶשׁ חַיָּה הוּא שְׁמוֹ:
וַיִּקְרָא הָאָדָם שֵׁמוֹת לְכָל־הַבְּהֵמָה וּלְעוֹף הַשָּׁמַיִם וּלְכֹל חַיַּת הַשָּׂדֶה וּלְאָדָם לֹא־מָצָא
עֵזֶר כְּנֶגְדּוֹ:
וַיַּפֵּל יְהֹוָה אֱלֹהִים תַּרְדֵּמָה עַל־הָאָדָם וַיִּישָׁן וַיִּקַּח אַחַת מִצַּלְעֹתָיו וַיִּסְגֹּר בָּשָׂר תַּחְתֶּנָּה:
וַיִּבֶן יְהֹוָה אֱלֹהִים אֶת־הַצֵּלָע אֲשֶׁר־לָקַח מִן־הָאָדָם לְאִשָּׁה וַיְבִאֶהָ אֶל־הָאָדָם:
וַיֹּאמֶר הָאָדָם זֹאת הַפַּעַם עֶצֶם מֵעֲצָמַי וּבָשָׂר מִבְּשָׂרִי לְזֹאת יִקָּרֵא אִשָּׁה כִּי מֵאִישׁ
לֻקְחָה־זֹּאת:
עַל־כֵּן יַעֲזָב־אִישׁ אֶת־אָבִיו וְאֶת־אִמּוֹ וְדָבַק בְּאִשְׁתּוֹ וְהָיוּ לְבָשָׂר אֶחָד:
וַיִּהְיוּ שְׁנֵיהֶם עֲרוּמִּים הָאָדָם וְאִשְׁתּוֹ וְלֹא יִתְבֹּשָׁשׁוּ:

Now the LORD God said, "It is not good for the human to be alone. I will make for him a fitting helper."

So the LORD God formed from the ground all life of the open field and all flyers of the heavens, and he brought them to the human to see what he would call each one, and whatever the human called each living being was its name.

And the human gave names to every behemoth and to flyers of the heavens and to every life of the open field, but for the human no fitting helper was found.

So the LORD God caused a trance to fall over the human, and he slept. And he took one of his ribs and closed the flesh under.

Then the LORD God fashioned the rib that he took from the human into a woman and he brought her to the human.

And the human said, "Now this is bone from my bones and flesh from my flesh! Regarding this one, she will be called woman, because from man was she taken."

Therefore, a man leaves his father and his mother and unites with his woman and they become one flesh.
Now these two were naked, the human and his woman, and they were not ashamed (Gen. 2:18–25).

The human confirms his interdependence with creation and his liminal existence between God and creation as he gives his life in service to creation, opening his life to the other in conscious reiteration of the divine life-act and thus participating in God's Spirit. He perceives beauty in the way of the Spirit; he intuitively values the harmony that he observes, affirming its productivity and enrichment over against disharmony. He does not resist the fact of his interdependence with the world but embraces it as good and right. Aligning productive action with moral evaluation, the human lives ethically, seeing and contributing to the coming of a world in which all life gives of itself freely in behalf of new life.

The human glimpses Eden, not as a lost locale but as a reformed tomorrow. Revelation cultivates expectation of creation redeemed, not creation vanished. It cultivates hope, namely, for life to emerge anew out of this life, beyond the horizon of death. It institutes a new time in time. In the time(framing) of revelation, the creature lives between the present and the future, seeing the present in the light of the future and orienting her "now" accordingly. Revelation empowers and invites the human to exercise her graciously endowed free agency in further acts of grace.

This chapter examines human constitution in the free act of selfless association with other humans. It construes authentic human existence to take place in the event of such association and considers the order of "freedom," which underwrites it: the capacity for otherness consciously actualized in the giving of self is the freedom of the Spirit.

EXEGESIS OF GEN. 2:18–25

With these verses, the first revolution of the wheel of the canonically (not chronologically) second creation story finishes. Another turn is to come, apart from which the total narrative remains incomplete. The story of God's making does not end with the fashioning of the creature, but with God's continued determination to fashion the creature in the midst of creaturely unfashioning. There is not one story of building and then a second of destroying (which occasions a later, third story of divine response). The one story of creating is not finished without the second story of God's preserving, exactly in the face of humanity's self-destruction. Genesis 2 and 3 are a whole (and the ensuing stories in Genesis and beyond rehearse their themes).

But the first turn of the total story finishes in Gen. 2:25, and that merits observation. The movement that began by consideration of the human culminates when both male and female are on the scene. There is not creation of man and derivation of woman or primary creation of man and secondary creation of woman. There is not independent man and dependent woman, but only the interdependent human as man and woman, woman from the stuff of man, מֵאִישׁ . . . אִשָּׁה, and man whose condition is, emphatically, "not good" (לֹא־טֽוֹב) without woman.[1]

Whether each man and each woman consummates his and her respective existence in conjugal unity is not the point. The point is that by virtue of their sexing man and woman stand in a relation of readiness for the other. Each, as it were, awaits the other. There is something primitive in this regard about Gen. 2:18–25. The primitiveness can be obscured by modern translations. These, for instance, sometimes follow midrashic readings of vv. 22–25 and bring water to the mill of thousands of wedding preachers by giving the more domesticated "wife" for אִשָּׁה in v. 24. Formal marriage is of course implied here, but the text depicts a primal environ in which אִישׁ is fretfully adrift among the sea of creatures, only finding release when at length he alights upon אִשָּׁה and turns toward her. Similarly, the landscape of beasts and flying things—quite literally, *every* other living thing—enhances the human's isolation in his state thus far described.[2]

There is an urge at work, not merely sexual, although that is intimated, too. More deeply, there is an impulse to the other that is nothing short of vital. Barth stresses the essentially associable character of humankind:

> In isolation man would not have been good. That is, he would not have been created good. He would not have been the being with whom God later willed to enter into relationship and to have intercourse. . . . We might say that it would not be good because solitary man would not be man created in the image of God, who Himself is not solitary. In the account itself, however, the reason is to be sought in the future. Solitary man would not be good because he would not as such be the subject presupposed as the partner of God in the history which follows.[3]

"Goodness" connotes symbiotic relation, not only because the eternally relational God is the ground of goodness but also because the intentions of this God for the creature, that existence which God sees and values as right for the creature, suppose the quality of relationality. Humanity is outfitted for life with an Other and *as such* is "good." Except that it is poised for fellowship, *Homo affinitas*, humanity is not good, or, it is not good for the human to be alone.[4] Barth insightfully describes humankind along a covenantal, Edenward trajectory: humanity exists as "the subject presupposed as the partner of God."

And humanity's partnering with God, its standing in responsibility before its Maker, takes shape according to its interhuman partnering. "To be God's partner in this covenant, man himself needed a partner. . . . What is sought is a being resembling man but different from him . . . so that in it he will recognize himself but not only himself, since it is to him a Thou as truly as he is an I, and he is to it a Thou as truly as it is an I. It is in this way that God Himself will confront man."[5] To be fit for encounter with God, the human requires עֵזֶר כְּנֶגְדּוֹ, a "fitting helper" (lit. "helper as counterpart to him"), a life corresponding to his own.[6] The man requires one in whom he identifies himself, yet who stands as other to him, as God will stand.

A "fitting helper" can only refer to another agent ready for mutuality, to an agency of the same free order as the human's, thus one who must, at the same time, remain distinct from *this* human:

> When the context is taken into consideration, the emphasis obviously falls on the fact that man was placed by God before a choice and decision which he was consciously to make and verbally to confess. Not only was he to receive his partner or helpmeet, but he was to discover this helpmeet as such, and freely to accept her. She was to become to him in his own recognition what she really is, and to be acknowledged and welcomed as such by his own free word. The recognition of the I in the Thou which rests on the recognition is possible only in freedom.[7]

In the context of the parade of species in vv. 19–20, a distinguishing feature of quintessentially *human* being emerges. In fact, it is the point of these verses to surface this feature, to show that *among all living things* לְאָדָם לֹא־מָצָא עֵזֶר כְּנֶגְדּוֹ ("for the human no fitting helper was found"). Humanity's relational existence cannot be fulfilled among the beasts, because the order of associative affinity proper to the one is not proper to the other. The difference resides in reflective freedom. What makes all else to be unfit for that companionship which completes man is that it lacks this one order of determination, which the woman has—that the woman knows and understands the man as he knows and understands himself, that the man knows and understands the woman as she knows and understands herself, that each knows and understands the primal urge of the other as his and her own, that each sees this mutual knowledge and understanding in the other, each reflexively perceives that the other has this possibility as she and he does, and that without compulsion, indeed joyfully, each decides in favor of realizing this possibility in communion with the other.[8] It is inbuilt predilection for *responsible* relation, which makes humanity what it is. This is indicated by the fact that only the human receives the breath of God *in a face-to-face encounter*, which is not said of the animals. The human is made within an act of volitional companionship. That accounts for the gushing response of the man in finding the woman: the finding quite literally reiterates the ground of his existence. The companionship calls forth total surrender and deep exultation;[9] in finding it, the human *rejoices*.[10]

It is not that the beasts bear no similarity to the human with respect to companionship. They are made of the same earth as the human (מִן־הָאֲדָמָה), and although not in a face-to-face encounter, each animal receives God's breath and is a living soul, נֶפֶשׁ חַיָּה. Although humanity's primal call for companionship, for a companion-*seeker* alike to him, cannot be answered among the beasts, they share his biological interconnectedness, manifested for many of them, as for humanity, in sexual reproduction. Thus, human responsibility extends to the beasts, in recognizing their order of relational goodness, however much it differs from that of humankind.

The human sees in the animals a defining association with regard to humankind and to other animals, which it affixes in speech by the act of naming. The act itself reflects the lack of reciprocity characteristic of this order of commerce, as the beasts do not affirm or accept the name, or offer a rejoinder.[11] Moreover, the name communicates that it is characteristics of import to human perception, which are most determinative in identifying the particularities of association, not the animal's self-consciousness personally conveyed. To wit: the word "leopard" is a compound of λέων πάρδος (leopard), a "lion panther." A leopard is *panthera pardus*, πάνθηρ πάρδος, a "panther (πάρδος) of the whole/class of preying beasts (πάν+θήρ)."

Nevertheless, in naming the beasts, the human begins to act responsibly concerning them, positing herself as an I among Its, if not Thous. The human knows himself as "This Kind" among "Those Kinds," as sharing, albeit idiosyncratically, in their biochemical structure and, even more, in their animating breath. Even though the beasts come no closer to him than this, even though they do not share his prefiguring in communion with God and so also his affinity for *reflective* fellowship, he perceives himself as having life with them, identifies them in a relation to him and each other, and thus takes them into his field of accountable action (in a way they cannot do for him), conducting his life with conscious consideration for theirs.

This accountability takes place not only spatially, with regard to lives about one's environment, but also temporally, with regard to lives yet to come. The human participates in the succession of life, experienced locally in the succession from parent to child. He exists as a from-which and a for-which, crudely, a product and a producer. He recognizes himself not only to receive life but also to receive with this gift the potency to give life, to become a secondary life-giver in the manner of his parent. He authenticates his humanity and takes responsibility for non-human lives when he consents to this situation as good and right, when he consciously wills it for himself. "Therefore, a man leaves his father and his mother and unites with his woman and they become one flesh" (עַל־כֵּן יַעֲזָב־אִישׁ אֶת־אָבִיו וְאֶת־אִמּוֹ וְדָבַק בְּאִשְׁתּוֹ וְהָיוּ לְבָשָׂר אֶחָד).

In sexual union, humanity perpetuates the gift of life that it has received. The ethics of responsible choice obtain here: the freedom to participate in the succession of life can never be forced upon or denied to a human, for it is of the essence of her humanity to confirm her place in relation to God and creation by consciously recommencing the giving of life. It is a violation of her humanity, of the divinely given permission to enjoy the tree of life, to refuse volitional openness in this area.

The ethics of covenantal life also severely interrogate certain features of modern genetic science. Reproductive cloning problematically abstracts the human from the good of sexual reproduction. Evolution has rewarded safeguards against such abstraction of life from other lives, reinforcing life's covenantal trajectory, such as the "genetic shuffle," the random contribution of traits from both parents, which takes place at conception and which contributes over the long run to a more stable genome. It is not at all clear that it would be to humanity's profit to forfeit such a safeguard.

More problematic is the presumption that, in a science like cloning, evolution has given rise to its own transcendence, to an organism (the human), which might now exempt itself from at least some of the environmental determinations that made it to be, and long survive the exemption. It is not straightforwardly clear that by way of such constructive gene science humanity will simply enter the next phase of its evolution, which entails coordinated direction of the process. Evolution has never entailed such intelligent design. One cannot have it both ways: either evolution just is or is susceptible to blueprinting.

Can the human be both evolved and evolver, ship and captain? Or is it that in the instant the human extracts himself from the evolutionary process in order to guide it, he ceases to affirm the web of life as primordial and thereby forfeits his humanity? The human imagines a second order of origination detached from the order of interdependence. In this void of his own making, separated to an extent (but only to an extent) from threat, yet also from mutual sustenance in the web, the human can only negate its own condition of being. Such word of caution is worth sounding in a generation, which seeks to extract and take custodial command of its generative potential. The human not only lives by the code of genes, but also, in this day more than any of its others thus far, the human reflects genetically; by his particular genetic heritage, the human makes genes the object of thought and research, as well as design and engineering. The human alone takes his very constituents in hand.[12]

The human realizes her humanity in perpetual acts of free communion, as each I sees and respects in the other his and her own constitution in distinct form, by virtue of which distinction the I gladly bears no control over the other, and seeks instead to share life with the other; that is, as I humbly and joyfully relates once again to Thou. In this regard, while detailed consideration of the continuums of sexual and gender identity is beyond the scope of this book, enough has been said to apply the above conclusions concerning binary sexual and gender identity to those who are intersex, homosexual, transgender, or queer. Binary sexing *con-figures* (gives coordinated shape to) the reflective action by which humanity realizes its existence as willed partner; it correlates the fulfillment of conscious companionship with biophysical structure. It does not, however, collapse human realization into that structure. Humanity is realized in reflective, free communion. Even when the erotic takes alternative shape among subjects of intersexual chromosomal structure, or of homosexual metaphenomenal attraction, or when it is muted in aromantic lifestyles, the volitional responsibility by which humans are not animals, by which I relates not just to It but also to Thou, still applies.

While valuing and promoting human being as male and female, and recognizing the goodness and rightness of its procreative nature, we cannot to make sexual reproduction the exclusive condition of authentic humanity. Authentic humanity stands as a genuine prospect for those whose decision not to take part in the progenitive quality of human existence transcends strictly Self-realization.[13] One can still assent to the goodness of this succession and have a share in it that is distinct from procreation—by, say, advocating against sexual exploitation. One can perceive the beauty in covenantal companionship and espouse conscious commitment to the inviolability of uncoerced sexual reproduction without taking part in such reproduction. In fact, coercing characteristic participation in predominant male/female patterns of existence would itself violate the Spirit of responsible, covenantal union.

Even our trustworthy guide, Barth, points down a misleading trail by confusing presumptive characteristics of malenesss and femaleness with realization of authentic humanity:

> The point of the name given by the saga [אִשָּׁה] is that woman is of man. This does not mean that she is really mannish. Nor does it mean that she is man's property. Nor does it mean that unlike him she is not a human being in the full sense. What it does mean is that in her being and existence she belongs to him; that she is ordained to be his helpmeet; that without detriment to her independence she is the part of him which was lost and is found again—"taken out of him." It is proper to her to be beside him. This is her humanity.[14]

To the reflective associability, which makes the human authentically human, Barth adds the qualities of needing and belonging, seeking and accompanying, to man and woman, respectively. He takes this to be the singular significance of the apparent linguistic closeness between *'ishah* and *'ish*, "woman" and "man," that is, that as *'ishah* is from *'ish*, so "in her being and existence [woman] belongs to [man]."[15] But the observation fails linguistically. As Sarna notes, *'ishah* and *'ish* have become "associated through folk etymology by virtue of assonance," but they are "actually derived from distinct and unrelated stems."[16] The author likely intends to affirm with the assonance the inherent interrelation between man and woman, as I have emphasized above, but one cannot extend this affirmation into corroboration of presumed, psycho-social characteristics of interrelation (which often turn out to be culturally specific).[17]

The point is that authentic humanity takes place in conscious repetition of divine self-giving, in freely leaving one's inheritance, what one takes as rightly and properly one's own, and opening oneself, including one's inheritance, to mutual determination with an other. It is to live within the constitutional interdependence according to which humanity is created as man and woman, which is the same as living in the covenantal constitution of God revealed in Christ Jesus, who left his divine inheritance and took on humanity's lot. It is to live within the Spirit of Christ—after the manner of his life and according to his capacity for otherness. It is to enact a freedom for communion among the communally constituted, or affirming the goodness of covenantal existence. The remainder of this chapter focuses on this peculiar spiritual freedom.

HUMAN ASSENT IN CONTEXT

Theological reflection on the question of human freedom has taken something of an elliptical orbit around two poles. The first asks whether the possibility of consciously rejecting the "from-for" order of life's succession amounts to an exercise of freedom or of bondage. Is it part of humanity's authenticity to be able to say "no" to life's interdependence, or is saying "no" itself a casualty of already having forfeited that authenticity, the convulsion of a will that has lost its ability to function as it should? The second, and opposite, asks whether refraining from this rejection and assenting to the "from-for" order of life's succession as right and good amounts to an exercise of freedom, or of bondage. Is it part of humanity's authenticity to be able to say "yes" to life's interdependence, or is saying "yes" an imposed restraint upon the authentic will, a reduction of its range of individualistic opportunity?

In classical parlance, the question is whether, on the one hand, the potential to sin is a matter of human freedom, or whether, on the other, human freedom entails the capacity not to sin. The verdict of the Augustinian-Reformation tradition, with which I am in broad agreement, is that, perhaps as something of a third particle, the capacity not to sin, or the ability to say "yes" to the "from-for" succession of life, is part of authentic humanity, yet the human is at odds with itself, living inauthentically in sin, and so inclines to say, "no." Assenting to life's interdependence (and more, to its dependence on God) does not amount to restraining or reducing what is natural to the will, but achieving it through the gift of grace.

Although I am in broad agreement with it, the Achilles weakness of the Reformation tradition is that it seeks humanity's authenticity in return to a paradisiac state. It suggests that there was a "time when," then a "time when not"; a lost era of pure human freedom and the rest of time in which we are bound to sin. It makes much better biblical sense to look forward, as I have been arguing: to see in Christ Jesus the prototype of authentic covenantal existence and to experience this existence anticipatively in the interdependence of man and woman. The human lives authentically as he lives into the self-giving way of Christ by giving himself to another in covenantal union and, in the classical terms of binary sexuality, consensual reproduction. It may be too much to construe marriage and procreation sacramentally, but it is not too much to identify them as primary ways of living in the Spirit of Christ.

There is no evidence in the sum total of its history that the human species underwent a transition from free encounter with God and fellow humanity to bounded insularity (and in this, as we will discuss, from innocence to culpability). The only human that has ever existed is the same as the one that we now know: the *adam* who by self-inclination compromises communion with God and fellow humans. However else evolutionary adaptation may have introduced change to human makeup, the pre-reflective, contrary impulse against assent to life's covenantal framework remains primordial and unadapted; we are as we were. God has created humanity to be realized in communion, not to return eventually to an alleged communion and be unrealized in the meanwhile.

Second, it is not clear how we ever could know an alternative order of humankind by looking rearwardly. Would it not be of the nature of sin to posit a sinless Self as most natural and encourage its recovery? Revelation does not show a sinless self, but the tendency of the sinful self to consider itself sinless. It thus points forward, not backward, to a Christomorphic alternative. It introduces the sinless self as *promise*, not as artifact. Once again, the primal couple are descriptive and emblematic; their lives are to be understood as placeholders for the true *adam*, causing us not to fix on them, but always to turn away from them to him.

Third, assuming a prior, primordial condition of blessedness in which the human acted freely toward God and fellow humans raised the impossibility of accounting for the transition. Humanity inexplicably forfeited freedom freely or acted as bounded freely. How it should do so has never been satisfactorily answered. For, either the created human actualized a latent potency to sin, which God would have had to put there, which impugns the character of "God" or antecedently restricts the range of options available to God in creating ("only a creature who could reject God can also love him"), or, the human actualized a potency that did not exist. It made something out of the void, as it were, with which God must now contend, a scenario that also destroys any meaningful consciousness of "God."[18]

I have been arguing that there is no such distinction between "once-created" and "then-fallen" humankind, but only humanity as intended, as created *for* covenantal union. There is only authentic and inauthentic human existence; humanity in motion toward bona fides, turning away from the artifice of Self toward its covenantal constitution, toward the true freedom of conscious interdependence. God determines to have life with the creature and so in-time.[19] Execution of this determination generates time; "moment" happens as con-sequence of the act of God and as its willed medium. Time is fundamentally the condition of creaturely realization insofar as its movement supplies the rhythm and cadence required for interpersonal encounter.[20]

To further make this argument, we will analyze a *locus classicus* of theological reflection on human agency, specifically in relation to divine agency: the controversy over synergism. I contend that the divine act of giving (grace) is indeed an imposition against an inauthentic will (life-taking and life-withholding), but that this transpires cynosurally, not in linear-sequential response to a rearward fall. It is thus the ongoing condition of possibility for human freedom, that is, the moment-by-moment condition of assent to life's succession (to receive and then to give), or to enter into reflective, covenantal communion.

In this, I further argue that the solution to the synergist dilemma, and the answer to the question of human freedom, is found by replacing substantialist ontological suppositions with an actualistic account of being. To make that case, I commend the thought of the nineteenth-century German theologian, Isaak Dorner (d. 1884). In the broader context of this book, it is worth noting that Dorner is a principal exponent of "mediating theology," or the school of thought which attempted, in part, to negotiate between the modernism of a figure like Schleiermacher and a more classical orthodoxy, as well as between religion and science.

Isaak Dorner and the Willing Human

"If the older metaphysical doctrine of God was demonstrably supposed to suffer from a lack of idealism and so removed God into an abstract beyond, contemporary theology will perform appropriate service if it vindicates for the concept of God a powerful worldly realism that will repristinate the almost

impotent representations of God and fill them with life and spirit."[21] Against
the metaphysics of classical dogma, and in keeping with his own place in the
tradition of *Vermittlungstheologie*,[22] Dorner argues for an account of God that
affirms God's reality with-us. Such a "realist" account, he contends—that is,
a view in which God is self-determining, yet just so in a concrete redemptive history—not only fills the doctrine of God "with life and spirit," but also
constructively meets the secularism of his age. "The strengthened secular
consciousness of our present age," Dorner writes, "hungers and thirsts for
realism to replace our accustomed idealism."[23]

Dorner argues for a doctrine of God that avoids the extremes of metaphysics and idealism, or, stated positively, that takes seriously *both* divine self-
constitution *and* reciprocal determination by human agency (thought, speech,
action). In doing so, he helps to dissolve one of the most rigid difficulties
posed to Christian theology: the relationship between divine sovereignty,
specifically in the gift of saving grace, and human freedom.

Rather than treating "God" and "humanity" in terms of characteristic oppositions (immutable and mutable, infinite and finite, eternal and temporal),
or, on the other hand, in terms of sameness, ("God" in some way completes
"humanity"), Dorner dialectically understands "God" as persistent alternative
to humanity, yet existing only in relation to humanity. God makes God's self
to be the future of humanity, giving new structure to each generation's present. Thinking of God in terms of moment-by-moment redemptive activity
allows Dorner to identify the divine as existentially determinative without
collapsing the divine into human existence; God compels and orients ethical
human activity but is never simply the sum of such activity.

The Reformation-era debates about human agency in view of the divine
act of salvation, particularly within Lutheranism, supply essential background to Dorner's perspective. We must therefore consider these if we are
to profitably unpack Dorner's insights. Because the older theologians posited
characteristic ontological oppositions between God and humanity, they could
not reconcile self-determinative human operation with God's determinative
action upon the human.

Synergism I: Background

"Synergism" (Gk. *syn* + *ergon*) refers to the belief that the human cooperates
with grace toward salvation, or more narrowly, that human reason or will
or some natural ability works alongside or in concert with God as a *causal
factor* in redemption.[24] Jörg Dierken observes that "the 'working-together'
of God and the human was, for early theologians of the Eastern church like
Origen, Basil, John Chrysostom, Cyril of Alexandria, John of Damascus
or Theophylactus of Achrida, broadly self-evident."[25] In the Latin church,

"cooperative relational allotments [*kooperative Verhältnisbestimmungen*] between divinely gracious dealings and humanly willed activity in the accord of salvation [*Heilsaneinigung*]" played a role in the thinking of Tertullian, Cyprian, Arnobius, Hillary, and Ambrose, and in the scholasticism of the Middle Ages.[26] It is only with Augustine, by way of his disagreement with Pelagius, that "varying, somewhat contradictory claims" about God's action over against human agency surfaced, taking distinctive hold "especially in the 16th century."[27]

A noteworthy development set the stage for the sixteenth-century debates.[28] The late medieval scholastic conception of grace served as the formulation par excellence over and against which Protestantism defined itself. The school of thought represented by Gabriel Biel (d. 1495) emerged as one of the Reformation's chief polemical targets.

Biel identified a significant role for the human to play toward its own redemption from sin and death. Thomas Aquinas (d. 1274) had argued that without the aid of grace, the human could not undertake even works of "congruous merit" (i.e., works of reason and will that are not deserving of reward in themselves, but which God, out of God's goodness, accepts and rewards nonetheless), let alone those of "condign merit" (works of the Holy Spirit, which are meritorious in themselves). Biel demurred, contending that one can, by one's natural powers prior to any supernatural aid, perform works of congruous (although still not condign) merit.[29]

Biel took a weakened view of the effects of sin on all human action. He conceived of sin like a stone weighing down a bird trying to take flight. If the bird receives the right amount of nourishment and tries consistently to fly, strengthening its wings through the effort, eventually it will overcome the impediment of the stone: "grace weakens the remaining power of sin, not . . . because it forgives or wipes out sins, but because it strengthens human power. We could use the illustration of a bird that has a stone tied to it so that it could scarcely fly away. Now if this bird's wings were strengthened, then we would say that the impediment to flight had been lessened, although the weight of the stone had not been lessened."[30] It is not that God counteracts sin in giving grace to the human, but acting on the other side of the ledger, so to speak, God injects strength into a functioning human will. God does not unbind a bounded will, but further empowers a free will to act as it ought. The human, then, overcomes sin in large measure by its own impulse and direction, albeit with some requisite divine assistance.

Erasmus of Rotterdam (d. 1536) held a similarly favorable view of the functioning power of human agency in a state of nature. In his 1524 treatise, "On the Free Will" (*De libero arbitrio*), Erasmus observed, as Dierken signaled above, that the substantial witness of the historic church, east and west, identified a determinative role for the human to work alongside God.[31]

That is, by the power of the human will "man can apply to or turn away from that which leads unto salvation."[32] In line with Biel, Erasmus did not view sin to be a catastrophic problem. "Our power of judgment," he contended, "has only been obscured by sin, and not extinguished."[33] Erasmus considered "too severe" the view of Augustine and the Reformers, which saw so-called "morally good deeds" done in a state of nature as "detestable in God's sight no less than criminal deeds."[34] He defended the perspective of Pelagius and the Nominalists by appealing to a four-fold scholastic hierarchy of grace: the human by birth is viewed to be in a state of "grace by nature" (i.e., created as such by God) and so, even acting naturally, to exercise free will, and to enjoy the added benefits of "extraordinary" or "operative" grace (whereby one acknowledges sinfulness), "efficient" or "cooperative" grace (which promotes the salvation already initiated and enables good works), and "a fourth grace" (which consummates saving cooperation).[35]

In 1525, Martin Luther wrote an irascible rebuttal to Erasmus's treatment of human freedom entitled, "On the Bondage of the Will" (*De servo arbitrio*), which categorically rejected the synergistic heritage of late medieval scholasticism.[36] Luther's argument contained three principal features—mutually supportive, like legs of a stool. These are the catastrophic character of sin, the ineffectiveness of human works, and the conclusiveness of predestination.

Luther's exegesis of Paul's Epistle to the Romans gave shape to his argument.[37] He read Rom. 1:18 ("for the wrath of God is revealed from heaven against all ungodliness and wickedness of those who by their wickedness suppress the truth") as pronouncing "the general verdict on all men, that they are under the wrath of God."[38] Far from being oriented to God in a state of birth, human beings stand opposed to God, suppressing the truth of God from their origin. Even thinking themselves to be in a state of "grace by nature" is a twisted form of just that suppression. They thus "do nothing but what deserves wrath and punishment."[39]

For Luther, the human is so confounded by entrenched rebellion against God that she cannot recognize her entrenchment (but must be made conscious of it; cf. Rom. 3:20). She does not know that she does not know God. "Are not the words entirely clear [Rom. 3:10ff], and do not they teach us just this, that all men are devoid of the knowledge of God . . . ? Such ignorance and contempt are beyond doubt not in the flesh and the lower and grosser passions but . . . in the reason and will, and therefore in the power of free choice itself."[40] Understanding the human according to the older view of hierarchical faculties, Luther rejects any easy solution to sin that relegates it to the baser realm of bodily impulses, whereby it might be overcome by rigorous application of higher faculties like reason and will, and instead identifies sin's grossest corruption to occur in these higher faculties. Because of its own corruption, the will could never become the means of sin's defeat.

Willfully ignorant of its ignorance, what can the human achieve by its efforts except further evil? "What now can reason dictate that is right when it is itself blind and ignorant? What can the will choose that is good when it is itself evil and worthless? Or rather, what choice has the will when reason dictates to it only the darkness of its own blind ignorance? With reason in error, then, and the will misdirected, what can man do or attempt that is good?"[41]

In this dark condition, divine grace clearly cannot be an endowment that perfects an already functional human freedom. Quite the contrary, grace must oppose the boundedness of the will. It must be the work of God over and against sin-soaked human works: "so little can grace tolerate the power of free choice or even the slightest hint of it."[42]

Luther acknowledges that humanity acts freely with regard to quotidian realities (what and when to eat, who to marry, when to plant and harvest). But "what we are asking is whether he has free choice in relation to God."[43] The answer to this is a decisive, "no!" When it comes to conscious, covenantal relation with God and neighbor, Luther is clear that God must act against human will; human redemption is a matter of God's willing. "God has taken my salvation out of my hands into his, making it depend on his choice and not mine."[44]

Luther thus opposes the synergist trajectory of much of the tradition.[45] He rejects as sinful the notion that in its created state humanity possesses a libertarian freedom to will or not to will in favor of God. Indeed, even in a state of grace, Luther views the power of sin to be strong enough to corrupt our decision-making. If we are to have any certainty of salvation, it must come from revealed knowledge that God gratuitously condescends to humankind and acts mercifully toward us. There is, in all of this, an element of hope for Luther: recognition of our inability instinctively invites receptivity to God's re-creative work (whether or not the will can act upon that receptivity); God's Law can force the human to confess its need.

A word of assessment before we look at a more refined version of the synergist debate: Luther's formulation is to be preferred to scholasticism and Erasmian humanism if on no other ground than the seriousness with which it addresses the human condition, especially vis-a-vis the self-limiting length to which God goes in assuring its correction. Luther can be considered a bellwether of the actualistism for which I am arguing even though, as the next conclusion demonstrates, he never draws such conclusions himself. There is a logical thread to trace from the extremity of humanity's need to the constancy of God's provision, that is, to the life and work of God's Spirit.

Yet for all of his disagreements with the scholastics, Luther operates within their same deleterious assumptions. When he thinks and speaks of God and humanity, he does so as given entities, quanta already standing opposite one another. God's electing is construed as being an indescribable rearward decision upon a *massa peccati* ("mass of sin") as Augustine famously put it. Problematic inquiries necessarily followed. What kind of "love" is this that restricts God's favor to an already-existing group, no better or worse than any other group, and damns every other group? What kind of justice is it that arbitrarily excludes a huge portion of human beings?

Luther ought to have argued that because of the extent of sin, there is in fact *no* authentic humanity. There is, from the perspective of divine agency, only inhumanity.[46] The verdict against the human is total. Therefore, God must do again what God has always done: give life. God must reiterate in time God's action "in the beginning"; God must self-consistently be who God is, Lord and Giver of life, so that the human might reciprocally come to be what God intended for it to be, determinative recipient of the Giver's gift.

In this, Luther might have opened up the scope of God's redemptive agency. One might at least hope that saving grace is for everyone, because it is not apportioned to a select group but coordinated with God's very creative action (in which, as we have discussed, God is God); no arbitrary temporal or spatial boundary could be set to it. Reverberations of Word and Spirit might undergird all things, however remote those things are from God. As God rejects what opposes God's will—which is sin, not finite being—and makes that rejection actual in time, does the human qua human come to exist.[47]

From within the thought-structures of metaphysics, Luther could not consistently construe humanity's dying and rising as existential realization of judgment and forgiveness coordinated with the *event* of God's eternal self-giving. He still posited characteristic oppositions between God and humanity, eternity and temporality, and so could not allow for God and the creature to be defined *entirely* in the relation of grace. He still had a self-existent God opposed in essence to a self-existent creature. Consequently, he engendered continued disagreement about the functionality of human agency "by nature, prior to" grace.[48]

Synergism II: The Formula of Concord

Philip Melanchthon (d. 1560) supplies our point of entry into the synergist dispute that unfolded among Luther's followers. Classically trained in philosophy and theology, Melanchthon was the first among the Wittenberg evangelicals to set forth their emerging doctrines in a systematic way. Melanchthon issued his *Theological Commonplaces* (*Loci communes theologici*) in 1521, just three years after he had joined the Wittenberg faculty; significant revisions were published in 1535, 1543, and 1555.

Setting these revisions next to each other, one easily tracks a shift in Melanchthon's thinking vis-a-vis divine grace and human action in salvation. In 1521, Melanchthon, reflecting Luther's influence, directly asserted that "since everything that comes about happens necessarily according to divine predestination, our will has no freedom."[49] He acknowledged that the human enjoys "some freedom in external works," but with regard to our covenantal relation to God, we cannot command our hearts to trust and love God.[50]

By 1555, Melanchthon's views differed notably.[51] He retained the teaching that "all good virtues toward God in the heart and will were . . . lost" in the fall.[52] It is true, he wrote, that "as far as external works are concerned, there remains in man a free will," but with regard to the weightier matter of salvation, "no man by his natural power can take away death and the inborn evil tendency of [his] nature."[53] Moreover, "we cannot continue to produce obedience without the Holy Spirit, for we cannot in and of ourselves ignite in our hearts a firm belief in God."[54] However, Melanchthon no longer worked from these convictions to the conclusion that God exercises a saving choice *over and against* the bounded human. He became concerned that if God were to predestine in such a way that human choice is completely devoid of influence, then God must be the author of every state of human existence, including sin. Such determinism would so degrade the knowledge of "God" as to render it senseless.

In addition, sticking with the plain sense of passages like 1 Tim. 2:4 and 2 Pet. 3:9, which indicate that God's salvific intention is broadly inclusive, the later Melanchthon found it logically necessary to maintain a causal role for human decision. "If the promises of God to have mercy are universal," Clyde Manschreck writes of the evolution in Melanchthon's thinking, "then the reason some are saved and others damned must be that man is in some way responsible" for his eternal condition.[55] The human must exercise some kind of determinative agency in receiving grace or it is impossible to explain why some are saved and others not, since God wishes for all to be saved. Either that, or Scripture is mistaken in its declaration of God's wish.

For Melanchthon, Scripture is not mistaken. God does actually will salvation for all, and as God, can achieve it. The only reason, then, that salvation is not universal is that humans, as they were created by God, enjoy the ability to accept or reject God's work. Their freedom in relation to God still functions at least at the level of some basic, responsive instinct, which God recognizes and to which he responds. Human agency is thus a causal factor in salvation. Melanchthon famously wrote, "we should not think that a man is a piece of wood or a stone, but as we hear the word of God, in which punishment and comfort are put forth, we should neither despise nor resist it. We should immediately arouse our hearts to earnest prayer."[56]

Of course, this assumes that the human *can* arouse its heart in a repentant attitude. At this point, Melanchthon finds himself caught in a thicket. On the one hand, sin binds the human will so that it cannot respond favorably to God, either incipiently or in any lasting reiteration. Yet on the other hand, the human is a human and not a block of wood and so is expected not to respond in mute silence to the Word of God. "This [contradiction] led Melanchthon to his famous *causa concurrens*: the Holy Spirit and the word are first active in conversion, but the will of man is not wholly inactive; God draws, but draws him who is willing, for man is not a statue."[57] God does not act against the human but engages the human as a third cause alongside (and in response to) Word and Spirit in a cooperative fashion. Those who are saved, while not generating grace, do gladly receive it. In fact, they *must* receive it. Word and Spirit only work with this receptivity.

By positing receptivity of human will not just as Luther did (as appropriate response to recognition of the human predicament, which nonetheless may not be acted upon), but as a third factor alongside Word and Spirit in salvation, Melanchthon softens Luther's bleak account of the human condition. But he does not depart from Luther's conceptual framework. Melanchthon, too, speaks of the human as a standing entity toward which a standing deity directs himself. To his credit, Melanchthon makes the response of faith central to realization of that human before her God. But doing so from within the assumptions of a basically substantialist ontology, he splits the human into a meaningless contradiction: at once unable to respond to the Word of God, yet respons-ible (able and accountable) for doing so.

Against the views of Melanchthon and his students, who became known as the party of Philip or the "Philippists," clustering in Wittenberg, a second group reasserted "pure" Lutheran doctrine concerning sin, human agency, and grace. Matthias Flacius (d. 1575) took zealous lead of the "Gnesio-Lutheran" party, clustered in Magdeburg.

Matija Vlačić Ilirik[58] (Latinized: Matthias Flacius Illyricus) was born in Venetian Albona, present-day Labin, Croatia, a city along the eastern edge of the Istrian peninsula in the northern Adriatic. Istria was part of the pre-Roman kingdom of Illyria, a heritage reflected in Flacius's assumption of the designation, "Ilirik." Flacius determined to serve the church already as a young man and to study theology. Wishing to follow the path of his uncle-by-marriage, the prior Baldo Lupetina, he intended for his theological training to take place in one of Venetia's Franciscan monasteries.[59] But Lupetina, having come under the influence of Lutheran doctrine, instead steered his eager nephew to schooling in Reformation lands. Flacius studied in Basel, Tübingen, and finally, from 1541 to 1543, in Wittenberg.

Beyond giving doctrinal orientation to his theological formation, Lupetina's own circumstances (as a Franciscan in Venetia sympathetic to Luther) influenced Flacius. Preaching bondage of the will, predestination, and the ineffectiveness of works for salvation, Lupetina was reported to the Inquisition and imprisoned in November 1542. Attempts at intervention by princes of the Smalcald League and even Luther himself, whose correspondence in behalf of Lupetina Flacius delivered personally, proved ineffective. Lupetina remained in prison until 1556, when he was drowned. Oliver Olson notes that "the root of [Flacius's] polemical zeal" can be traced to the Lupetina affair.[60] Both Flacius's strident opposition to political interference in churchly matters and his commitment to doctrinal purity in the face of exile and threat were no doubt galvanized in part by his intimate connection to Lupetina.

Equally galvanizing was a three-year bout of spiritual depression, which Flacius suffered initially in Basel. According to Wilhelm Preger, he was lifted from existential despair finally by the pastoral care of Luther, who identified in Flacius something of his own faith struggle as an Augustinian, and who thus stressed the certainty of justification by faith alone.[61] Flacius's lifelong effort to protect this teaching against any adulteration by the supplement of human works undoubtedly reflects his conversion to it. Indeed, I share this brief biography of Flacius to indicate that of all the Lutherans, except Luther himself, Flacius was perhaps best positioned to appreciate the existential decisiveness of Luther's teaching. But Flacius, too, was victimized by the ontological presuppositions of his era.

The synergist fight between Philippists and Gnesio-Lutherans began earnestly in 1555 when the Philippist Johann Pfeffinger published a series of propositions defending free will. The Magdeburg theologian, Nicholas von Amsdorf (d. 1573) first responded, and Flacius quickly joined the lists. The highwater mark of disagreement came in 1560 at Weimar, where Flacius debated Viktorin Strigel (d. 1569).[62] Having trained and lectured in Aristotelian philosophy, Strigel employed the categories of substance and accidence to human being. He argued that sin is accident-al to the human, part of humanity's alterable form, not part of the unchanging substance that makes the human to be *human*. Flacius countered that sin is too potent and determinative to be mere accident. The created substance of the human must be corrupted itself. Human nature had been effectively supplanted by a kind of sin nature. Flacius tried to distinguish between kinds of substance so as not to divorce the human so completely from God as to make the devil its creator. But the distinction seems to have been without force. If Melanchthon split the human into a bounded state of sin, on one side, and a capacity of receptivity, on the other, Flacius, despite his intention, conflated the human in total into bounded sinful nature. Sin was effectively the essence of the human.

The later concordists settled on a mediating position.[63] On original sin, they concluded against Flacius, contending that "the corrupted human being cannot be sin itself, without any distinction between the two. Otherwise, God would be the creator of sin."[64] They affirmed, in other words, the Philippist concern that a complete nullification of responsible human being and doing (and corollary, absolute divine determinism) demeans God by contend-ing that sin originates with God (or turns the human into a creation of the anti-god, the devil). Moreover, one must differentiate between human nature and sin, lest in forgiving sin God obliterates the human.[65]

But how strong should we understand that differentiation to be? On free will, the concordists concluded against the Philippists:

> We reject and condemn . . . the teaching that, although human beings are too weak to initiate conversion with their free will before rebirth, and thus convert themselves to God on the basis of their own natural powers . . . nonetheless, once the Holy Spirit has made a beginning . . . the human will is able out of its own natural powers to a certain degree, even though small and feeble, to do something, to help and cooperate, to dispose and prepare itself for grace, to grasp this grace, to accept it, and to believe the gospel.[66]

The human is so bound in sin that she cannot cooperate with God unto salvation; even subsequent to an initial endowment of grace, the human remains in bondage. She needs the continuing work of divine mercy on her behalf, never relying on a latent capacity to set herself into a positive relation to God. She lacks, unto the end, a natural capacity even of receptivity to divine grace.[67] The concordists thus separate human nature in its created state from its sin nature, yet construe the former to have become so corrupted by the latter as to be rendered ineffectual. For all intents and purposes, humanity is dead in its sin, not merely wounded.[68]

In this, the Formula of Concord (1580) largely restates Luther's position, albeit in a more refined way. It leaves the discussion with the same, long-standing tensions. It confesses the existence of a created nature apart from sin, but only as hypothetical. In the actual fact of all human beings, sin nullifies the created condition. It acknowledges the need for decisive intervention by God, but it denies determinism. It refuses the human a role to play in salvation, but it insists that God does not so act against the human as to nullify its nature; the human qua human must act as a responsible party.

Can these conclusions be reconciled? I have begun to argue that the underlying problematic, enduring beyond Concord, is unexamined commitment to a static ontology in which divinity and humanity are conceived *a priori* to subsist in and of themselves. What is needed is a thorough subordination of ontology to epistemology and ethics. That is, God and humanity must be redefined according to the perception and operation of charity; God and humanity come to exist in conscious, moment-by-moment establishment of covenantal relationship—life freely given and joyously received.

Once More, Isaak Dorner

We catch a glimpse of the needed subordination of ontology to epistemology and ethics in Isaak Dorner. Of principal relevance for us is the way that he describes God and humanity to exist in a coordinated event.[69] As indicated above, Dorner expresses dissatisfaction with the traditional, metaphysical account of God.[70] A God whose God-ness is necessarily "above" or "beyond" the physical, in a "simplicity" that absorbs all ethical attributes into substantial perfections—is straightforwardly not the Christian God. Such a God can only be conceived "deistically," as unconcerned with creation, or "acosmically,"[71] entirely one with creation so that any self-determination of the world (with its change and complexity) is an illusion.

But in rejecting traditional, static metaphysics and its corollary deism or pantheism, Dorner still does not find a solution in the kenotic Christology favored in his day (e.g., in Gottfried Thomasius and the Erlangen School). For Dorner, the only way that one can consistently carry through the notion of a radical divestiture of divine predicates—in Christ's kenosis or self-emptying (Phil. 2:7)—is by extending the divestiture into God in God's self, a move that reduces the Son to the status of a creature and represents another kind of pantheism.[72] Dorner thus charts a path between metaphysics and kenoticism. He tries to retain the primal objectivity and self-determination of God even as he understands "God" only in the terms of a definite relation to the world.

Dorner begins by raising a series of objections to the classical teaching, central to metaphysical theological speculation, concerning divine "simplicity." Asserting that God is "simple" meant to resist the idea that God is composite, made collectively of parts or characteristics. Stated positively, it intended to explicate the truth that God is a unity; God is one, not a collection of subdivine qualities or sub-divine entities that only together comprise divinity, but are not each fully divine in themselves, and not a tribunal of divinities whose cumulative counsel amounts to divine will. Rather, the ancients wished to ground God's unity in the most basic possible oneness (judged from within the scope of their Hellenistic context), a singularity of *being*.

Confessing such singularity, the tradition sought to deny every real distinction in God that might be conceived. God is *actus purus*, pure act, not part potential and part act. God's attributes are varied from the perspective of the human but are undifferentiated in God's self. God is not subject to shift from one state of existence, will, knowledge, or emotion to another. God is similarly not constrained by sequence or location, as if God could move from one moment or space to the next, or as if part of God was located in one moment and space and another part elsewhen and elsewhere.

In the attempt to arrive at a mediating doctrine of God, between metaphysics and kenoticism, Dorner does not dismiss such teachings about divine simplicity out of hand. Rather, he reinterprets them constructively, that is, in such a way as to take more seriously the reality of God's existence in and among the contingencies of space-time, suffering, and above all, love.[73] For the sake of space, I will focus on just two of the ways that Dorner constructively rethinks divine simplicity. One has to do with the life of God; the other with humanity as the creature intended by God. Together, these insights compose a dynamic picture of God in relation to humanity, which conceptualization helps to dissolve the synergist dilemma.

In the first place, Dorner corrects the contention that God is pure act. "The distinction of *potentia* and *actus*," Dorner argues, "if aseity is to be taken seriously, may not be so annulled that God is conceived only as one of the two, as if perfection lay in that one [*actus*] alone."[74] As indicated, Dorner does not forfeit the truth of divine aseity, the teaching that God's deity is entirely sufficient in itself. Quite the opposite, he argues that this teaching must be taken seriously, but he concludes that this can only be done if God's essence is both potential and actual:

> If [God's] Trinitarian self-establishment is an enduring one and not something once occurring and now past, then God is to be conceived as eternally both absolute potentiality and absolute actualization by virtue of the eternally self-rejuvenating divine life-process. This, to be sure, will only be possible, figuratively speaking, in that the life of God constitutes an organism and cycle of life, or logically speaking, in that the eternal and absolute self-actualization of God eternally wills and confirms its own ground.[75]

Dorner reasons that if God is the only ground of God's life, then God's Trinitarian essence is something over which God must exercise a kind of right of establishment. But if this is to endure, which is to say, if this self-establishment is "not something once occurring and now past" and God is to be again who God is, then God must moment-by-moment will and enact God's life. God cannot be trapped, as it were, by an abstract "eternity" of self. To say that God is eternal cannot be to say that God is not vital, or, to speak figuratively, "organic." Rather, God forever wills and enacts who God is, which means that God is both fully potential and fully actual; God is *God* by continuing exercise of a comprehensive power of self-determination.

If this is so, then we must conceive of God's relation to the world as being coordinately established in and with the fullness of God's vitality. The world is not a problem to God in God's self, a realm of contingency over and against static immutability. If God's aseity is instead thought of as "a fullness of divine powers . . . whereby the divine life appears not as an endless indeterminate ocean, but as an infinitely determinate and structural organism,"[76] then the world can be seen to exist simply in and through divine self-determination. God establishes God's self as the ground of all possibility, including the world in its every variation (and the human in its freedom), this, once more, moment by moment.

Dorner retains affirmation of the consummate uniqueness of God's existence but recasts it in terms of active priority. What makes God of God is not a particular substance out of which God acts, which as an infinite substance common-alizes God's acts, if you will, or reduces them to an ontic unity (while still affirming distinction as to form). But rather, Dorner construes the self-differentiating, self-determining character of God as a maximal event: God exists as such in the coordinated reoccurrence of self-establishment and other-establishment. God exists as God causes God's self to be *means* and *telos*, becomes *primus* to a *secunda*. Or God exists as Creator, Redeemer, and Sanctifier. "God thinks and wills himself as the beginning, the means and final goal of the world."[77]

In this, God subjects God's life to the vicissitudes of the contingent other. "The world is conceived by God as fluid and changeable . . . ; consequently, the divine understanding (even if originally through itself) is also afflicted with the changeable, and indeed not merely as spectator but also as ideationally productive of it."[78] God knows, and by virtue of the knowing, causes God's self to be afflicted with the changeability inherent to the world. God not only sees God's self in this way but reiteratively makes it so; he is no mere spectator of his mutuality relative to the world. God understands God's self as an organic origin of all reality. This *is* God's existence: *as* Source, Sustenance, and Goal, *as* bringing about a world and entering into dynamic interplay with it, culminating ultimately in charitable communion.[79]

Recognition of the dynamic interplay between "God" and "creation" brings us to the second way that Dorner constructively reconsiders divine simplicity, which is instructive for our treatment of the synergist problem, namely, his understanding of humankind. "Man is not destined to rest merely embraced by the divine power," Dorner observes, "like a child in its mother's lap; he is rather to become a proper causality of a secondary sort."[80] God creates a living existent, an other with whom God exists in *actual* relation. "A reality that is . . . absolutely passive, would be only an altogether dead one, a nothingness . . . so that the divine actuality would be no causality at all, would have effected nothing."[81] If God exists in productive *self*-establishment, a selfhood that is defined by *causal relation*, then of necessity the effected other must possess a measure of corollary self-determination; the human must, paradoxically, come to be what it is, "an effect which is self-effecting, an act which becomes active."[82] As we discussed in our exegesis above, the human is at once product and producer, willed participant in the "from-for" succession of life, secondary life-giver after the manner of the Giver of Life.

The crucial point is that just as "God" is that in which humanity lives and moves and has being, so also—again, contingently—"humanity" is that in which God dwells and moves:

[God] does not will to stand merely in the relation to [human beings] of a purely determining power; no more does he will to be in the mere relation of law objective to them. Rather, on the grounds that they live, move, and are *in him* whether they will it or not, he wills to dwell and move *in them* as the beings they have themselves actually become, willing and knowing themselves to be what they are recognized [*erkannt*] by God to be, that is, what is God's eternal idea of them.[83]

By exercise of its received self-determination, the human comes to be what it is intended by God to be, the occasion of *God's* self-determination. That is, as the human knows and wills itself in relation to God, it exists as the covenant partner known and willed by God, which primal knowing and willing is, once more, the self-establishment of "God."

Neither God nor humanity is a given, a quantum, or a datum, to which the other somehow enters into relation. Rather, "God" and "humanity" come to exist per se only in the event of relation to each other, which is not a *purely* reciprocal affair (as if one might start with either God or the human). God is always first, or God is not God; indeed, it is the first-ness, the absolute precedence, that makes it to be *God's* knowing and willing. The productive efficacy of human knowing and willing begins as *product*. *God* exists as subject-determining object of the human.

But God does will only to *be* in and with the human, subjected to creaturely subjectivity. It is the determination of physics, historically conditioned thought and will, not un-determinable metaphysics, that makes God of God.

CONCLUSION

Dorner supplies the kind of conceptual resources needed to unravel the classical tangle of synergism: denial of any native human potential or capacity for God, and with this, affirmation of the comprehensiveness of divine action on humanity's behalf, yet at the same time, affirmation of authentic *humanity* in the event of the covenant, and so a non-deterministic account of *God's* life and work. He achieves this by locating the content of "God" and "humanity" in a concrete, historical activity, God's *moment-by-moment* self-giving in Christ.

The question of human freedom in relation to God's act is resolved when God's act is understood as both self-determining and continuing. God wills to live as Life-giver in each creaturely generation, as the reiterative ground of that generation's authenticity (i.e., in the act of creation-preservation). The human is thus regenerated, made free to be by the freedom that God is, which freedom it at once enacts by saying "yes" to its relational constitution.

There is no linear chronology here, only dynamic living-after in the sense of living-in-the-manner-of. As I have argued, the human discovers that her life is not a given but a being-given, which discovery (in revelation) obliges her to embrace the giving. She sees goodness and rightness in the action of giving herself for the sake of others as, for her sake, God gives. The human exists authentically when she consciously becomes a secondary life-giver, joyfully entering life's "from-for" succession by living according to the ethics of interdependence. The capacity for otherness consciously actualized in the giving of self is the freedom of the Spirit.

NOTES

1. "The idea here is that man is recognized to be a social being"; Sarna, *Genesis*, 21.

2. A parenthetical observation about interpretation is worth making: according to the parallelism of Gen. 1:20–23 and 24f, the flying creatures (עוֹף) were made not of הָאֲדָמָה as here in 2:19, but from the waters (הַמַּיִם). Such textual inconsistencies can be gainfully understood only if our hermeneutical procedure accords appropriate flexibility to the writing of ancient creation myths and does not seek hidden scientific (in the modern sense) information, as we said in chapter 1.

3. Barth, CD III.1, 289–90.

4. It is worth noting that the first "not good" in the biblical canon occurs in v. 18, when the LORD God says, לֹא־טוֹב הֱיוֹת הָאָדָם לְבַדּוֹ ("it is not good for the human to be alone"). The goodness of humanity is thus characterized by the opposite state of things, not by aloneness but by communion.

5. Barth, CD III.1, 290.

6. "The whole phrase (Heb. *ezer kenegdo*) could be rendered 'a helping counterpart.' At any rate, the Hebrew does not suggest a subordinate position for women"; Fox, *The Five Books of Moses*, 20 n. 18.

7. Barth, CD III.1, 292.

8. On the man's sense of isolation apart from another like him, see Sarna, *Genesis*, 22: "The review of the subhuman creation makes the man conscious of his own uniqueness, of his inability to integrate himself into that whole biological order or feel direct kinship with the other animate beings. At the same time, by observing the otherwise universal complementary pairing of male and female, he becomes aware of his own exceptional status and of his loneliness."

9. Thus the, "at last . . . ," the ecstatic proclamation of 2:23 in which, over against all the animals, man finds the partner who completes him, who makes him to realize his manhood. Wenham notes that "in these five short lines [of 2:23] many of the standard techniques of Hebrew poetry are employed: parallelism . . . assonance and word play . . . ; chiasmus . . . ; and verbal repetition"; *Genesis 1–15*, 70. The joyous self-discovery of man in discovery of woman is highlighted by the intricate aesthetics of its narration—syllabic progression (one line of four syllables, one of six, and three

of seven), assonance and wordplay between "*ishah* and *ish*," parallels between "bone" and "flesh," "woman" and "man."

10. The interpersonal intimacy between man and woman is further signaled by the bemusing account of vv. 21–22, in which the woman is depicted as being derived from the very corpus of the man. Although I have followed the standard interpretation, rendering צֵלָע as "rib," the word has a flexible range of meaning, including "side chamber" (of a building), or just "side," (see BDB 5th ed. p. 854), perhaps "midsection." It is not clear what exactly the author intends.

Sarna associates the imagery with *theotokic* narratives, in which gods are birthed from that particular body part, which corresponds to the deity's distinguishing character (e.g., the Mesopotamian god of wisdom, Ea, is associated with "the ear of Ninurta," and the Greek goddess of love and fertility, Aphrodite, sprung from the sea foam collected around the severed penis of Uranus [*Genesis*, 22]). One obvious shortcomings of this view is the lack of any clear, corresponding quality obtaining to the male rib or side, which would distinguish the woman as such (except, so Sarna, a very general sense of "equivalent structure").

Reacting against readings that take the author to be making reference to some feature of human anatomy, such as the popular but mistaken view that men have one less rib than women, Wenham looks for meaning above the level of corporeal description. "The whole account of woman's creation has a poetic flavor: it is certainly mistaken to read it as an account of a clinical operation or as an attempt to explain some feature of man's anatomy. . . . Here the ideal of marriage as it was understood in ancient Israel is being portrayed, a relationship characterized by harmony and intimacy between the partners" (*Genesis 1–15*, 69). That the text lauds marriage as humanly ideal is true enough, but lacking in explanatory force. The passage is concerned to locate interpersonal union at a primal level, the outcome of which is, quintessentially, marriage, yet it is not clear that marriage per se is the impelling motive behind the passage's logic.

If Sarna's line of reasoning is basically aetiological, and Wenham's symbolic, a third approach understands vv. 21–22 to form a wordplay or pun. Whereas צֵלָע means something like "side," צָלַע (different vowel pointing) means "stumble." Is there a veiled reference here to the way that woman is at once essential to man, yet in view of Genesis 3, a cause of stumbling? Probably not. As G. P. Hugenberger notes, the text makes the opposite point, stressing "the supreme adequacy of the woman as a suitable helper"; see Hugenberger, "Rib," *The International Standard Bible Encyclopedia* rev. ed. vol. 4, ed. Geoffrey W. Bromiley (Grand Rapids: Eerdmans, 1988), 183–85 (citation on p. 184).

Setting aside aetiological, symbolic, and wordplay, Hugenberger focuses on the woman's derivation: just as *adam* is not made *ex nihilo*, but formed from the *adamah*, so is the woman not derived out of nothing, but "built" (בנה) from the man. Thus, just as "Adam's creation answers an expressed need with respect to the ground . . . [so also] Eve's creation answers a prior need in Adam" ("Rib," 184). Continuing along this trajectory, Hugenberger considers whether the "cutting" involved in the formation of woman is meant to echo the "cutting" of the covenant with Abraham. The fact that the *adam* is put into a trance (תַּרְדֵּמָה) like Abraham may be relevant. The woman represents a primary locus of covenant partnership apart from which man is unfinished.

However they are understood, the critical point of these verses is that there is inbuilt correspondence between man and woman. So Westermann: "the process of creation itself explains how man and woman belong together" (*Genesis 1–11*, 230).

11. It is often remarked, in fact, that in naming the animals the man stands in a position of authority over them. Language use itself is a medium of human power. "Because man gives names to the animals, his sovereignty over them is asserted," Westermann writes (*The Genesis Accounts of Creation*, 29). This is certainly true, but the text is not to be pressed into a general theory of language—either with regards to use or origin. Moreover, it has to be noted that at least at this point (the situation may be different in Genesis 3, concerning Adam's naming of "Eve"), the man exercises no authority over the woman in calling her "woman," for with this "name" the man simultaneously expresses his own identity as "man" (אִישׁ appears for the first time here), and so establishes the inherent equality of the woman. "Of an entirely different order from this objective knowledge," Westermann continues, "is the 'jubilant welcoming' (as Herder put it) of woman by man. . . . The name that he selects for her is a name of love and is at the same time a thanksgiving for God's gift"; (ibid.).

Sarna expresses the matter succinctly:

> Insofar as the power of naming implies authority, the text voices the social reality of the ancient Near East. Yet the terminology used here differs from that employed in verse 20 for naming the animals. Here the man gives her a generic, not a personal, name, and that designation is understood to be derived from his own, which means he acknowledges woman to be his equal. Moreover, in naming her *'ishah*, he simultaneously names himself. Hitherto he is consistently called *'adam*; he now calls himself *'ish* for the first time. Thus he discovers his own manhood and fulfillment only when he faces the woman, the human being who is to be his partner in life. (*Genesis*, 23)

It is too much, in my judgment, to stress a distinction between "generic" and "personal" naming, as this already supposes a good deal about language. Furthermore, animal "names" indicate that personal names are often generic descriptions that have become refined by usage. But the essence of Sarna's point is well-taken: in its intended condition, man cannot name woman without naming himself, and so cannot exercise some language-conferred authority over woman, since he effectively "discovers his own manhood" only in reflective awareness of his person in relation to hers.

In respect of this reflective awareness, a final point about language: although the text does not supply a general theory of language, by placing language on humanity's lips precisely at the point of self-discovery ("Now this is bone from my bones and flesh from my flesh!"), the text correlates the reflective companionship constitutive of human existence with language. Or more precisely, it introduces language as the medium of that companionship by which humanity is realized.

However much word functions as the medium of sin, of humanity's dislocation vis-a-vis God, creation, and itself (we will consider this with reference to the work of Paul Ricouer in chapter 5), it is also, and more so, the means by which sin is defeated, and so at once the means of human reconciliation (on each level). In word, the self-contradictory impulse to isolation is named, that is, identified and condensed in thought and externalized in speech—the act of confession. In turn, the human may set himself in relation to this articulated impulse: he may embrace and revel in it, or disavow it and repent. And in turn, the human may hear a word of response to his confession; he may receive judgement and forgiveness. Indeed, the human word may be met by the divine Word. Acknowledged and taken up by it, the human word may answer the Word of grace and pardon, which now becomes the condition by which the thinker and speaker is freed to seek an alternative construction, a life in relation to God and fellow humans.

12. *Therapeutic* cloning is another matter. As we will discuss in chapter 5, it may well be the responsibility of humankind so-evolved to bring the full weight of its reflective heritage to bear against threats to life resident in the web of life, and so to put its growing command of genetic processes to the work of repairing and replacing compromised organs and tissues.

The line between reproductive and therapeutic cloning is not easily drawn, as the same techniques are used in each case (the difference residing largely in the degree of cellular specification). Moreover, in both cases the issue of identity is complexified: also in therapeutic cloning the individual begins to take on a mechanized hue, functioning as a collection of interchangeable parts. Nevertheless, it strikes me that a line can and should be drawn between life *extracted from* and life *willfully embedded in* the web.

Reproductive cloning extracts this one species from the web and definitively sets it above all others by way of self-derived mastery of the generative potential of others. Therapeutic cloning just as definitively imbeds the human in the web as its servant (as the growth and replacement of new organs and tissues is not only tested among but also enhances the viability of various species). Mechanizing the individual may prove avoidable (practice alone will tell) by virtue of the interdependence of organs and tissues in the body; therapeutic cloning can only succeed insofar as it can overcome the crucial obstacles of immune rejection and holistic functionality. Mechanizing might also be overcome by the continuity of memory, although scope prevents further discussion of that prospect for the time being.

13. It is too much to claim, as Augustine does, that "holy virginity" represents a higher order of existence than sex within marriage (which he deems nonetheless honorable, or not sinful, so long as it is done to produce children, by contrast to marital sex for pleasure and extramarital sex for children, both of which are venial sins, as well as extramarital sex for pleasure, a mortal [!] sin; see Augustine, "The Excellence of Marriage," in *Marriage and Virginity*, The Works of Saint Augustine 1/9, ed. John E. Rotelle, O.S.A., trans. Ray Kearney [New York: New City, 1998], 41–43). Augustine argues this on the unstable ground that reproduction is no longer necessary to populate the kingdom of God: "at earlier times, before Christ became man, there was need to have descendants physically for a large nation, for it to be the bearer of prophecy. Now, however, since members of Christ to be God's people and citizens of the kingdom of heaven can be brought in from the whole human race and from every nation, *Let anyone who is able to accept it, accept* sacred virginity (Mt. 19:12), and only those who are unable to be continent should marry; *for it is better to marry than to burn* (1 Cor. 7:9)";

Augustine, "Holy Virginity," in *Marriage and Virginity*, 72. No further reproduction among Christians is necessary, only conversion among pagans, and growth in physical restraint (which is the same as progress in spiritual maturity) among the converted.

Besides the fact that many generations and much time have passed since Augustine's, and many more pagans than converts have lived and died, which makes God's historical aims seem either ill-conceived or poorly executed, Augustine's exaltation of celibacy as spiritually ideal reflects more Neoplatonism than biblical insight. "The freedom from all sexual intimacy that comes with the devout practice of celibacy, belongs with the angels, and in corruptible flesh it is a foretaste of eternal incorruptibility. All physical parenthood, all married chastity, must give way to this"; (ibid., 74). In the light of his treatment of Matt. 19:12, Augustine's thinking here borders on veneration of the epicene.

Luther's elevation of the marital estate, including its conjugal practice, to the same level of monastic spirituality—in certain respects, to a higher level—is to be preferred. Luther reasons that there is no better context than the Christian home in which to participate in God's dearest labor: "the greatest good in married life, that which makes all suffering and labor worth while, is that God grants offspring and commands that they be brought up to worship and serve him. In all the world this is the noblest and most precious work, because to God there can be nothing dearer than the salvation of souls"; Luther, "The Estate of Marriage," in Luther's Works 45: The Christian in Society II, ed. Walther I. Brandt (Philadelphia: Fortress, 1962), 46. Man and woman realize God's intention by having children and raising them to know and love God. (There is clearly a divergent soteriology in play for Luther as well, one that is more "existential" than, as for Augustine, "sapiential"; on this, see the classic work by Otto Hermann Pesch, O. P., "Existential and Sapiential Theology—The Theological Confrontation between Luther and Thomas Aquinas," in *Catholic Scholars Dialogue with Luther*, ed. Jared Wicks [Chicago: Loyola University Press, 1970], 61–81.)

Although his view is exegetically sounder (esp. vis-a-vis Gen. 2:18–25), and better accords with God's continuing work of redemption through the long generations, Luther rightly qualifies it. "I do not wish to disparage virginity, or entice anyone away from virginity into marriage. Let each one act as he is able, and as he feels it has been given to him by God" (*The Estate of Marriage*, 46.). For Luther, it is the freedom reiteratively to confirm in marriage and childbearing the covenantal union for which he was created that is critical to human being. He defends the spirituality of the estate of marriage not as an ideal for everyone, but as the conventional setting for the vast majority of human beings in which to realize their humanity as servants of God's creation.

Indeed, Luther considers the passage cited by Augustine above (Mt. 19:12), which concerns categories of "eunuchs." In each case, he acknowledges exceptions to the command to "be fruitful and multiply" (Gen. 1:28; 9:7). He criticizes only those who would elevate the category of voluntary virginity to highest order spirituality, and so expand it to include those incapable of achieving such a thing, whereby undue elevation of the goal renders the ardor of the task mercilessly involuntary (see ibid., 18–22).

14. Barth, CD III.1, 301.

15. See ibid., 300–301: "the simplest and most comprehensive definition of woman is that she is the being to which man, himself becoming male [שׁיא], can and must say in the exercise of his freedom that 'this' is now the helpmeet which otherwise he had sought in vain but which had now been fashioned and brought by God."

16. Sarna, *Genesis*, 23.

17. In fairness to Barth, his exegesis here is, typically, more theological than linguistic.

18. The tradition supposes a linear sequentialism, treating Eden as a "once-upon-a-time" condition, subsequent history as a fall from that condition, and subsequent Paradise as restoration of Edenic existence. This view supposes a continuing, stable substance, called *"adam,"* fashioned at creation then enduring through fall and redemption, as well as an equally enduring divine substance (extending even "before" creation). I argue for a cynosural temporality, such that time is a collective, spiraling movement from promise to fulfillment, from the pledge of life to acceptance, then again from its culmination to commencement, then again from its prospect or hope to its source or ground, and so on. Proper human freedom is not yet, even though it is already achieved; we experience it in Spirit.

19. God's determination is "in-time" in the sense that it anticipates the fullness of relationship in which God and creation are meant to exist, that is, it comes in (due) time. It is "in-time" in the sense that it rescues the human from rendering itself timeless and nonexistent, that is, it arrives (just) in time. And it is "in-time" in the sense that it transpires according to temporal framing, that is, it unfolds (with-)in time, within the time that it creates.

20. This movement, time, is coordinated with the determinative movement of God: time is and comes again to be (as) both the theater of life and means of its relation, just as "God" is both the field of life and its condition. The event of time is reiterative of the event of God; with time, as primarily with God, life is co-determinative. Its appearing, as primarily with his, is only among the living (cf. Mk. 12:27; Matt. 22:32; Lk. 20:38): as life knows itself in being given, it at once is conscious of Giver, and in turn, it seeks and finds the Giver in the act of giving—as it turns to other lives in support and encouragement, in grace, it finds what it knows, what first found and encountered it, the God of grace—and so also, in just this seeking and finding, makes real its time. Time is neither more nor less than measure of the events that make up the living. It is either, therefore, a fixed artifice of linear life, or a dynamic modality coordinate with life in truth. In fact, in the transition from bondage to freedom, it is both.

21. Isaak A. Dorner, *Divine Immutability: A Critical Reconsideration*, trans. Robert R. Williams and Claude Welch (Minneapolis: Fortress, 1994), 42. This text is a collection of three essays, which Dorner published between 1856 and 1858 in *Jahrbücher für deutsche Theologie* under the title, "Über die richtige Fassung des dogmatischen Begriffs der Unveränderlichkeit Gottes, mit besonderer Beziehung auf das gegenseitige Verhältniss zwischen Gottes übergeschichtlichem und geschichtlichem Leben."

22. "Mediating Theology" broadly refers to the attempt in the nineteenth century to reconcile theology and science, and more narrowly to bridge between Protestant

orthodoxy and liberalism (in both cases, between traditional Christianity and modernity). More narrowly still, Dorner charts a path between what he takes to be the last
in the line of metaphysical theologians, F. D. E. Schleiermacher, and the quintessential idealist, G. W. F. Hegel, that is, with regards to immutability, the inability of
Schleiermacher's God to be impacted by the world, and Hegel's ever-evolving God.

23. Dorner, *Divine Immutability*, 42. To say that a "strengthened secular consciousness" is a product of idealist religion is to say that secularism, or the effort to
think and construct society in its various organizations and conventions absent religious influence, correlates directly with an accounting of "God" that is deliberately
constrained to self-reference and self-consciousness, apart from revelation considered
objectively. Dorner cites Ludwig Feuerbach's diagnosis of self-projection in idealist
theology and a rise of materialism as evidence of a strengthened secular consciousness in his era. Cf. Feuerbach, *The Essence of Christianity*.

24. The crucial verbiage is "causal factor." Human agency in some way contributes to the actualization of God's redemptive work; cf. Werner Joest, "Synergismus,"
RGG VI, 561–62 (*der Mensch als ursächlicher Faktor* neben *der Gnade vorgestellt
wird*). See also Jörg Dierken, "Synergismus," *TRE* XXXII, 508–24: "In a general
sense, synergism signifies various conceptions, which see the cause, that is the
underlying principal of the reception of salvation (*den Grund bzw. die Ursache
des Heilsempfangs*) in a spiritual or ethical cooperation of the human, or rather, in
the 'working-together' of God and the human (*im Zusammenwirken von Gott und
Mensch*)" (509).

25. Dierken, "Synergismus," 509.

26. Ibid. There's something of a wordplay here, as *Heilsaneinigung* connotes both
a salvific agreement between parties (as between God and the human) and the reaching of a mutual conclusion (as between theologians on the doctrine of salvation).

27. Ibid.

28. German mysticism supplied a second stage-setting factor. Dierken observes
that through the "theology of passion" or "suffering" of the *Devotia moderna*, "the
foundation of justification by human faith witnessed, in the [person's] yielding to a
takeover of the discipleship of the cross, a dispositional prerequisite to the receiving
of grace, or in . . . 'calmness'/'letting go' (*Gelassenheit*), deliberate coordination of
divine and human wills." In this way, redemption was construed synergistically, over
and against the more monergistically-oriented notion that God deals with humanity
in the external means of Word and Sacrament alone; see "Synergismus," 510.

29. The infusion of grace, for Biel, is a subsequent addition to works of congruous merit, a reward for such works itself, which allows humans to perform works of
condign merit, acts of cooperation with the Spirit that receive the ultimate reward of
eternal life. Biel envisioned salvation to occur via participation in a sort of symbiotic
back-and-forth between God and humanity, which system God has ordained. This
salvation is "by grace" in the sense that the human is graced with life, out of which
it performs good deeds (via the conscience), for which it is rewarded with additional
aid from God, and so on. For a helpful introduction to late medieval theology, and
specifically to Biel as representative of its Pelagian elements, see Denis R. Janz,
"Late Medieval Theology," in *The Cambridge Companion to Reformation Theology*,

ed. David Bagchi and David C. Steinmetz, Cambridge Companions to Religion (Cambridge: Cambridge University Press, 2004), 5–14; see esp. pp. 10–13. For a more expansive overview of this background, see Steven Ozment, *The Age of Reform 1250–1550: An Intellectual and Religious History of Late Medieval and Reformation Europe* (New Haven, Yale University Press, 1980), 22–72, 231–39.

30. Biel, "The Circumcision of the Lord (ca. 1460)," in *A Reformation Reader: Primary Texts with Introductions*, ed. Denis R. Janz (Minneapolis: Fortress, 2008), 55.

31. Erasmus, *Discourse on Free Will*, Milestones of Thought, trans. and ed. Ernst F. Winter (New York: Frederick Ungar, 1961), 13–16.

32. Ibid., 20.

33. Ibid., 22.

34. Ibid., 27. Arguing that even morally good deeds done *extra gratiam* are "detestable in God's sight" was a way for the Reformers to express the extent to which the human will was bound in sin: in sin, the heart and mind do not even know how to operate righteously, let alone to how to execute that will. They must be shown what righteousness is and enabled to do it. The noetic and volitional effects of the fall are as utter as the behavioral.

35. Ibid., 28–30. Erasmus defended Pelagius, even though he recognized the judgment of the "orthodox" against him.

36. See *Luther's Works vol. 33: Career of the Reformer III*, ed. Philip S. Watson (Philadelphia: Fortress, 1972).

37. It was his treatment of Romans, famously 1:17, which Luther credited as catalyzing his conversion to the doctrine of justification by grace through faith alone (apart from works); see Luther, "Preface to the Complete Edition of Luther's Latin Writings, Wittenberg, 1545," in *Martin Luther's Basic Theological Writings* 3rd ed., ed. Timothy F. Lull and William R. Russell (Minneapolis: Fortress, 2012), 496–97. Luther's strong view of sin and even stronger view of God's action in behalf of the sinner was no "merely doctrinal" perspective. It was existentially decisive. The personal significance of his doctrinal development helps to explain, I think, Luther's resolve in confronting so much of the traditional understanding vis-a-vis human agency in salvation (idiosyncrasies of personality, as well as psycho-social factors, notwithstanding).

38. LW 33, 247.

39. Ibid.

40. Ibid., 254.

41. Ibid., 255. See also 271: "man's works and endeavors themselves are condemned, no matter what their nature, name, or sign may be."

42. Ibid., 280. Luther considers the necessity of Christ to be antithetical to human free choice. If the human could reason and will her way toward salvation, he concludes, then the mission of the Son to humanity becomes superfluous.

43. Ibid., 285.

44. Ibid., 289.

45. Late Medieval Scholasticism hardly represents the sum total of Roman Catholic tradition. One finds a more subdued form of synergism, perhaps even a light

monergism, in the Augustinian-Thomistic branch. Critical for this branch is the doctrine of *prevenient grace*. For Augustine, the creature is not able to overcome concupiscence in her natural state, but must receive antecedent supernatural assistance. The Holy Spirit balances the scales of free agency, which are naturally inclined to evil. Once balanced (in baptism), the human may cooperate with God by performing works of virtue. Among Augustine's anti-Pelagian writings, "The Spirit and the Letter" is especially important to Luther; see Augustine, "The Spirit and the Letter," in *Answer to the Pelagians I*, The Works of Saint Augustine: A Translation for the 21st Century 1/23, ed. John E. Rotelle, O.S.A., trans Roland J. Teske, S. J. (Hyde Park, NY: New City, 1997), 139–202.

46. Wolfhart Pannenberg summarizes the matter exactly: "there is no real biblical basis for the emphasis of the older Protestant dogmatics on a paradisiac perfection and integrity of human life before the fall in consequence of Adam's original righteousness." Human perfection does not appear until Christ: "it was left to Schleiermacher to recapture this insight [already in Irenaeus] in his pertinent formula that we must see in Christ for the first time the completed creation of human nature." See Pannenberg, *Systematic Theology* vol. 2, trans. Geoffrey W. Bromiley (Grand Rapids: Eerdmans, 1994), 212.

47. I take this to be what Karl Barth is after in his constructive treatments of Election and Nothingness. See Barth, *Church Dogmatics* II.2, 3–508; CD III.2, 289–368. So far as I can tell, in these we have Barth's own attempt to actualize what Luther rightly concluded, that is, to set Luther's conclusions into a post-metaphysical, yet not idealist framework.

48. Pannenberg echoes this conclusion along the registers of a natural knowledge of God in human conscience and of reason and idolatry versus revelation and faith; see *Systematic Theology* vol. 1, trans. Geoffrey W. Bromiley (Grand Rapids: Eerdmans, 2009), 108–13.

49. Melanchthon, *Commonplaces: Loci Communes 1521*, trans Christian Preus (St. Louis: Concordia, 2014). Kindle edition.

50. Ibid.

51. Clyde L. Manschreck contends that the 1524–1525 debate between Erasmus and Luther impacted Melanchthon, so that already by his 1527 commentary on Colossians Melanchthon softened his commitment to predestination. "In the first *Loci*," Manschreck writes, Melancthon "asserted that God controls everything through the mystery of divine predestination ... After 1527 and when he wrote the last editions of the *Loci*, he rejected the idea that 'God snatches you by some violent rapture, so that you must believe, whether you will or not'"; Manschreck, "Preface," in *Melanchthon on Christian Doctrine: Loci Communes 1555*, trans. and ed. Clyde L. Manschreck (New York: Oxford University Press, 1965), xii–xiii, citing vol. 15 of the *Corpus Reformatorum*.

52. Melanchthon, *Loci Communes* 1555, 52.

53. Ibid., 53, 57.

54. Ibid., 57–58.

55. Manschreck, "Preface," xiii.

56. Melanchthon, Loci Communes 1555, 60.

57. Manschreck, "Preface," xiii; see also Joest, "Synergismus," 561.

58. The biographical information presented here draws principally from Oliver K. Olsen, "Flacius Illyricus, Matthias (1520–1575)," *TRE* XI, 206–13; idem, "Flacius, Matthias," *RPP* 5, 137–38; Henry W. Reimann, "Mathias Flacius Illyricus: A Biographical Sketch," *Concordia Theological Monthly* 35:2 (1964), 69–93. Reimann summarizes the classic two-volume biography by Wilhelm Preger, *Matthias Flacius Illyricus und seine Zeit* (Erlangen: T Bläsing, 1859–1861). More contemporarily, see Olson, *Matthias Flacius and the Survival of Luther's Reform* 2nd ed. (Minneapolis: Lutheran Press, 2011).

59. As a Franciscan, Lupetina was not married. His relation to Flacius is by the marriage of his sister to a brother of Flacius's mother.

60. Olson, "Flacius Illyricus, Matthias (1520–1575)," 206.

61. As reported by Reimann, "Mathias Flacius Illyricus," 70–71.

62. Friction between Flacius and Strigel began a few years earlier, not long after Flacius joined Strigel on the faculty at Jena (1557). In 1558, Flacius secured a commission to draft a "Book of Confutations" setting out genuine Lutheran positions on a series of debated topics, including free will, the role of the Law, justification, Zwinglianism, Anabaptism, Schwenckfeldianism, adiaphora, and good works. Strigel took part in the initial composition of the *Konfutationsbuch*, but after a series of revisions undertaken by Flacius, which strengthened opposition to those who deviated from "pure doctrine," Strigel refused to accept it. He was arrested and imprisoned for his opposition by the then-Gnesio-minded Jena political leadership, and relieved of his teaching duties; see Reimann, "Mathias Flacius Illyricus," 79–81.

63. See "The Formula of Concord" Articles I and II, in *The Book of Concord: The Confessions of the Evangelical Lutheran Church*, ed. Robert Kolb and Timothy J. Wengert (Minneapolis: Fortress, 2000), 487–94 (Epitome), 531–62 (Solid Declaration); Hereafter FC, article, paragraph, page (Ep.), and FC, article, paragraph, page (SD).

64. FC I.38, 538 (SD).

65. The concordists considered Flacianism to tend toward Manichaeism, the fourth-century heresy that understood the human person to be a material concoction of an evil deity, designed to trap the divine light, thus not responsible for its sinfulness; see FC I.26–30, 536–37 (SD). On the concern about destroying the human in forgiveness, see FC I.46–47, 539 (SD).

66. FC II.11, 493 (Ep.).

67. The concordists explicitly reject Melanchthon's third cause: "Before the conversion of the human being there are only two efficient causes, the Holy Spirit and God's Word as the instrument of the Holy Spirit, through which he effects conversion; the human creature must hear this Word, but cannot believe and accept it on the basis of its own powers"; FC II.19, 494 (Ep.).

68. FC I.60, 542 (SD): "original sin is an indescribable impairment and a corruption of human nature so deep that nothing pure and good remains in it or in any of its internal and external powers. Instead, all is so deeply corrupted because of this original sin that human beings are truly spiritually dead in God's sight, having died, with all their powers, to the good."

69. See esp. Dorner, "The Reconstruction of the Immutability Doctrine" (*Divine Immutability*, 131–95). This is the third of the three essays mentioned at the outset.

70. Dorner deflects concerns about the use of the term, "metaphysics"—that is, objections that it denotes various philosophical conceptualities that should not be unfairly caricatured in the way that Dorner does, as static, aloof, and so on—by discussing various such conceptualities in a sweeping history of the doctrine of immutability. See his second essay, "The History of the Doctrine of the Immutability of God from the Patristic Period to Schleiermacher Set Forth Historically-critically according to Its Main Tendencies," in *Divine Immutability*, 82–130. Dorner's attack on metaphysics in his third essay assumes the conclusions of the survey conducted in his second.

71. On acosmism, see *Divine Immutability*, 95 esp. n. 30, 133–34.

72. Kenoticists developed basically two ways of understanding how God "emptied" (*ekénōsen*) God's self of those attributes that, if retained, would have prevented the Son from genuinely becoming human. (The following remarks summarize part of Robert R. Williams insightful introduction to Dorner's immutability essays; see Williams, "Introduction," in *Divine Immutability*, 6–9.) First, they introduced the notion of a *temporary* divestiture, for the period of Jesus's life, of specifically those qualities that would prevent him from living humanly. This entailed a twofold distinction: between use and possession, and between relative and absolute attributes. As Christ, the Son retained possession of the full range of divine attributes, but did not use all of them. Particularly, he eschewed use of the relative qualities, that is, those that express God's relation to the world (omnipresence, omnipotence, and omniscience), but not the absolute ones (freedom, eternity, holiness, love).

The second way that kenoticists construed the Son's self-emptying was by appealing to the difference between actualization and potentiality. Divine powers were limited in Jesus to potency; they could not be actualized in the flesh.

Dorner faulted both ideas. As to the first, he observed that omniscience is not merely a relative attribute in God, but includes God's knowledge of God's self. To set aside its use is in fact to set aside what makes God of God in each instant, thereby reducing the Son to something less than God. (Of course, on the other hand, not to set aside the use of omniscience would seem to compromise Jesus's true humanity. The problem is not so much in the kenotic interest to exploit a dynamic God-world relation, but with the unrecognized, or at least unstated metaphysical suppositions out of which even the kenoticists were operating). Similarly, to reduce the divine attributes in Christ to mere potency is to return to an Arian sort of demi-god. As Athanasius argued and Nicaea affirmed, full, *actual* divinity and humanity operate symbiotically in the one person of Jesus (e.g., when as God Jesus heals, he does so with a human hand, or when as God Jesus forgives sins, he does so with human speech).

73. Dorner recognizes that "a change in the old ecclesiastical dogmatics is required by scientific thought [*Wissenschaft*] and religion"; *Divine Immutability*, 131. If theology is to speak meaningfully in a world whose ideas and values are increasingly informed and shaped by science, and in which the religious imagination is existentially (and not supernaturally) focused, then it must rethink its doctrine of God.

It is also worth observing at this point that Dorner's essay is not composed in a strictly deductive fashion. In dealing with metaphysics broadly, and here, simplicity, Dorner marshals a series of observations concerning the God-world relation, which function together to form a kind of alternative picture. I cannot redraft that image in its details, but endeavor instead to sketch enough of its outline to convey the crucial impression, specifically in contrast to a classical doctrine of God.

74. Dorner, *Divine Immutability*, 137. Later (see 157–61), Dorner argues against the pantheistic alternative of reducing God to mere potency.

75. Ibid.

76. Ibid., 139.

77. Ibid., 142.

78. Ibid., 142–43.

79. If God's knowledge, which again includes knowledge of God's self, is changeable, then the doctrine of immutability must be recast. It must now be thought of along the lines of a constancy of fidelity in God to remain Lord of creation, or covenant partner to creation, in the midst of creation.

80. Dorner, *Divine Immutability*, 144.

81. Ibid.

82. Ibid.

83. Ibid., 145.

Chapter 4

Evil as Event among Humans

וְהַנָּחָשׁ הָיָה עָרוּם מִכֹּל חַיַּת הַשָּׂדֶה אֲשֶׁר עָשָׂה יְהוָה אֱלֹהִים וַיֹּאמֶר אֶל־הָאִשָּׁה אַף כִּי־
אָמַר אֱלֹהִים לֹא תֹאכְלוּ מִכֹּל עֵץ הַגָּן:
וַתֹּאמֶר הָאִשָּׁה אֶל־הַנָּחָשׁ מִפְּרִי עֵץ־הַגָּן נֹאכֵל:
וּמִפְּרִי הָעֵץ אֲשֶׁר בְּתוֹךְ־הַגָּן אָמַר אֱלֹהִים לֹא תֹאכְלוּ מִמֶּנּוּ וְלֹא תִגְּעוּ בּוֹ פֶּן־תְּמֻתוּן:
וַיֹּאמֶר הַנָּחָשׁ אֶל־הָאִשָּׁה לֹא־מוֹת תְּמֻתוּן:
כִּי יֹדֵעַ אֱלֹהִים כִּי בְּיוֹם אֲכָלְכֶם מִמֶּנּוּ וְנִפְקְחוּ עֵינֵיכֶם וִהְיִיתֶם כֵּאלֹהִים יֹדְעֵי טוֹב וָרָע:
וַתֵּרֶא הָאִשָּׁה כִּי טוֹב הָעֵץ לְמַאֲכָל וְכִי תַאֲוָה־הוּא לָעֵינַיִם וְנֶחְמָד הָעֵץ לְהַשְׂכִּיל וַתִּקַּח
מִפִּרְיוֹ וַתֹּאכַל וַתִּתֵּן גַּם־לְאִישָׁהּ עִמָּהּ וַיֹּאכַל:
וַתִּפָּקַחְנָה עֵינֵי שְׁנֵיהֶם וַיֵּדְעוּ כִּי עֵירֻמִּם הֵם וַיִּתְפְּרוּ עֲלֵה תְאֵנָה וַיַּעֲשׂוּ לָהֶם חֲגֹרֹת:
וַיִּשְׁמְעוּ אֶת־קוֹל יְהוָה אֱלֹהִים מִתְהַלֵּךְ בַּגָּן לְרוּחַ הַיּוֹם וַיִּתְחַבֵּא הָאָדָם וְאִשְׁתּוֹ מִפְּנֵי
יְהוָה אֱלֹהִים בְּתוֹךְ עֵץ הַגָּן:
וַיִּקְרָא יְהוָה אֱלֹהִים אֶל־הָאָדָם וַיֹּאמֶר לוֹ אַיֶּכָּה:
וַיֹּאמֶר אֶת־קֹלְךָ שָׁמַעְתִּי בַּגָּן וָאִירָא כִּי־עֵירֹם אָנֹכִי וָאֵחָבֵא:
וַיֹּאמֶר מִי הִגִּיד לְךָ כִּי עֵירֹם אָתָּה הֲמִן־הָעֵץ אֲשֶׁר צִוִּיתִיךָ לְבִלְתִּי אֲכָל־מִמֶּנּוּ אָכָלְתָּ:
וַיֹּאמֶר הָאָדָם הָאִשָּׁה אֲשֶׁר נָתַתָּה עִמָּדִי הִוא נָתְנָה־לִּי מִן־הָעֵץ וָאֹכֵל:

*Now of all life of the open field that the LORD God made, the serpent
was most shrewd, and it said to the woman, "When God in fact said,
'you are not to eat from every tree of the garden . . . .'"*
*But the woman said to the serpent, "We eat of the fruit of the trees of
the garden,*
*but of the fruit of the tree that is in the middle of the garden, God said,
'you are not to eat from it and you are not to touch it, lest you die.'"*
"You 'surely will not *die,' the serpent said to the woman!*
*"In fact, God knows that on the day you eat from it, your eyes will have
been opened and you will have become like gods, knowing good and
evil."*

> *Now the woman saw that the tree was good for food, and that it was*
> *desirable to the eyes, and that the tree commanded close attention,[1] so*
> *she took from its fruit and she ate, and she gave also to her man beside*
> *her, and he ate.*
> *And their eyes were opened, and they knew that they were naked, so*
> *they sewed fig leafage together and made loin coverings for themselves.*
> *Now they heard the sound of the LORD God walking in the garden in*
> *the breeze of the day, and the human hid himself and his woman from*
> *the face of the LORD God, in the middle of the trees of the garden.*
> *And the LORD God called to the human and said to him, "Where are*
> *you?"*
> *And he said, "I heard the sound of you in the garden and I feared,*
> *because I was naked, so I hid myself."*
> *And he said, "Who reported to you that you were naked? Did you eat*
> *of the tree that I ordered you to refrain from eating?"*
> *And the human said, "The woman that you gave for my company, she*
> *gave to me from the tree, so I ate" (Gen. 3:1–12).*

So begins the second revolution of the wheel of the single creation myth
of Gen. 2–3. We noted that these chapters do not present two creation
stories, but one story in two twists or turns. The story of creation does not
finish with description of humanity's making in Genesis 2, but with God's
creative constancy in the midst of humanity's unmaking in Genesis 3.
Creation and preservation, making and redeeming cannot be neatly separated. Indeed, we will now see how much the former must be understood
in terms of the latter.

This chapter concerns sin—its basis and character. It contends that sin
is an event corresponding to the exercise of humanity's perceptive agency,
namely, the event in which the human does *not* perceive interdependence *as*
good and right and seeks a consciousness *alternative to* participation in life's
"from-for" succession, which entails consciousness of *freedom from* God (or
in Schleiermacher's language, only relative and not absolute dependence on
God). That the human should incline this direction and exist inauthentically
evidences the continuing need for God's creative efficacy: by not participating in life's "from-for" succession, the human takes part in the nothingness
and disorder outside of life's covenantal grounding. The human dies.

The human perceives its Self beyond the web of life, as alone necessary to
its own existence and the existence of others, not mutually contingent upon
them. The human ceases to be life-receiving and becomes life-withholding
and -taking, falsely conscious of himself as a god. He seeks unlimited existence and like all else must be renewed in his proper limit in order to live.
In this respect, sin is not the consequence of inexplicable ancestral infidelity,

but an existential happening across the arc of human generations. Humanity births sinfully (and thus may also be said to be born in sin).

This chapter critically assesses one of the Western tradition's most influential treatments of sin and evil: Augustine's. Although Augustine is inconsistent in carrying through the protological insight that humanity is created seminally or emergent-ly, and indeed, his Neoplatonic background must be updated into a more thoroughly actualistic frame of reference, he nevertheless offers a way of thinking about sin as a continuing inclination away from God and each other, which must be defeated for authentic humanity to be realized. For Augustine, the human comes to its intended existence as it lives by reflex, so to speak, in the Spirit of God.

EXEGESIS OF GEN. 3:1–12

Four exegetical observations immediately commend themselves from the opening verses of Genesis 3. First, a mournful and tragic tone now inflects the score, a creeping discord—distressing yet inevitable, resistance and acquiescence taking turns—as the serpent offers and the woman gives in, the woman offers and the man gives in, the man turns on woman and gives hostility its reign in his life and hers. The contrast between the mythopoeic harmonies of ch. 2 and the terse, perfidious breach of relation in 3:12 is dramatic and lamentable.

"At last! Bone of my bones and flesh of my flesh!" becomes "the woman that you gave," as if man had no primal desire for woman and her existence was discretional, not interdependently vital.[2] As the man turns on woman, he turns against God, no longer begging but *blaming* him for her. "The repeated verb [נְתַן, 'the woman that you *gave* . . . she *gave*']," Alter writes, "nicely catches the way the first man passes the buck, not only blaming the woman for giving him the fruit but virtually blaming God for giving him the woman."[3]

Ecstatic fulfillment and human realization in covenantal union give way to cheap self-preservation and disregard for the other. "The narration of Gen 3 takes us in a different direction [than Gen. 2]," Arnold writes. "The preceding paragraphs have explained why humans have an intimate relationship with the earth, the animals, with each other as sexual partners, and especially with God. [The beginning of Gen. 3] continues the etiological interests by narrating how all of these relationships changed dramatically from their original conditions."[4] Aware that creaturely reality bears only shadowy resemblance to that depicted in Genesis 2, the narrator continues in Genesis 3 to describe what has cast the pall. The narration takes the shape of progression from idealized original to compromised aftermath, although as we have seen the transition should not be read as a one-time historical crisis, for it describes recurrent human history. The possibility of self-consciousness *with* another gives way in each generation to consciousness of Self *against* another.

Why? This is the relevant question. It is not the case, as Arnold suggests, that the narrator's interests in Genesis 3 are entirely etiological. However causative at the surface level, the account is simply too mythologized to be read as providing explanation for the darkened state of things. The account does not offer reasoned clarification, but tragic narration: Genesis 3 dramatizes the human condition.[5] It invites the reader to identify himself in the temptation, to feel the lure to disobedience and self-interested action as his own, to recognize the contradiction on the page as the condition of his soul and thus to interrogate his own motives. "Why!?" Why must my constitutional need for covenantal union so readily give way to a contrary urge toward self-preservation and, ironically, self-destruction? The reader knows that the question does not concern whether such fall might happen, but assumes that it is happening.

The second exegetical observation is that Genesis 3 incisively imbeds the human condition in the very perceptive agency by which the human might confirm its place in creation. Sin transpires within the functioning of human consciousness. The canny language of vv. 4-5 grabs attention. In the first place, the serpent responds to the woman in words reflective not of her own in 3:3, but of the LORD God in 2:17. Rather than simply contradicting what she said, that is, rather than simply saying "you will not die," (תְּמֻתוּן לֹא), the serpent says that "dying you will not die," or "you surely will not die" (לֹא־מוֹת תְּמֻתוּן). With this construction, the serpent effectively answers *God's* claim in responding to the woman, denying its truth and thereby perching as divine rival. The serpent not only demonstrates awareness of the divine prohibition but also claims truer understanding of the consequence of its violation, and so represents another account of reality next to God's. The serpent rises up before the human, in her perceptual faculty, as alternative to the divine way.[6]

Although the claim is false, for the serpent's alternative does prove to be wrong, the serpent does not seem to be knowingly deceiving. Nowhere does the text indicate that the serpent postures at an understanding, which in fact eludes it. On the contrary, it depicts the serpent to be acting with utmost confidence in possession of genuine comprehension. If the serpent is wrong, suggests the text's depiction, then it will come as a surprise also to the serpent. The deceiver would be self-deceived.[7] By making this claim *for itself*, to be the arbiter of what is and what might be, and to judge rightly—what is "good" or best—without reference to the divine account, indeed in opposition to it, the creature forces itself on to the plane of deity and will have to prove itself there.[8] Its consciousness will have to be self-authenticating. Of course, the serpent does not manage this. Already by v. 7, the humans' eyes are opened to perceive the serpent's error and impotence. In this eye-opening, the serpent typifies the self-consciousness of the human in recognition of its sin, the standing contradiction, which threatens the human across time—total dependence on God confronts its inclination to know and act as god.

The threat facing the human is that she will obtain the quality of יֹדְעֵי טוֹב וָרָע (knowing good and evil). Now, the human is capable of knowing; her humanity entails readiness, unfixed in scope, to acquire and master, to assimilate and digest, and so to become other to herself through learning, that is, to be in the next instant one and the same as in the prior instant yet also new, with altered awareness and judgment. The human exists as dis-coverer. In the etymological sense of the Greek word for "truth," ἀλήθεια (*a-lethe*), she exists in "un-concealing." The human lives into truth as she excavates herself and her world.

The human naturally enjoys an appetite for self-enlargement. This is obviously not sinful; it is as God wills. But in consciousness of her knowing prowess, which is to say, in her very self-consciousness, the human faces a choice: either to conduct her learning in gratitude for its potential, undertaking its activity in conscious affirmation of its source—knowing her knowing to be a knowing-after God's—seeking its application toward the will of God in behalf of the world, or to conduct her learning in entitlement, undertaking its activity in studied ignorance of or even antagonism toward its source—knowing her knowing as knowing-against God's—seeking its application toward the imagined good of Self over the world and God. She cannot decide whether to be a knower, for she must be that, but she must decide whether to practice her knowing in faithfulness or disobedience.

In receiving life, the human receives perpetual opportunity to be God's partner who takes covenantal responsibility for God's creatures. As we have discussed, this opportunity takes the form of obedience to command and acceptance of permission. But the fact that the human exists in perpetual encounter with command and permission means that disobedience and denial always appear before her.[9] Disobedience does not lack appeal; the serpent's account presents itself as having a certain probability, a certain likelihood of success.[10] If it did not, it would amount to little more than concession to the only evident prospect, which is not at all the same as constitutional affirmation of humanity's place as right and fit. (The beasts, too, reflex to the only perceived course of action.)

Humanity dis-covers its place by conscious participation in the redemptive history of God, which ongoing discovery becomes *intrinsic* to the human in the act of conscious obedience, or faith. By the operation of his unique faculty of perception, the human reiterates the self-giving of "God," that is, the self-displacement by which place is made for another. The human sees and seeks his fit place after God on behalf of creation and moves toward his rightful, redeemed existence there. "Sin" is interruption of this biorhythmic event-constitution, in the form of giving in to the serpentine alternative.[11]

This brings us to our third exegetical observation. Sin is transgression of humanity's constitutional limit: it is to see the self not as recipient first and life-giver second, but as life-giver first and recipient second, as god, and at once to desire this order of things, to perceive it (precisely in contrast to the divine account) as right and proper. It is to prefer the evil to the good.

Knowing "good and evil" does not refer to gaining pieces of knowledge, but to a kind of Self-consciousness, a perception of self as All-knower at least by potential, and thus as the center of world-existence. The prohibition against such knowledge is not an arbitrary imposition, which restricts growth opportunity. "The prohibition does not have the purpose of confining man," Westermann writes, "in the sense that it takes away or deprives man of something."[12] It is not a casual test—not setting the table for a hungry creature then giving the command not to eat—by which arbitrary submission the human strangely proves faithful. God does not invite the human to be human, to learn and grow, only to disallow it in some vaguely stated area or manner, so that God might maintain a knowledge-gap, or the like, between him and the human and provide motive and justification for punishing the human when the human (inevitably) breaches the gap. "God" does not seek motive to destroy what God has made. Quite the opposite, as *God* the Creator seeks reason and occasion to secure the flourishing of what God has made.

Prohibition presents limitation to consciousness as *productive*. "It does provide a limit," Westermann continues, "it is true, but by this limitation God is entrusting to man something which relates him to the eternal, namely, obedience."[13] The divine command situates the human in the living condition of *response*. The matter of whether the human will grasp after the knowledge of good and evil is not a matter of whether she will strive for a variety of comprehension, which she does not possess (moral, social, perhaps sexual). It is rather a matter of whether human consciousness consents to God's account of the world and her place therein. It is a matter of whether the human perceives herself to stand as *secunda* to *primus* and rejoices in that perception.

The serpent threatens the woman with the blessing that "your eyes will be opened" (וְנִפְקְחוּ עֵינֵיכֶם), and that she (you) will come to know (ידע) good and evil. But the woman's eyes are already blessed with openness; she already perceives the prospect of goodness. She already knows the permission of God, that she may eat of the trees in the middle of the Garden (in the intimacy of God's presence?), in receipt of God's permission, *and* that she may not eat of this one tree, in receipt of God's command. She already perceives how to enact her authentic self.

But she also perceives the possibility of an alternative "goodness." Before she eats of the fruit, she already "sees" (ראה) that the tree is "good," טֹוב הָעֵץ.[14] Yet her seeing restricts the tree's goodness to her self-reference. It is good only in respect of *what it can give to her*: it is good "for food" (לְמַאֲכָל). The tree is already instrumentalized in the event of her perception. Quite apart from giving in and eating, then, just by the action of perception, sin creeps; the human is ready *not* to care for creation, to treat creation as mere implement of her survival. That does not make the act of perceiving to be sinful, or the human sinful specifically as the agent of perception, but it does imbed sinfulness within the defining agential activity in which creation's harmony might instead be realized, within the constitutive perception of humankind. Once more, Genesis 3 gives a tragic description of the human in her state of contradiction.

The fourth exegetical observation to be made is that, in keeping with his nature as learner, the human must be confronted with a right self-consciousness; the human must perceive that he is known in the fullness of his potential, better than he knows himself. God must reenter the Garden and seek out the human: וַיִּקְרָא יְהוָה אֱלֹהִים אֶל־הָאָדָם (v. 9). Within I-referenced history God must make a time of grace, redemptive divine pursuit. Within the framework of human self-perception God must institute a new way of perceiving the self—now again as object of God's activity. And God must make real within human existence a life defined by its favorable response to this activity, a human that confirms his humanity in conscious affirmation of absolute dependence on God. God must make covenantal life with the human and create the conditions for the human to enter that life, grant to the human the obedience and acceptance that the human otherwise does not achieve. God must fulfill the covenant among humanity so that humanity might come to its own fulfillment.

A few secondary exegetical remarks augment these four principal observations. The text plays on the linguistic proximity in Hebrew between "shrewd" (עָרוּם) and "naked" (עֵירֹם).[15] Nakedness communicates innocence, blamelessness even before God, but the sinful human dissembles this innocence; he perceives himself as naked (וַיֵּדְעוּ כִּי עֵירֻמִּם). He sees this in the deceptive light of the serpent's account: now he is the maker and the product of his own knowing—cunning and shrewd, on the one hand, yet conscious of his precariousness, on the other, vulnerable. He not only can make himself, but also must do so. He must set the measure of his life and guard it against all assault, including the judgment of the God against whom he has turned.

In the eating, in the transgressing, God's account stands before the human not in a benign sense, but as obstacle and threat. "God has not changed," writes Gowan, "but the human has, and from his position of independence God now looks different, threatening."[16] The human is conscious of "God" as *menace* from which he must hide. As creation's ground, God is friend and companion to the human, indeed, God unites himself with the human, so thoroughgoing is his love for creation. But in sin, God appears as foe; God springs to life in Self-consciousness as antagonist.

Still, God is not and will not be humanity's enemy.[17] As just noted, God comes to the human even when the human turns from God. "Where are you?" This question on the lips of the Creator at once expresses the lost-ness of the human in her disobedient hiding (see n. 5) *and* the faithfulness of God in the self-consistency of gracious pursuit. It is not God playing at ignorance and forcing the human, like a cookie-thieving child, to come clean. It is a rhetorical inquiry meant to confirm the human in her factual estrangement (from God and creation) and to re-settle the human (after God among creation) in covenantal dependence.

To come full circle, just as interpersonal unity serves as the context in which humankind primarily confirms the self-giving character of its Maker, so also interpersonal discord serves as the context in which humankind confirms the self-withholding character of sin. The human inclines to Self particularly against other Selves.[18] By this, I do not mean that interpersonal disharmony is the principal *order* of sin; transgressing the divine command is sin's principal order. I mean, rather, that in the quotidian experience of humankind, it is above all in crimes against one another that humanity transgressively exercises its free agency. "The woman that you gave." It is in discord among humans that sin against God takes historical shape, and it is in redemptive love among humans—the offer of grace and forgiveness to those who would otherwise be our enemies—that the restorative work of God finds concrete expression.

To explore these exegetical conclusions further, we will hear for the remainder of this chapter from Augustine. I will interact critically with Augustine's commentaries on Genesis, at times disagreeing, but for the most part demonstrating that the existential relevancy of the divine command, the intricate connection between humanity's perceptive modality and sin, and the transformative potential of the human in the event of self-consciousness are all latent, and occasionally explicit, in Augustine's thinking.

Two prevailing currents guide Augustine's treatment of humankind, one protological and one eschatological. Protologically, Augustine understands the human to come to exist in and through a *dynamic* process of creation. The human, as we will see, is *both* made whole stock, so to speak, in the instant that all things are created, *and* progressively. Eschatologically, the human obtains her authentic being in Paradise, which is to say, in receipt of the beatific vision. Between her creation and coming to exist in heaven, she lives in sin (preferring lower goods to God, the highest good), and thus in a process of training her soul to receive the true vision of God.[19]

DISCUSSION OF AUGUSTINIAN ANTHROPOLOGY I: PROTOLOGICAL CONCERN

Augustine locates the sapiential hominid along an interlinked chain of existence: a hierarchy of being that derives from God. Humanity's link on the chain of being is as something of an intermediary between immaterial and material existence; a soul situated between its Source and lower emanations from the Source. Authentic humanity is conscious of itself among a world of goods yet willingly concentrates its focus on the highest Good, on God. Inauthentic humanity directs its consciousness away from God to objects of the world. The inauthentic human exists as a candidate for condemnation or grace (as God sees fit to apportion them). He may be consigned to the lot of God-rejecters forever, to damnation, or helped to resist temptation and return to God, elected to grace.

Augustine's account of humankind as a liminal creature between immaterial God and material world assumes Neoplatonic distinctions between immutability and mutability, and between eternity and time.[20] Augustine asserts a basic atemporality apart from which God is not *God*. We discussed this in chapter 2: to be "God" is, by definition, not to be subject to time, for time charts "the movement of creatures from one state to another"[21] and "to be what once was not the case is to be subject to change and variation,"[22] which cannot be true of "God." Within the operative thought structures of Augustine's day, for God there can only be "the simultaneity of eternity."[23]

Like we disagreed with Schleiermacher, we cannot agree with Augustine on this absolute distinction between God and time; we cannot let the meaningfulness of our account of "God" be predetermined by commitment to ontic immutability (as a way of preserving either the absoluteness of our feeling of dependence or of God's transcendent goodness). In the first place, time not only means change but also *generation*. With time comes new opportunity, new con-sequences attend the old sequences, and new sequences beget yet further consequences: new "ifs" beget new "thens" and "becauses" illicit new "wherefores" as well as "therefores." Every resource given to the human to recognize and affirm God's redeeming work, to know God in the event of right self-consciousness (to know God in the event of the *new* covenant), takes temporal shape, and this fact does not intrinsically turn the human away from God, or it is not the temporality of consciousness that accounts for its sinfulness.

It is in time, not a contrived, static "eternity," that things become otherwise than as they are. It is in time, not a projected, static "eternity," that God is who God is: Lord and Giver of Life. God makes God's Kingdom in time, and thus elects time to God's self. To make and maintain a history that is alternative to the history of self-interest is to be of time. To die is to be of time, and to live again is to be of a new time. Concern for Neoplatonic immutability cannot overtake the patterning of thought given in God's redemptive life and work.

"Eternity" cannot be the conceptual opposite of time insofar as it applies to God's existence. It can designate the constancy of God in the act of assuming time, in giving God's life to and for another (regardless of the constancy in receptivity of that other), but not the absence of time. As a creature of his time, if I may, Augustine assumes an ontological break between what is eternal and what is temporal, which Christian faith today must severely interrogate.

But Augustine's distinction is not without some enduring relevance. By making it, Augustine rightfully wishes to establish a definite relation in consciousness between "God" and "creation." For "God" to be a meaningful designation, it must signify something other than creation, something from which creation comes, around which it orients, and to which it heads; it must signify the condition of creation's becoming, that which is not of creation (in classical parlance, "uncreated") even as it exists only in and with creation. Augustine wishes to uphold divine precedence along the lines of what I have argued here: God is "before" creation (or creation is "after" God) not chronologically, but archetypally: "it is not in time that you [God] precede times. Otherwise you would not precede all times."[24] We agree with Augustine's concern for God's primacy, if not with the way that he tries to uphold it by appeal to a-temporality.[25]

If "God" connotes archetypal and not sequential precedence to temporality among the temporal, then we cannot think of God's activity as taking place along a linear timeline. Creation cannot occur along a progression of six, 24-hour days. God is free for these units of time, to work in and with them, yet this freedom entails a continuing divine precedence among them; the time units themselves come to exist in and through the creative work that transpires on them. God must have "made all things simultaneously together," Augustine writes.[26] That is, God "does not will one thing at one time, and another thing at another time. Once and for all and simultaneously, he wills everything that he wills. He does not need to renew his resolution."[27] Although, again, the language of "simultaneous" problematically assumes time (as it denotes "things happening at the *same time*"), and for Augustine serves as a too-blunt tool for upholding Neoplatonic immutability, Augustine rightly seeks to avoid forcing God to work according to a particular time-framing ("days"). God gives life in time, but time comes into existence with the giving.

In speaking, "Let there be light"—which speaking Augustine frequently observes cannot be an actual vocalization of a syllabic series, as this would, once more, imply "this-then-that" in God, but instead, has to be a kind of instantaneous intellectual conveyance—God creates not a modality within a temporal (24-hour) structure, but the very structure of temporality *per se*. "I have come to think that time is simply a distension. But of what is it a distension? I do not know, but it would be surprising if it is not that of the mind itself."[28] We have considered how time recurs in human perception, now we might consider the same on the divine side: God *opens* God's mind and in this act "initiates" the modality of time—the "beginning" just is the happening in God's consciousness of opening, the newness inherent in distention.[29]

In the opening of God's mind (which is equivalent to saying "in the speaking of God's Word), God conveys openness, newness. For Augustine, the light of Day One is foremost *illumination* of the divine will, which at once instantiates Day One. Augustine understands that it is by light that we reckon a world of happening, that space opens in which events and entities interface (pertinently for us, that a fundamental relation is set in which entities and events interconnected-ly emerge), and this "light" is not merely a thing "out there," but is at once a revealing "in here," the condition of perception.

The creative distending/illuminating takes place firstly—firstly, once more, not in sequence, but in proximity to God's self—in the hosts of heaven. "The idea of a creature to be fashioned came first in the Word of God, when he said, *Let light be made*; and then light itself followed, in which the angelic mind was formed, and made in its own nature."[30] The communication of God's mind involves a communicant; by its very operation the Word of God generates a recipient, which in its own proper way or "nature" becomes a further communicator. The angels/heavenly messengers are born.

In their creation, God communicates to the angels consciousness of creation, of their own reality as that which God said, "let it be," and enacting that self-consciousness (i.e., in contemplation) they confirm the goodness or propriety of creation. They praise God, and this continues reiteratively for all the things created in God's Word or communicated by God. "Day," "Evening," and "Morning" take rise as affirmations first in angelic consciousness of God's creative work:

> That "day which God has made" is itself repeated through his works, not in a bodily circular motion but in spiritual knowledge, when that blessed company of angels before anything else contemplates in the Word of God that about which God says *Let it be made*; and in consequence this is first made in their own angelic knowledge when the text says, *And thus it was made*, and only after that do they know the actual thing made in itself, which is signified by the making of evening. They then refer this knowledge of the thing made to the praise of that Truth where they had seen the idea of making it, and this is signified by the making of morning.[31]

Time recurs in triadic ordering of angelic knowledge, in contemplation of the thing made according to the divine idea of it (contemplation of it in the divine Word), then understanding the thing as it exists (its nature), then in appropriate appreciation of the Creator in relation to the thing created. It is in this movement of understanding that we have the light of day, followed by evening, followed by morning. And it is this intellectual movement in repetition that constitutes the six days of creation, until the morning of the seventh, which of course has no evening.[32] As Edmund Hill, O. P., summarizes, "the narrative of the six days of creation (and the seventh day of rest) tells of a kind of serial projection of the basic elements of the divine work onto the screen of the intelligence of the spiritual creation."[33] The illumination of the heavenly agents anticipates the illumination of humankind: human consciousness repeats in its way the revelation-infused consciousness of the angels, and as such, reiteratively confirms, or takes its own part in, "creation." The "day which God has made" is repeated also in *this* work.

God "first," most proximally, brings forth spiritual reality (angels and the "heaven of heaven"),[34] and "second," at the distant end of existence, so to speak, God communicates material entities (earth and the celestial realm). This latter substance of terrestrial and celestial being is shadowy, not in the sense of being morally dark, for it, too, is the good product of the Good Lord, but of being unformed and therefore difficult to define. "If one could speak of 'a nothing something' or 'a being which is non-being', that is what I would say."[35] Formless matter is the barely existent, lower-order correlate to the higher order spiritual realm. Within these two poles, as it were, is all of creation.

Although Augustine tirelessly strives not to allow *time* to co-structure divine existence, he does here allow space to creep in instead. *Distance* conceptually structures the relation by which "God" and "world" exist: material creation is as far down the chain of being from its immaterial Source as can be thought. But by Augustine's own refusal of any creaturely antecedent with respect to God-consciousness, such spatial reasoning should not obtain. In fact, precisely in God's eternity, all things should be equally proximate to God just as they are temporally "present" (simultaneously extant). God should have to be always and equally right next to every aspect of creation, material included.

Even though it should not obtain, Augustine's spatial reasoning frames his protological understanding of the human in a way that merits assessment. God gives a material creature a kind of animation, a soulishness by which the creature may know *and* acknowledge its Creator. As is proper to its ensouling, the human must enact within its consciousness the triadic knowledge and praise that first took place among the angels. But for creatures who are not angels, creatures farther down the chain of being, such self-consciousness can only be seeded and cultivated:

The truth is that those things which were due to be "unwrapped from their wrappings" in the course of subsequent ages, and which God created simultaneously with all things when he made the world, were both completely finished then in a certain way and also started off in a certain way . . . ; started off . . . since they were seeds in a sense of future realities, destined to germinate in suitable places from hidden obscurity into the manifest light of day through the course of the ages.[36]

Created in-between the higher and the lower, humanity by its nature exists in a state possibility. Its authenticity comes through growth (in choosing to move toward rather than away from the immaterial, immutable Good). Human existence can be likened to that of "seeds."[37] Humanity exists *proleptically*.[38] It will take *time* for the *adam* to become what he is, that is, to be conscious of himself before God, to delight in that situation, and to praise God as the angels do: "when he [*adam*] is said to have been made among them [the six days], it was, surely, the actual cause that God made, by which the man was to come to be in his own time, and in accordance with which he was to be made by the one who both finished what he had started on account of the perfect completeness of the causal formulae, and started what was to be finished on account of the ordered march of time."[39] From the perspective of God, or in regard to the atemporal eternality of God, or as to the causal-formula contrived by God, humanity is complete in the instant of its creation. But as to what "the man was to come to be in his own time," or in regard to the way things unfold through "the ordered march of time," or as to what the human might become as the divine formula is worked out temporally, the human is made to develop, or to employ contemporary vernacular, to *evolve* into that which God intends.

Now we confront a complication. When Augustine illustrates what he means by forms of creation emerging according to the prescriptions of their causal formulae, he appeals to things like a grapevine receiving water and nourishment from the earth, eventually yielding grapes, which in turn yield wine. The seed, vine, grapes, and wine are all contained completely in the divine formula, but only come by as these things over the arc of a temporal lifespan. Likewise, he observes that it takes a set period of time for animal reproduction, for instance, for a "snake to be conceived, formed, hatched, [and] reach full growth."[40] God's creation entails each stage, or each stage is in a sense, "created."

What, then, about the specific Adam of Gen. 2–3? Does Augustine mean by appeal to the causal formula of *humanity* to suggest that it is written into the fabric of human beings to emerge over perhaps quite lengthy time through dynamic interplay within the broader creation? Or, does he mean that God created a fully formed human prototype and parent in whom the causal formula of all humans was exhausted, so that humans "emerge" by procreation from this parenting—that they are conceived, born, and grow to adulthood like grapevines and snakes?

Augustine suggests both. In reading Genesis, Augustine's Manichaean opponents contended for a quasi-mystical admixture of biblical saga and esoteric speculation: bound to sequence in creating, God is finite; another exists alongside God. Room for another next to God helps to account for the origin of evil. An adversarial divine force brings it forth in the specific form of matter. The Manichees took Neoplatonic distance between immaterial and material to the extreme of ontic opposition, construing the latter as the means of entrapping light (goodness). The stuff of this world in its many sensate pleasures is illusive and ill-omened, the product of a deity who wishes to shackle the truth. The real prophet of Eden turns out to be the serpent, for it supplies humanity with secret knowledge of its inner, immaterial divine spark, which it must set free.

Against this, Augustine argues for a "literal" reading of Genesis, that is, one that is unencumbered by eccentric, cryptic speculation that has to be interpreted by the initiated.[41] The reader is to progress directly, albeit reflectively, from one line to the next, without arcane admixtures. Augustine's simultaneous/emergent schematic derives from the sheer challenge of reconciling the two accounts of Gen. 1 and Gen. 2–3, read in sequence. How can creation take place over *six* days in Gen. 1 and "in *the day* [singular]" when God created the heavens and earth of Gen. 2:4? How can God have created vegetation in Gen. 1:11–12 and yet "no shrub of the field had yet appeared on the earth and no plant of the field had yet sprung up" in Gen. 2:5? How can humanity, male and female, be created at the simple Word of God in Gen. 1:26–27, then be created by God breathing into the mud of Gen. 2:7, then be differentiated by sex as woman is taken from the man's side in 2:18f?

Augustine's answer, as we have seen, is that God created all things at once, including formless matter endowed with a biogenic power and set of principles according to which all living things would take form. Plants, in their full essence as plants, are sown as seeds into creation. Whatever plant-ness proves to be over the arc of time is there in the "beginning." And whatever *each* plant proves to be in the arc of its lifespan is there, too. Humanity is, likewise, sown into the fabric of formless matter with all things in the six days; whatever humanity will be over the arc of time is already there. And each human peculiarly instantiates this formula across the arc of its distinct lifespan.[42]

God prescribed both that the human should be fashioned from the earth or mud and born of parents: "If in those first causes of things which the creator originally inserted into the world he not only put that he was going to form the man from mud, but also in what manner he was going to form him; whether as in the womb of a mother, or in the form of a young man, there can be not the slightest doubt that he did it as he had prescribed there; he would not, I mean, go against his own program in making him."[43]

The human comes to be in a manner consistent with the prescription of God's created formula.[44] That formula is flexible enough for a creature to be fashioned out of the earth either as an adult or as an infant in a parent's womb. Of course, Adam had no parents, so in fact, he was formed as an adult or at least, thinks Augustine, as a young man. But regardless, Augustine has it in mind that it was God's intent to form *this* human from which others would emerge as offspring. "God multiplied the human race from one man whom he created first [which] was much better than if he had started it from several."[45] God's causal agency both in the shaping of body from earth and in-breathing of a soul, to which we will turn shortly, was directed toward the *end* of producing this one man. The action of humanity's causal formula is fully manifested in his lifespan. There might be other orders of such manifestation (in brain size, reflective capacity, kinesis, and so forth), but any further happening of human existence is by participation in what this first human is. For Augustine, the human population is merely the offspring of one called "Adam."[46]

It may seem in this that in one single motion Augustine opens and closes the door on species development through a prolonged period of environmental adaptations. But in fact—and here is an added complication—the flexibility inherent in Augustine's notion of causal formulae forces him to construe creation as unfolding through the operation of a coordinated divine providence rather than just through instantaneous fiat decree. In one of his more challenging formulations, Augustine writes:

> Perhaps the necessity of [a hypothetical] man actually growing old is written into the world, while if it is not in the world, it is in God. For it is what he wills that will of necessity be in the future. . . . Many things, you see, will be in the future as determined by lower, secondary causes, while if they are also in God's foreknowledge like that, they really will be in the future. But if they are there in a different manner, they will rather be in the future as they are there. . . . Thus old age, we say, lies in the future for this young man; but for all that it is not in the future if he dies before reaching it, while this will happen as determined by other causes, whether ones woven into the world or ones reserved to the foreknowledge of God.[47]

Humanity's causal formula prescribes a certain scope to human life. A certain age that we would describe as "old" lies in each human's future. It is part of created nature. But this is the case only if, one, certain secondary causes (disease, famine, war) do not interfere, and, two, if God himself does not intervene—intervene, importantly, not by overriding the exigencies of the formula, as this would amount to God (in history) acting against God (in eternity), but by actualizing certain potentialities latent in the world that would cut life short.[48] With regard to every human, God foreknows which eventuality will take shape.

But that means, minimally, that God not only allows but even causes, by virtue of the character to which he gives it, creation to participate in the formation of creation. (This fits, we recall, with what Augustine taught concerning the event of day's creation: it is reiterated in creaturely self-consciousness.) Although the human is said to be made on the sixth day, he is only *formed* out of the mud by the undefined action of God's sculpting; Augustine does not, indeed cannot specify what degree of this sculpting entails God's acting specially upon the earth, and how much he leaves to the earthling to develop according to its seeded potentiality. The question is necessarily unanswered: just how much development did God allow nature to contribute to the formation of the first *Adam*?

Clearly, Augustine thinks that the human species is populated linearly through the procreation of Adam and Eve. Adam is the teleological product of humanity's emergence from the ground; he alone is formed from the mud. In this respect, Augustine's teaching runs against the grain of modern evolutionary science. But even though he restricts the emergence of the race to a single commencing figure, Augustine allows for the development of the human progenitor out of the *adamah* to have occurred in a deliberately ambiguous, undefined way.[49] Similarly, Augustine is aware that Gen. 1:24 has the land bringing forth animals, his discussion of which gives no indication that this should be otherwise than through a gradual process of development.[50] Indeed, in an instructive passage, Augustine thinks it absurd that maggots should be thought to have been created prior to the death of the animals on which they feed; they rather must have emerged *as such* only with the dying of animals.[51] And as we now look briefly to his account of the soul, we will see that if he was cautious about proscribing the extent or timeframe of *corporeal* development, Augustine is downright diffident about such proscriptions vis-a-vis *spiritual* development.

Augustine is clear about what it is that God intends to create in making humanity: a covenantal partner whose understanding of self and world is ordered entirely around God. Rather than locating authentic humanity in any size, shape, or kinetic motion, Augustine insists that humanity's true self, its divine image, is in exercise of a uniquely free operation of judgment, which is to say, a rational faculty or rational *soul (anima)*. "[The Apostle] makes it plain enough just in what part man was created to God's image—that it was not in the features of the body but in a certain form of the illuminated mind."[52] This "certain *form* of the illuminated mind" is challenging to describe. "The soul is not corporeal," nor is it even made "out of the corporeal elements of the universe," say, air.[53] But then, what is it? And if it is not formed out of formless matter, then where does it come from?

Augustine dedicates a fair bit of reflection to the question of where the soul comes from, that is, the nature of God's "blowing" the breath of life into the *adam* in Gen. 2:7 and ensouling of human beings.[54] He rejects any suggestion that this breath is a self-impartation of the divine. The human is a creature of God, not a god itself. But what then? Are all souls created simultaneously in the six days? That would suggest that there is a causal formula for souls to emerge "in some primary creature" just as Adam is the primary bodily entity. Or perhaps "only the first man's soul was made among those primary works, and from it all other human souls derive." Or perhaps "new souls are made subsequently, without any formula."[55]

He weighs each possibility, dispatching the first (a distinct causal formula just for souls) as lacking biblical support, but ultimately not deciding between the latter two (traducianism and creationism, respectively).[56] Augustine concludes that while he might speak with confidence about bodily creation both happening all at once and progressively emerging, "I will affirm nothing as certain about the soul."[57] The soul's character, if you like, can improve, but as for the soul's origin and nature, Augustine has little to say. He is content simply to insist upon the following: that the soul "is not a body, but a spirit;" that it is "not begotten of the substance of God . . . but made of God;" that it is not made "in such a way that the nature of any kind of body or of non-rational soul can be turned into its nature"; hence, that it is "made from nothing;" that it is "immortal as regards life in the ordinary sense," but "as regards a kind of mutability" it can "also be seen as mortal."[58]

Beyond these (sometime-paradoxical) conclusions, Augustine understands the human as an integrated unity. Although the soul is not corporeal, it is also not a free-floating entity entrapped within the body. The soul interpenetrates the body, or something like that. "All that was meant where it is said: *the man was made into a live soul* (Gn 2:7), is that he began to have sensation in his body."[59] The body, he continues, is not moved solely by external action upon it, but also by an "inner motion."[60] The soul is the body's animation, that reflexive capacity of the human to be aware of itself within the world as well as the power and bearing to act upon the world; to receive from the world and react.

"The soul . . . being something non-bodily, first activates the kind of body which is nearest to being non-bodily, like fire (or rather light) and air; and then through these the other coarser elements of the body, like moisture and earth, which constitute the solid mass of the flesh."[61] Reflecting his classical context, Augustine thinks of light, like air, water, and earthen material, as not only external to the human but also internal. Eyes not only receive light but also generate it. Moreover, Augustine's Neoplatonic affinities condition his view that the non-corporeal soul acts first through the less-material elements of light and air and through them affects mass and flesh.[62]

But in this instance, too, the classical and Neoplatonic details need not detain us. The critical point is that Augustine construes the soul not so much as a ghost inhabiting a body, but as the dynamic seat of human agency. It is the animated animation of the human person. What Augustine distinguishes as "soul" can thus be correlated with what I have been developing as the fulsome operation of *self-perception*. The soul exists in the most integral interface with the body, affecting it and being affected by it, moving and being moved, animating everything from will to limbic action and reciprocally learning and growing in response to them. For instance, "the soul feels and is vexed by the body's afflictions, it is offended at the activity with which it governs and cares for the body being thwarted through the body's constitution."[63] Pain, pleasure, hope, anxiety, achievement, failure—all are states that take root in the soul and that develop in nuance and complexity over time as the soul experientially develops. Pain yields vexation, or reflective exasperation, which as a second-stage condition betrays a kind of developmental capacity alongside a self-regulatory function.

Unlike the animals, who also have souls and react as agents in the world, the human does so in a way that is *fitting*. It "*administers* the body"[64] through cogitative scrutiny and not brute reflex. The soul adjudicates what it takes in and how it might respond according to sense of potential, scale, and propriety. It is only in such a creature (and in the higher-order cogitation of angels) that the goal of covenantal unity with creation can be achieved. The soul must take in not only sensory data but also the higher-order light of God's Word. It is the latter knowledge by which all other knowing, willing, and acting have to be adjudicated. Human understanding, desire, and activity in the world are only rightly ordered in view of revelation. With this insight, we may at length transition to Augustine's complementary eschatological concern.

Discussion of Augustinian Anthropology II: Eschatological Concern

The ensouled human participates in its own realization. By virtue of her peculiar animation, the human realizes her seeded existence in constructive response to the stimulus of God's voice. She is conformed in and through her soul to the image of God in Christ. As we have seen, Augustine assumes as right and proper a measure of human form-ability. The human is made to be otherwise in the next moment than as she is in this one.

Augustine is not entirely consistent, however, in this way of thinking. Augustine's hope for the human is that she will ultimately transcend *change*, or the ability to change; that she will achieve a kind of otherness, which halts the potential for alteration. The human can be otherwise in the next moment than as she is in this one, but only until the eschaton, or for the sake of being otherwise in the eschaton than she is in the present; she exists then not only in conformity to the will of God, but also, strangely and not entirely convincingly, in conformity to the atemporality of God. Eschatologically, Augustine hopes for stasis, existence beyond the restive mutability of time: "things which are not in their intended position are restless. Once they are in their ordered position, they are at rest."[65]

This hope stands in tension with the seed-conception informing Augustine's protological view of creation, especially ensouled humanity, and gives further reason not to follow Augustine in rigidly distinguishing between eternity and time. As Caroline Walker Bynum summarizes, "for all his interest in process and his creative use . . . of Stoic seminal reasons to explain it—Augustine rejects the Pauline seed metaphor with its attendant implication that body is fluid, dynamic, potential, open to infinite development."[66] For Augustine, the goal of human existence is to share in the immutability of its Source; the animating potential of the soul is not to set the body along a process of ever-growing, upward-spiraling transformation, but of restoring the cadaverous creation to a (yet-more?) natural[67] condition of rest.

Augustine's inconsistency, besides problematically assuming Aristotelian mechanics, evokes the squishy subjectivity latent in restorationist views of creation (those which would restore a lost Edenic state). For instance, he concludes that each person will be raised to a size in keeping with his actual frame—not to a common size instantiated in, presumably, the risen Jesus—yet proportionally. His posture (and by extension weight, hair length, etc.) will be perfected: he will be restored to his youthful dimensions if the individual reached old age, or to what would have been his proper, mature dimensions if he died in childhood.[68] But why not, for the sake of argument, the height that the person would have enjoyed in youthful maturity had he been nourished with more calcium?[69] Is there a dietary mix that would somehow contribute to a corporeal "perfection," which humans are slowly learning about, and will enjoy in the resurrection? Augustine could argue something like this: Adam had the offer of corporeal perfection through right diet in the Garden (the tree of life?; see the discussion below), but forfeited it, and so his offspring likewise have failed to enjoy that perfection. But then, the argument about proper posture, and so on, based on an alleged age of perfection is senseless: no human at any age has ever enjoyed the fullness of corporeal life, because it has been denied them by Adam's choice. In the end, a restored state of resurrected perfection proves to be nothing but arbitrary allegation, a bodily form set either by standards of measure that obtain to specific environmental and dietary conditions at a particular time, but not at other places and times, or by standards of measure that have never existed and can only be sheer conjecture.

Augustine understands the human, qua human, as ready for learning and growth, but identifies the achievement of the human with the achievement of a divine rest beyond learning and growth, which *ipso facto* would seem to undercut the human's humanity. If the animating principle of the human just is the potential for being otherwise—*corporis et intellectus per animam*—then removing her potency, or rather, taking "being-otherwise" as an achievable, fixed state beyond potency, would seem at once to destroy her causal formula.[70]

A little more exactly, to follow Bynum's construction, Augustine's open-ended protological views would be better suited to something like Origen's eschatological account of the body, which emphasizes the *goodness* of change. Augustine's difficulty is that, while recognizing that human change is good, he stresses the way that the goodness of change quickly is transformed into evil. While seeing the soul's susceptibility to otherness as humanity's condition of transformation, Augustine focuses on the body's susceptibility for otherness as humanity's condition of decay and death. In turn, rather than holding on to the good in mutability, rather than seeing in mutability not only evil but also evil's defeat, Augustine sees mutability as that which must *itself* be defeated.

Origen, by contrast, making much of the seed metaphor in 1 Cor. 15, thinks of body as *inherently* transformational, by its *nature* susceptible to development. It is "a substratum whose identity is guaranteed by a corporeal *eidos* [form]. This *eidos* is a combination of Platonic form, or plan, with Stoic seminal reason (an internal principle of growth or development). A pattern that organizes the flux of matter and yet has its own inherent capacity for growth, it is . . . a bit like a genetic code."[71] Humanity is realized not in transcending its mutability, but in seeing its change perfected or refined, which is to say, in being transformed (learning and developing) in keeping with the Good.

Bynum shows that Patristic thought about authentic human existence oscillated between identity across time and transformation through time: a figure like Augustine sought to stabilize authentic human existence; a genuine humanness can be identified, fixed, and achieved. Resurrection hope takes the shape of a broken statue being reconstructed. Origen, by contrast, thought of human being as intrinsically in flux, a substratum ready for form, which takes shape through assemblages of matter and especially mental formations, according to a divine plan. Resurrection hope takes the shape of a seed being planted, which initial form breaks down and gives way to new forming, to new life (however different this might be from the previous iteration). We will again take up the tension between human identity and transformation in the next chapter.[72] Suffice it to say that Augustine starts with the seed metaphor but does not finish with it, and this involves him in a contradiction. In a certain respect, Origen's eschatological vision better completes Augustine's protological thinking than Augustine's own eschatological vision does.[73]

Still, we benefit by lingering on Augustine's conviction that the human exercises genuinely determinative agency. Although he does not carry its implications through as consistently as we should like, Augustine does helpfully see that the human causes her un-forming, and at God's enabling and guiding participates in her re-forming. In this, we are met with Augustine's influential account of the origin and overcoming of evil.[74]

Against the Manichees, evil is not a thing. "There is no nature whatsoever that is evil; in fact, 'evil' is nothing but a term for the privation of good."[75] Again, "evil . . . is not a nature of any kind, but the loss of the good has been given this name."[76] In what sense has goodness been lost and evil eventuated? "I inquired what wickedness is; and I did not find a substance but a perversity of will twisted away from the highest substance, you O God, towards inferior things."[77] More fully, "the changeable good [humanity], which comes after the unchangeable good [God], becomes a better good when it clings to the unchangeable good by loving and serving it with its own rational will. . . . If it refuses to do this, it deprives itself of a good."[78]

Instead of being enraptured in the beatific vision of God, wherein it contemplates all things in praise of its Maker, humanity becomes ensnared in contemplation and enjoyment of created things, which are naturally mutable and temporary (and thus unable perfectly to satisfy). The will involves itself in a vicious cycle of deprivation, unmet desire. To turn to lower goods does *not* mean, importantly, to affix the gaze on an inherent evil, for God created nothing that is not good. What becomes known as evil—what emerges in the angelic and human realm as a force opposed to God—is neither more nor less than *disposition* away from God toward lower goods rooted in self-interest, or perceiving all goods in relation to oneself. "What else are we to call this vice but pride?"[79]

But if God is good, and creates nothing that is not good, then what is the cause of pride? "If we look for the efficient cause of this evil will, we find none."[80] Augustine thinks that it is futile, even absurd to try to give a positive account to the origination of sin. That is because, again, any positive account would posit some existing will, which moves the human will toward evil, which would itself have to be evil, leaving us in a self-defeating line of regression. "No one, therefore, should look for an efficient cause for an evil will. For it is not an efficient but rather a deficient cause, because the evil will itself is not an effect but rather a defect."[81] The search for evil's source ends in hollow emptiness. "To defect from what has supreme existence to what has lesser existence is itself to begin to have an evil will. And . . . to want to discover [its] causes is like wanting to see darkness or to hear silence."[82]

Evil happens (already) in the inexplicable instant that the will takes the shape of lower-grade preference. Evil is not created with the will, but it also is not extrinsic to the will in its good operation; it is characteristic deficiency of the will.

Nothing more can be said of "evil" than that, paradoxically, it is the nothing, which is just there in the moment-by-moment sensations of the soul. "Those things that are known not by perception but by lack of perception are somehow known by not-knowing them, with the result that, by knowing, they are not-known—if such a thing can be understood."[83] As silence can only be known as the absence of sound, evil is only "known" as absence of good. Its origin, then, can only be described as self-contradiction, defective turn away from the good (since "in the beginning" there is only the good).[84] Any other account of evil, as a thing which origin is known positively, renders it certain that the knower is mistaken, that by her "knowing" it, she remains unknowing.

Thus, even in creating the agents of evil, angels and humans, God is not the cause of evil. Evil arises out of a nature that is good living among other good natures, in the form of self-contradictory predilection for lesser beings/lower goods. "Evil" designates transgression of the will of God by the will of man, which taking place across history forms an aggregate threat, but which is, in the time of God, nothing. Evil is not a creature or thing of standing; it is an event, the anti-God-event. It is rejection of the covenant by the creature who only exists because of the covenant, which is predestined to overpowering by the will of God, unable, in the end, to endure. In time's culmination, evil will be shown for its factual nothingness.

There is much worth retrieving in Augustine's account of evil, particularly in support of the argument made in this book. However metaphysical Augustine's speculations otherwise are, he does not account for evil in such terms, or more exactly, it proves futile not only to account for evil among metaphysical existents, but even as a metaphysical construct. Rather, remarkably, Augustine construes it *actualistically*. "Evil" *happens* as self-perception alights on the serpentine alternative and values it, or as the soul turns in directions other than the way of God; that is, evil simply is so-alighting and turning. It is *betrayal*, disloyalty to the other and therefore to the self as companion, to the good of faithfulness. ("The woman that you gave.") This turning-away cannot be characterized other than as deficiency latent in the perceptive act/soulish sensation, or as we now will see, as disobedience resident as a possibility within the agency of obedience.

Augustine understands the Tree of Life as a "sacrament," a *sign* of God's gift of life, which takes part in the reality signified. "So then the tree of life also was Christ."[85] (In construing the Tree of Life as a type of Christ, Augustine is not, in his view, rendering it allegorically. Rather, the tree refers the reader to the holy Wisdom in and by which all of creation comes to have life.) Like the body of Christ, the tree held mystical, life-giving properties. "While the tree did indeed provide bodily food, it was of such a sort that the man's body would be fortified by it with enduring health . . . by some hidden infusion of vigorous well-being."[86]

Not so the second tree. Eating of the Tree of the Knowledge of Good and Evil did not induce death in the same way that eating of the Tree of Life produced "vigorous well-being." "I am of the opinion that it was not a matter of that tree having poisonous fruit—the one who had made all things *very good* (Gen. 1:31) would not have planted something bad in Paradise—but of the man's transgression of the commandment having been bad for him."[87] Once again, Augustine rejects any hint that God created evil in any form. The divinely planted Tree of the Knowledge of Good and *Evil* must be of a different significance than the Tree of life; it must be important not because of the poisonous nature of its produce, but as supplying occasion for the human to enact obedience.

"It was necessary that the man, placed under God as his Lord and master, should be prohibited from doing something, so that obedience might itself be his virtue by which to deserve well of his master."[88] The Tree of the Knowledge of Good and Evil was thus given to *adam* as a kind of opportunity really to be the ensouled creature who knows and approves of God's will:

> The man . . . would have had no reason to reflect that he had a Lord and master, and to feel it in his bones, unless he had been given some order. And so the tree was not evil, but it was given the name of the knowledge of discerning good and evil, because if the man should eat of it after being forbidden to do so, there was in it the future transgression of the commandment, as a result of which the man would learn through his experience of the penalty what difference there was between the good of obedience and the evil of disobedience.[89]

Augustine comes close to the misjudgment identified in our exegesis above of treating the knowledge of good and evil as a sadistic object lesson, that is, an arbitrarily imposed quarantine zone established for no other reasons than to test humanity's discipline and justify divine punishment when the human exercised insufficient restraint. But I think that he narrowly avoids this misstep. Augustine is saying that the human must existentially realize; must "feel . . . in his bones" the primal relation in which he exists as human. The human must actually come to know himself as *secunda* before *primus*. Only as he does this is he in fact human. Thus, the Tree of Knowledge of Good and Evil is not an arbitrarily imposed test, but a foreordained (in the fullness of that wisdom communicated in creation) chance for humanity's self-confirmation, the means of its obedience. If the Tree of Life signifies the mystical gift of life, then the Tree of the Knowledge of Good and Evil signifies creaturely realization through obedience. The one tree is the divine permission, and the second is the divine prohibition.

One either refuses to eat of the second tree (obeys the divine command) and is given to eat of the first or one eats of the second tree (disobeys the divine command) and is barred from the first. For, the human cannot have the means of growth without its occasion. One cannot have the divine permission without the divine prohibition; the human cannot realize its existence apart from obedience to God.

This, finally, is why the gap between Augustine's seed-protology and statue-eschatology disappoints: a dynamic eschatology better expresses his insight that the human comes to authenticity through obedience, through actively perceiving the self in relation to God and neighbor and preferring this to the serpentine alternative. His conception of seeded causal formulae otherwise dovetails nicely with his understanding of the obedience of faith signified in the first and second trees: to become what it was intended, the human must consciously refuse every alternative to the divine way and accept the gift of covenantal life. Nonetheless, while a contradiction remains for Augustine between the seed of human creation and the reconstructed, body-soul statue of the eschaton, it is modulated somewhat by a second distinction, which he posits between the seed of human creation and the resurrected, body-*spirit* of the eschaton. The latter is still a kind of stasis, but more clearly thought of in terms of perfected obedience than static rest—this precisely in the event of self-perception. We will conclude this chapter by trying to harvest some of what Augustine has to say in this latter respect.

Augustine distinguishes between the ensouled and enspirited body, between *corpus animale* and *corpus spiritale*. Both are forms of bodily quickening, but the latter is superior to the former; soulish quickening is earthly, whereas spiritual quickening is heavenly. Augustine draws the distinction and ordering from 1 Cor. 15:45–49. There, Paul speaks of the "first human Adam" (ὁ πρῶτος Ἀδαμ) being a "living soul" (ψυχὴν ζῶσαν), and the "second" or "eschatological Adam" (ὁ ἔσχατος Ἀδαμ) being a "living spirit" (πνεῦμα ζῳοποιοῦν). According to v. 46, "the first human is from dust of the earth" (ὁ πρῶτος ἄνθρωπος ἐκ γῆς χοικός) and "the second human is from heaven" (ὁ δεύτερος ἄνθρωπος ἐξ οὐρανοῦ).

Paul of course speaks of the relationship between the created *adam* and Jesus of Nazareth, the obedient, true *adam*. In this, Paul supplies for Augustine a Christocentric picture of authentic, redeemed human being. In view of Christ, the question rises whether *adam* was created earthly or heavenly, an ensouled body or enspirited body, that is, "whether it was an embodiment of soul that was first formed for the man out of mud, such as we now have, or an embodiment of spirit, such as we shall have when we rise again."[90] After some wrestling with the possibilities, Augustine decides that if we are to take seriously the fact that the human was placed in a garden among trees bearing food, then we have to conclude that the human was created as ensouled and not enspirited, earthly and not heavenly, indeed, mortal and not immortal. "Who, I mean to say, would ever suppose that food of that sort from fruit trees could have been necessary for immortal and 'enspirited' bodies?"[91]

The human was not created with an immortality that it forfeited by disobedience, but mortally, or *potentially* immortal. Immortality had to be actualized by obedience:

> Before sin, in fact, the body could have been said to be both mortal for one reason and immortal for another; mortal, that is, because it was able to die, and immortal because it was able not to die. It is one thing, after all, not to be able to die [created like the angels] . . . while it is quite another to be able not to die; and this is the way the first man was created immortal, something to be granted him by means of the tree of life, not by his natural constitution.[92]

Augustine believes that had Adam and Eve not sinned, they would have procreated offspring (which act of procreation would have been freed of the lust that all such acts now exhibit), and these children would have had children, and so on.[93] And each ensouled generation would progress through successive stages of maturity, receiving spiritual bodies in due course, until such time as the full measure of God's people would have been achieved. Now, in its state of sinfulness, for the human to become what it was created to be, for the soul to yield finally to the spirit, the human must proceed through death[94] and enjoy resurrection.

In salvation, then, the human is not restored to a state of blanket immortality. It never possessed that. It is restored first and foremost to a condition of righteousness. "It is not the immortality of an 'enspirited' body that we get back, which the man did not yet have; but what we get back is the justice from which the man fell through sin."[95] That is critical, because the soul's transformation and humanity's enjoyment of immortality still runs through existential realization of its place in the divine order. The human actually must be the covenantal agent, which God intended for it to be. It must actually instantiate in the seat of its being a right knowledge and appreciation of God's account of things, God's will. "So then, we shall *be renewed in the spirit of our minds* (Eph 4:23), *according to the image of him who created us* (Col 3:10), which Adam lost by sinning."[96] The human realizes its humanity as it is conformed to its created image, an image that it *perceives* in Christ Jesus.

That brings us to the final piece of our puzzle. It is telling that Augustine ends *The Literal Meaning of Genesis* with a protracted discussion not of Genesis but of Paul's account of "a man" being raptured to the "third heaven" (2 Cor. 12), which Augustine takes to have been Paul himself, and the nature of heavenly paradise.[97] In assessing Paul's journey to the third heaven, Augustine identifies three types of *vision* particular to the human, "one with the eyes . . . one with the human spirit . . . a third with the attention of the mind."[98] In light of the foregoing discussion, we should note that Augustine does not mean by the second form of vision that of a resurrected, enspirited body. Rather, beyond sensate perception of objects (the first form), he recognizes that the human also retains images in memory and calls them to the mind as if they were physically there (but, of course, are only there "spiritually"). Beyond these two there is a third, which is perception of purely mental constructs, "observation" of a condition or idea that may be signified by a physical object or image, but is not that object or image itself.

For instance, Augustine cites Joseph's interpretation of the pharaoh's dream in Genesis 41.[99] There are actual cows and grain stalks (or in Augustine's translation, ears of corn) in the world, which as such are taken in by the ocular sense. Second, Pharaoh dreams of these things, wherein their image is imprinted on his mind as if they were there. Third, Joseph explains the significance of the dream, prophetically interpreting it to invoke states of famine, preparation, and wise leadership, none of which can be collapsed into any one image or series of images, but all of which can be "seen" by the mind.

As we might anticipate, Augustine arranges these forms of vision hierarchically. Each of the two lower forms assumes the next one higher, but neither of the two higher forms needs the next lower to occur:

> There can, after all, be no bodily vision without the spiritual, seeing that the moment contact is made with a body by a sense of the body, some such thing is also produced in the spirit. . . . Spiritual vision, on the other hand, can occur without the bodily kind, when the likeness of absent bodies appear in the spirit. . . . Again, spiritual vision is in need of the intellectual kind in order to have a judgment or assessment made of it, while the intellectual is in no need of this inferior spiritual kind.[100]

Pure intellection, so to speak, need not revert to brute imagination. Augustine dedicates some effort to demonstrating the ways that the two lower forms of vision become confused. It is part of the muddle of our fallenness for the soul to be susceptible to temptation and error vis-a-vis corporeal and spiritual matters. "The devil deceives people with bodily visions . . . [and] plays tricks on the soul by the images of bodies in spiritual vision."[101] Divination and the images of wet dreams are but two of the realities that Augustine considers in these regards.[102]

The point of this demonstration is to set up, by way of contrast, the reliability of pure intellection and the nature of the beatific vision. "While good spirits instruct and evil ones deceive by means both of bodily vision and of the images of bodily realities which are exhibited in the spirit, the intellectual kind of vision on the other hand cannot be deceived."[103] This seems like an incredible claim, but Augustine simply means that "the one who supposes [that the object of intellectual vision] means something different from what it actually does fails to understand."[104] By *exclusio per definitionem*, the one who errs in intellectual vision does not actually possess that vision. Actually to possess intellectual vision of something means "it is *ipso facto* true."[105]

This kind of vision, the content of which just is the case, is the only kind capable of authentic knowledge of God, as it is the only kind in which, circularly, there can be no error. In a vision, "without any bodily likeness the pure transparent truth is perceived, overcast by no clouds of false opinions."[106] The highest possible vision is a kind of stable comprehension of divine truth, pure possession of heavenly knowledge. It is untainted by bodily vicissitudes (even spiritual vision, once more, is of bodily images) of imprecision, temptation, and inequity. "It has been so secluded and removed and totally snatched away from the senses of the flesh and purified, that it is inexpressibly enabled by the charity of the Holy Spirit to see and hear the things that are in that [third] heaven, and the very substance of God and God the Word *through whom all things were made* (Jn 1:3)."[107]

Beatific vision is perfect comprehension of the Word of God. From within the life of the Apostle, this happened, as the immediate citation indicates, absent the senses. But Paul's rapture to the third heaven only *prefigures* the resurrected condition, because the human is raised *bodily*. What transpires, again, is that the human is transformed so that she may enjoy not just an ensouled but also an enspirited existence:

> If the body is such that the administration of it is difficult and burdensome, like this flesh of ours . . . deriving as it does from the handing on of the first transgression, the mind will be even more completely distracted from that vision of the highest heaven. That is why it had necessarily to be snatched away from the senses of this flesh, for that vision to be shown it in whatever measure it could grasp it. Accordingly, when it receives back this body, now no longer just 'ensouled' but thanks to the transfiguration to come 'enspirited,' it will have the measure of its proper nature complete, it will be both obeying and commanding, both quickened and quickening with such inexpressible ease, that what was once its burden is now its glory.[108]

In a body governed by a perfected will, obedience has been rendered effortless. It is the easy and constant preference of the human. But as willed

obedience, eschatological human existence is actual *human* existence: resurrected humanity's "immutability" is really just the constancy of its free
action in conformity to the beatific vision. The human perfectly receives and
embodies the Word of God.

Augustine still uses language of "getting back" or "return" to some previous state, but obviously enough, this verbiage is quieted to a degree by an
overtone of transformation. The human is not restored to any state of being
that it ever possessed; its "return" is only by the addition of a condition (a
spirituality), which it has never known, or which it had to learn and must, as
God's beloved, continually enact.[109] We had to walk an arduous path to arrive
at this insight, picking our way through Neoplatonism and, by turns, a rigid
literalism, but the journey has been worth it. Augustine helps us to think of
authentic human being as moment-by-moment, existential conformity to the
way of God by actively resisting evil (obeying the divine command) and joyfully affirming the gift of covenantal life (receiving the divine permission) in
and through God's Spirit.

CONCLUSION

Augustine remains a helpful interlocutor for the deep and detailed way that
he understands authentic human existence to mean actively living in the
Spirit of Christ. The human is made for the covenant, made as a creature that
can accept God's offer of life and refuse the alternative at each and every
moment, that can reiterate within its biorhythms the self-giving character of
its Creator. It is God's creative intention for humanity to exist this way. But
as such, as a creature poised to become, humanity is and is not yet. It exists
proleptically, in a present being fashioned after a future communion, perceiving life with God but as promise, as hope fulfilled in Christ but therefore also
renewed in him. In the light of Christ, humanity perceives what it is in the
light of what it can be, and seeks the latter. It experiences the reformation of
its desires, the repatterning of its interests as, indeed, the ground of its being.
The human hears the dissembling hiss of the serpent, the falsehood of a self-
given, all-comprehending life, yet as something that has been defeated and
thus as something that might be defeated again. The human perceives his life
within the victory of Christ's life over sin. On the one hand, he feels the pull
of betrayal, yet, on the other, he recognizes his true self within the free giving
of covenantal loyalty.

Sinfully, the human acts according to the baseless pride of a falling will.
He looks to goods that reinforce a sense of Self not with others but over and
against others, goods that help to construct an I not with Thous but opposed to
thous. He does this even in the sphere of his most primal desire, with respect

to the gift of a partner who is otherwise one with him. The man who experienced the joy of fulfillment in the divine gift of woman now fixes on the woman apart from the divine; she becomes impediment rather than complement, a means of Self-realization rather than a telos of mutuality. And in this primal infidelity, the man turns against the gift of his own life, not valuing and affirming the goodness of faithfulness but pursuing an alternative ground, to his own loss; the man rejects the from-for order of life and its productivity, and woman does the same, and together they stand under the curse of death.

Yet even in this sinful condition, man and woman receive God's mercy. God does not cease to give life, to have God's own life in the giving. God self-consistently seeks the human in the very place of his disobedience, within his falling soul. God calls him out of his death-bent Self-consciousness and turns his perception Eden-ward.

NOTES

1. "The tree commanded close attention" is not the most satisfying translation of וְנֶחְמָד הָעֵץ לְהַשְׂכִּיל, but the wide variety in modern renditions demonstrates the challenge of treating this phrase. The point is the transfer in perception from receiving to projecting, more exactly from taking in the desirable (what is beautiful, good, and true) to desiring it lustfully, or to "take pleasure" (חָמַד) in what the tree provides for oneself, or finding it right and good to possess it's fruit (wisdom) self-referentially. Alter renders לְהַשְׂכִּיל, "lust to the eyes;" *Genesis*, 12.

2. Is there an allusion to intercourse here, characterized specifically as male letdown after successful conquest of the forbidden? Perhaps, although with most interpreters, I take the meaning of these verses to penetrate deeper than carnal knowledge and the sense of remorse that may follow it. To the extent that Genesis 3 invokes the sex act, it depicts adulterous man, unfaithful man, man not content to live within the framework of covenantal relation.

3. Alter, *Genesis*, 13.

4. Arnold, *Genesis*, 61–62.

5. Midrash on Lam. 1:1 ("How lonely sits the city that once was full of people! How like a widow she has become, she that was great among the nations! She that was a princess among the provinces has become a vassal") helps to demonstrate the existential poignancy of the Genesis story: "R. Nehemiah said, 'The word "how" bears the meaning only of lamentation, in line with the following usage: "The Lord God said to the man, saying to him, 'Where are you' (Gen. 3:9)" [which uses the same letters as the word for 'how.'] 'Where are you' can be read 'woe is you.'" (Jacob Neusner, *Lamentations Rabbah: An Analytical Translation*, Brown Judaic Studies 193 [Atlanta: Scholars, 1989], 111). Rabbinic commentators observed a parallel between the catastrophe of sin in the Garden and the heart-wrenching devastation of exile (see also ibid., 20–21). Israel was banished from the land of promise like Adam and Eve from the Garden. Conversely, Adam and Eve's real crisis is estrangement

from their Maker and Lord; woe to sinful humankind, for like a nation in exile, it is lost. As Neusner's bracketed comment makes clear, the base form of the Hebrew interrogative (אֵי) is flexible. It can be prefixed to adverbs and pronouns that allow it to mean "where," "whence," "how," "in what manner" (see BDB 5th ed., p. 32). Thus, the commentator uses an indirect linguistic connection to associate Lam. 1:1 with Gen. 3:9 thematically.

6. Literature on the nature and function of הַנָּחָשׁ in Gen. 3 is abundant. For a helpful summary, see Westermann, *Genesis 1–11*, 237–39. Westermann relies on the landmark 1937 study by Th. C. Vriezen, *Onderzoek naar de Paradijsvoorstelling bij de oude Semietische Volken* (Wageningen: H. Veenman and Zonen). Vriezen categorized the interpretive options as follows: the serpent is Satan incognito; the serpent is symbolic; the serpent is a mythological creature; the serpent is an animal known for its cleverness. Westermann disagrees with Vriezen's own conclusion that the serpent is a magical "animal of life and wisdom," which the Jahwist has made into a tempter (237). The problem he sees with this line of interpretation is that the Jahwist expressly states that the serpent was made by the Lord God in 3:1, and there is no way that the narrator would make God responsible for the tempter.

Here again, I endorse Westermann's judgment: "the function of the serpent derives from the structure of the narrative. The couple's transgression in the garden where God put them is elaborated by the temptation motif portrayed in an action. . . . It is portrayed as a personal event spelled out in a dialogue" (238). The serpent appears as a kind of foil, a contra-locutor, so that the inward dialogue vis-a-vis disobedience is portrayed in external, mythical form.

In this respect, we might assume that the Jahwist constructively reworked aspects of a Canaanite serpent cult. Arnold relates the theory that "the Garden of Eden reflects an old Canaanite myth of a sacred grove, with a tree of life, living waters, guardians at the entrance, and especially a serpent. Thus it is possible an ancient story has been demythologized in order to expose the real nature of Canaanite Baalism, and not only to expose it, but to universalize the experience for all Israel so that obedience to Yahweh's voice and repudiation of Baalism becomes paramount for all"; *Genesis*, 63. The Jahwist takes over a common cultic figure, strips it of its pagan teaching, and makes it the expression of human sin, precisely in pursuit of a knowledge of God that is alien to that which is given by Yahweh.

The Jahwist might further reflect "a popular notion, often represented in the art of the ancient Near East, that the serpent originally walked erect. Having arrogantly aggrandized itself in a challenge to God, it is now permanently doomed to a posture of abject humiliation"; Sarna, *Genesis*, 27. Although backgrounds may be different, I take this line of interpretation to correlate logically with that which locates the serpent in the chaos myth; it represents the divine adversary (in the form of Leviathan, or Rahab), the standing threat to that order by which God brings life. The serpent signifies not only disobedience, but in this, death.

7. Fretheim gets close to the matter: in that the consequence of disobedience, death, is more complicated than merely eating of the one tree, that is, it also entails failure to eat of the other tree (command and permission work together), "the serpent speaks a word that has the potential of being true (at least at the physical level). . . .

The serpent is correct in saying the human would become like God(s), knowing good and evil, and that eating in itself would not necessarily mean death in at least some sense"; *The Book of Genesis*, 360–61.

8. Literature on the nature of יְדְעֵי טוֹב וָרָע is no less abundant than that on the serpent. Here, too, Westermann supplies a useful summary; see *Genesis 1–11*, 242–48. He generalizes a consensus on three points: "the knowledge is completely subordinated to the command," "the knowledge . . . does not mean moral knowledge," and "knowledge is [of] a broader and general sense," that is, following Wellhausen [*Composition of the Hexateuch*], "good and evil" are polarities meant to describe a whole (242–43). Beyond this, Westermann finds disagreement in the details of whether the knowledge is of a carnal variety, whether the knowledge connotes a root sin of hubris, whether the knowledge is magical in nature, and with this, whether the arts of fertility in the Canaanite serpent cult stand in the background, or whether some synthesis of all of these is intended, so that the human finds existence in a paradoxical state of having the potential to advance beyond the gods that gave it existence (243–45).

Westermann's own conclusion is again commendable. After considering cognate tales in which a divine prerogative is stated over against the creature (Job 15 and Ezek. 28), as well as ANE background myths in which conflict emerges between gods and humans (the Adapa Myth and the Enkidu Episode), Westermann reasons that humanity pursues a kind of wisdom that would displace God with self-mastery. "The promise 'to be like God' is not something over and above knowledge, but describes it and all that it is capable of. It is concerned with a divine and unbridled ability to master one's existence" (248). This is not exactly the same as saying that in seeking the knowledge of good and evil the human becomes a creature of *pride*, in the classical way of thinking. It is rather to suggest that the human pursues such a self-consciousness as would exclude from reality the authentic source and goal of its existence.

As I will argue in the discussion that follows, "knowledge of good and evil" should not be thought of in a quantitative sense, either with regards to a sum total of "knowledge," or with respect to discrete kinds of knowledge (say, scientific), or with regards to details of content (e.g., humanity might learn certain truths of physics, but be restricted by God from comprehending others). In each of these cases, the human is already pitted against God, quite apart from sinning. She has no choice but to sin, in fact, in that the very exercise of her knowing capacity involves her in a process of quantitative knowledge acquisition, of constantly moving into new territories of understanding; at some point, she inevitably must transgress the divine boundary. But God does not create the human to know only to deny her the opportunity. Indeed, insofar as God has created the human to know *God*, God involves the human in a ceaselessly progressive, ever-expanding act of knowing, precisely as she comes to perceive God in relation to creation and its creatures.

With Sarna (and, perhaps, Wellhausen), it is best to understand "knowledge of good and evil" as a *merism*, that is, "as undifferentiated parts of a totality"; *Genesis*, 19. (In this manner, "good and evil" is to be understood like the phrase, "heaven[s] and earth," which refer not only to sky and ground, but to the total cosmos.) "Totality" should not be taken in the sense of *comprehensive collection*, but of that order of knowledge which it is the prerogative of God, as God, to possess—we might say, *omniscience*.

9. A development in biblical interpretation favored especially in the modern era deserves comment at this point. This line of thinking contends that in Genesis 3 we can identify a subversive undertone, such that the fall of humanity is at one with its realization: in disobeying God, the human transcends itself and achieves the right and power of self-determination. The human recovers the autonomy for which it was always destined, freedom from the bondage of religious duty to enjoy the creative power of the mind. Michael Welker helpfully traces the origin of this (Neomarxist) development to Hegel, who, Welker notes, was especially fond of citing Gen. 3:22, "the man has now become like one of us." See Welker, *Creation and Reality*, trans. John F. Hoffmeyer (Minneapolis: Fortress, 1999), 74–82.

Certainly, I am operating with a contrary notion of "freedom"—not self-possessed independence, but self-realization in willful acceptance of factual interdependence. Entailed in this view is, obviously, assumption that authentic knowledge is realized in faith and not in unbelief. I recognize that already such a statement is an act of faith. Self-willed autonomy with regards to the subject matter and operation of faith, that is, with regards to biblical thought, can only be manifestation *par excellence* of that bondage diagnosed by biblical thought. So Welker:

> Through the fall autonomous human beings have loosed themselves from the community of creation, from the association of relations of interdependence grounded and intended by God. Now human beings are only autonomous, only self-determining. Now they follow only their own perspectives on what is beneficial and detrimental only to their life. At the same time human beings intersubjectively shore up and fortify themselves in their solitariness and isolation. At the same time they are able in their solitariness and isolation to perceive and to determine in their solitary and isolated way what is beneficial and detrimental to their life. Because of this, human beings fall into a situation *structured by enormous delusion*. They fancy themselves free, superior, secure, powerful, indeed equal to God. They think that they have their life fully in hand and under control. . . . They do not notice how in their relative power they destructively introduce themselves into creation, boring their way into it. They do not notice how in doing so they whitewash over and seek to repress their isolation and their being *echad* [like us]. (ibid., 80)

10. Gowan frames the situation nicely:

> The subtlety, the apparently perfect reasonableness of much temptation, is skillfully represented in v. 6. The woman does not condemn God; we hear no direct questioning of God's good intentions, no outright denials or expressions of doubt. She just begins to think for herself. And what (we may respond) is so bad about that? Was it not God who gave her (us) the ability to reason, to make decisions . . . ? [Eve faces] a temptation that is convincingly reasonable and thus unavoidable. (*Genesis 1–11*, 54)

11. I am not concerned to give a comprehensive, exegetically exhaustive account of the biblical concept of "sin," but only to indicate the nature of this reality in a primal sense as conveyed by the creation myth of Gen. 2–3. It goes without saying that there is no consensus among Bible students on the essence of *sin* (the word,

incidentally, is not used in the Genesis creation stories). "Interpreters have had difficulty identifying the nature of the primal sin," Fretheim rightly observes. That may be because "the story remains complex and devoid of abstract reflection" (*The Book of Genesis*, 366). Genesis 3 does not reflect philosophically on the character of sin, but moves descriptively through a narrative that describes it tragically.

I have already given some indication that, extrapolated from the descriptive tale of Genesis 3, sin is not exactly the classical notion of *pride*. Neither is it precisely *rebellion*, or *mistrust* (the latter is Fretheim's preference; see ibid.). It contains elements of these things, as well as of *disobedience* and desire for *autonomy*. The best way to describe it, perchance—and in this regard, Augustine remains a helpful interlocutor—is as *covetousness*, specifically for the self-authenticating place of God.

The question of sin's nature really is one with the question of sin's origin. Latent in humanity's consciousness of self as knower, specifically as dis-coverer, is the propensity to be conscious of Self as unbounded not so much in accumulation of knowledge but in justification for it, in pronouncing not only what is but also what ought to be on the shaky valuation of one's knowledge (as more than it is), and thus to be aware of one's Self as at least potentially an all-knower. But this propensity, again, is not itself sin; it becomes sin when admixed with desire for it to be so. When the Self is conscious of this standing as *good*, then the human sins. (At this instant, the human is prideful, rebellious, mistrustful of God's account, disobedient, and eager for autonomy.)

Critically, sin, and more broadly, *evil* is resident not in the world, but in humankind. According to Genesis 3, "there is no inherent, primordial evil at work in the world. The source of evil is not metaphysical but moral. Evil is not transhistorical but humanly wrought;" (Sarna, *Genesis*, 16). A hurricane, even a deadly one, is no more inherently "evil" than photosynthesis is inherently "good;" abstracted from the will of the Creator, both just *are*. Evil transpires from within the distinctly human capacity to distance one's person from harmfulness by externalizing it, by falsely describing the damaging effects of nature as "evil' in order to make oneself victim and not perpetrator, or even more sinisterly to ascribe these effects to the inscrutable will of a Creator (e.g., as strangely benevolent, or as judgement from on high).

The human manifests evil as she stands in opposition to the will of God in the knowledge of good and evil, percolating harmfulness as she becomes gladly conscious of herself in this opposition. At that point she might seem well-positioned to give right account of evil, but of course, her very standing in opposition prevents that from happening. Evil can only be described post facto, as confession made after the content of revelation.

Sin is only known as such, and enacted as such, in continuing encounter with revelation. Revelation confronts the human in sin and in so doing becomes, paradoxically, the occasion of sin: as opposition to divine will becomes a part of human consciousness, as the human now perceives herself withdrawn (and withdrawing) from God's history of redemption, the human confirms her sinfulnessand must take responsibility for herself as a sinner. The human recognizes herself in a predicament from which she cannot extricate herself; she exists as God-opposer in the manner of the serpent. Finally, then, it is left to revelation also to become the occasion for humanity's transformation; confrontation with God's redemptive history must be with effect, must locate the rebellious consciousness within that history precisely as its object, and thus restructure that consciousness as recipient of a triumphant grace, a persistently creative love. The human must take responsibility for herself as sinner, but she may *not* take responsibility for herself as savior, for the transformed consciousness knows the condition of its transformation to be a gift no less than her very life.

12. Westermann, *The Genesis Accounts of Creation*, 27.

13. Ibid., 27–28.

14. "A correlation between verbs of seeing and verbs of knowledge or understanding is common to many languages;" Alter, *Genesis*, 12.

15. "In the kind of pun in which the ancient Hebrew writers delighted, '*arum*, 'cunning,' plays against '*arumim*, 'naked,' of the previous verse"; Alter, *Genesis*, 11.

16. Gowan, *Genesis 1–11*, 56.

17. Exegetes of the OT have noted the undertone of grace in God's confrontation with *adam* in the Garden:

> After this transgression, the reader is prepared for swift and terrible annihilation of the human couple. Instead, they hear 'the sound of the Lord God walking in the garden' and subsequently they hear his voice calling to them (3:8–9). The grace of God was evident in the creation of the world and of Eden, with appropriate blessings and gifts (Gen. 1:1–2:4). But this is somehow different. There in Gen 1 and 2 we savor God's acts of power and grace, but this gracious forgiveness and divine mercy in the face of human recalcitrance is a new and somehow deeper insight into the character of God. (Arnold, *Genesis*, 66)

18. A word is in order concerning sin and pre-conscious sexual fit, which we considered last chapter. It should be clear by now that sex per se is not sin. Pace Augustine, that goes for sex outside of marriage, too. But with Augustine, sex absent interpersonal commitment, which marriage supplies, presents a powerful occasion for sin.

The sexual impulse anticipates consciousness of the covenantal interdependence in which creation takes place. Primal urge for another, even outside of marriage, is proper. But given the interconnectedness of the human person—that reflex and reflection inform one another—the pre-reflective urge is necessarily admixed with self-desire, that is, the conscious or at least semi-conscious want to gratify one's Self in the act of intimacy. The sexual impulse is susceptible to the same disgracing, or a better word in this case would be *perversion*, as is the total personage. Sex in the imperfect human is encoded with lust.

The instant of perception in which one desires another is cross-bred throughout the arc of human evolution. It is a hybridized, knotted entanglement of copious altruism/other interest and cupidity, each of which remains, in the natural flux of an evolving organism, susceptible to growth as well as training and restriction. Not only the purity of other-interested desire but also the cupidinous admixture can become more or less, a greater or lesser factor at the pivot point of sin. Cupidity can be restrained or encouraged, the latter to the point of rapacity and eventual deviancy.

Marriage provides a strong impulse in the former direction, toward restraint of cupidity and enhanced appreciation of the other in the instant of perception's desire. (Predatory marital arrangements, in which one "partner" is for whatever reason an un-conscious or un-willing participant, excepted.) Along these lines, we would have to conclude that lustful heterosexual intercourse consciously committed outside of marital (or similarly monogamous) commitment is an offense, whereas homosexual intercourse consciously committed within the marital (or similarly monogamous) commitment is not, in that it evinces the quality of self-giving love. Categorically denying the chance to marry to gay and lesbian couples cannot be considered ethical.

No proof-texting can overturn revelation's broader work of locating authentic humanity in the divine history of *agape*. To wit: one simply cannot assert a reading of Rom. 1 against the overwhelming drift of the biblical canon toward deliverance from the ruinous, in-evolved depth-lust facing all humans, heterosexuals included, which is responsible, beyond biological non-complementarity, for perverting what God has made good. This should be clear enough from Rom. 1. The vice list of that chapter, like the rest of the book, falls under the controlling motif of ὑπακοὴν πίστεως (the "obedience of faith"), which bookends the whole in 1:5 and 16:26. It is the obedience of faith that justifies, and it is not evident that homosexual behavior, let alone intuition, qualifies as disobedience.

The only way that resistance to homosexuality by homosexual persons could become a righteousness-instancing form of obedience is if it was of the same class of obedience as resisting lust by heterosexuals. But for both heterosexuality and homosexuality, lust presents itself as enemy of loving relational order. Homosexuality per se does not present itself as enemy of just relation, for again, just relation is simply that which refuses the impulse to Self and instead lives into the self-giving history of God. Genuinely covenantal love stands as a possibility not against homosexuality, but against the unjust order of lustfulness. The antidote to unjust, non-covenantal love is not heterosexuality, but faith.

In short, Paul's condemnations must be read as reiteration of a recognized vice list, which on the basis of Paul' own, broader logic, cannot stand across history as markers of righteousness. These targets of 1st-century condemnation must come to be seen as part of a creation that is in receipt of God's transformative Spirit and being brought into wholeness, a right order of things anticipated not in hetero-normativity, but faith: ὁ δίκαιος ἐκ πίστεως ζήσεται (1:17; Hab. 2:4), and δικαιοσύνη θεοῦ διὰ πίστεως Ἰησου Χριστοῦ εἰς *πάντας τοὺς πιστεύοντας* (3:22).

19. Augustine's discussion of the biblical creation accounts, from which I present his anthropology, is found mainly in three commentaries, the composition of which stretched over three decades. Beginning around 388, he composed a work on Genesis in opposition to the Manichees, *De Genesis contra Manichaeos*, trans. *On Genesis: A Refutation of the Manichees*. He restated his anti-Manichee polemic in a second commentary 5 years later, *De Genesis ad litteram liber unus imperfectus*, trans. *Unfinished Literal Commentary on Genesis*. The title of the latter demonstrates Augustine's conviction that the Manichean position could best be answered by appeal to a "literal" handling of the biblical text, over against the Manichees' "figurative" rendering. But he did not finish the work, feeling inadequate to the task of consistently carrying through the hermeneutic. Determined to succeed, and acknowledging progress in learning, Augustine wrote a lengthier, more systematic and constructive commentary between 401 and 416 called *De Genesi ad litteram*, trans. *The*

Literal Meaning of Genesis. All three of these commentaries in translation, along with relevant extracts from Augustine's later *Revisions*, have been collected and published: Material from Augustine, *On Genesis*, The Works of Saint Augustine: A New Translation for the 21st Century Pt. I vol, 13, ed. John E. Rotelle, O.S.A., trans. Edmund Hill, O.P. (Hyde Park, NY: New City, 2002) is reproduced here by permission from the Augustinian Heritage Institute. Subsequent citations from this volume will employ the following abbreviations: OG, ULG, and LMG, followed by book, section, and paragraph numbers.

In his revisions to the ULG, Augustine concedes that "to make a note of the things I find unacceptable in this book, or to defend things that may be unacceptable to others when they are not well understood, seems to me to be unnecessary. I prefer in a word to advise people to read those twelve books which I completed long afterward as a bishop" (*On Genesis*, 113). The following analysis takes his advice and, among his commentaries, focuses on the LMG.

Augustine began the LMG as he was finishing his *Confessions*, the final three books of which (XI-XIII) treat creation. See Augustine, *Confessions*, The World's Classics, trans. Henry Chadwick (Oxford: Oxford University Press, 1992); subsequently cited as *Conf.*

Additionally, Augustine took up the subject matter in his ranging opus, *de civitate dei*, especially in Books XI-XIV (ca. 416); see Augustine, *The City of God*, The Works of Saint Augustine: A New Translation for the 21st Century Part I vols. 6 and 7, (Hyde Park, NY: New City, 2012–2013); cited as CG followed by book, chapter, and page number. For a helpful orientation to this material, and indication of Augustine's discussion of creation in his more occasional writings, see Edmund Hill, O.P. "General Introduction," in Augustine, *On Genesis*, 13–22.

20. The most insightful and concise summary of Augustine's work on creation that I have found is William A. Christian, "Augustine on the Creation of the World," *HTR* 46:1 (1953), 1–25; repr. "The Creation of the World," in *A Companion to the Study of Augustine*, ed. Roy W. Battenhouse (New York: Oxford University Press, 1955), 315–42.

21. LMG V.5.12.

22. *Conf.* XI.iv.6.

23. *Conf.* XI.vii.9.

24. *Conf.* XI, xiii.16.

25. This discussion echoes Socrates' famous Euthyphro dilemma, wherein an attribute that is commendable in itself would *de facto* be greater than the gods who practice it (they would be beholden to it). Yet conversely, if the attribute is not universally commendable, but only commendable because the gods practice it, then all that is considered good is arbitrary, dependent upon the particular god who declares such and such to be the case, in which instance it is both good and bad at the same time. The solution, and it seems that Augustine's logic reflects this, is that while God is not subject to any pre-existent attributes, God's eternity comprises perpetual iteration of those qualities which God declares to be good.

26. LMG IV.33.52.

27. *Conf.* XII.xv.18.

28. *Conf.* XI.xxvi.33.

29. Augustine arrives here at a fertile insight with regards to time: he begins to perceive that "time" is a subjective modality, relative in character to perception in space. It will not be until the modern era, beginning with Newton, that the sway of classical mechanics (above all Aristotle's notion that the natural state of things is rest) yields to a more interactive accounting (the natural state of things is motion, as forces constantly act on bodies to accelerate, decelerate, and change trajectories), which opens the way to conceiving of time as interconnected with observed space. For more on this, see Stephen Hawking, *A Brief History of Time* (New York: Bantam, 1998), esp. pp. 15–35. Since, as Hawking observes, Newton resisted the pull of his own thinking and continued to insist upon an absolute "time," that is, continued to believe that independent observers would always measure the same duration of an event, it will not be until Einstein that the full relativity of time is appreciated. A readable translation of Einstein's theories of relativity is: Einstein, *Relativity: The Special and General Theory*, trans. Robert W. Lawson (New York: Three Rivers, n.d.).

30. LMG IV.32.50.

31. LMG IV.26.43.

32. Augustine understands the openness of the seventh day to constitute the open-endedness of divine rest, which in the light of Heb. 3–4 is the destiny of the redeemed human; see LMG IV.8–19.

33. LMG IV, n. 36, p. 262.

34. The phrase "heaven of heaven" is from Ps. 113 (114):16. Augustine opens *Conf.* XII with a lengthy discussion in which he differentiates this supracelestial existence from the celestial heavens.

35. *Conf.* XII.vi.6.

36. LMG VI.11.18.

37. Augustine here employs a famously Stoic category of thought. I will not attempt to adjudicate whether he is merely appropriating a convenient construct in an ad hoc manner or systematically engaging an integral feature of Stoicism. I will merely signal that the seed metaphor is pregnant not only protologically but also eschatologically. Indeed, as Caroline Walker Bynum demonstrates below, by employing the seed metaphor protologically (with respect to the event of creation) but eschewing it eschatologically (with respect to the event of resurrection), Augustine involves himself in a difficult contradiction. See Bynum, *The Resurrection of the Body in Western Christianity, 200–1336* (New York: Columbia University Press, 1995), 94–104.

38. God creates humans simultaneously, within the atemporal conveyance of the divine mind, and on the 6th day, i.e., with respect to the sixth repetition of angelic knowledge. The angels receive the mind of God, but again, as creatures, as entities that know God's knowledge not in the immediacy of God's self, but in receipt of God's communication. Therefore, the fullness of the divine mind is something toward which they, also, might move; through reiteration of the triadic mode of consciousness, they come to know what God gives them to know, or they become the knowers that God creates them to be. The purity of their consciousness is not predetermined,

but must occur. This is important for Augustine, because it means that the angels, too, can fail to confirm their rightful knowledge. They, too, can sin.

39. LMG VI.15.26.

40. LMG VI.13.24.

41. In one of history's more striking ironies, modern conservative readers of the Bible often appeal to Augustine for support of a shared, "literal" reading of the text. This appeal betrays substantial ignorance of what Augustine meant by "literal." In important respects, conservative literalism makes for a direct target of Augustine's criticism: by insisting upon 24–hour-length sequences in creation, conservatism reads the very succession into "God," which Augustine explicitly rejected but the Manichees celebrated. Eschatologically, moreover, insofar as its form of literalism inclines it to anything like dispensational premillennialism, conservatism also tends to conceive of salvation as Manichaean deliverance from the material world.

42. Augustine really does think that this amounts to a literal handling of the text. See LMG IV.28.45:

> And please let nobody assume that what I have said about spiritual light and about the day being constituted in the spiritual and angelic creation ... that none of this can be said strictly and properly, but that it all belongs to a kind of figurative and allegorical understanding of day and evening and morning. Certainly it is different from our usual way of talking about this bodily light of every day, but that does not mean that here we have the strict and proper, there just a metaphorical, use of these terms. After all, where you have a better and surer light, there you also have a truer day.

43. LMG. VI.15.26.

44. Either, Augustine continues, because God seeded the actual means of formation into the fabric of formless matter, as the previous citation indicates, or because he withheld to himself the means of formation, and rather simply decreed a formula that prescribed open-ended potency whereby the human could have emerged by any number of means, then actualized the one that he did according to his good pleasure; see LMG VI.15.26.

45. CG XII.22, p. 62.

46. We might say that the causal formula is such as to have allowed for multiple kinds of human emergence, but upon the actual appearing of humanity it restricts itself to the single mode of procreation. This way of putting it strikes me as being both faithful to Augustine and as correlating his ideas, at the same time, with modern thinking. Although the latter does not collapse human origins into a single instance, it does, of necessity, understand eventual species-emergence to take place by way of successful procreation of a luckily well-suited population (and not ongoing instances of inter-species transition). The question is whether Augustine restricts Adam's offspring to a narrowly-defined set of criteria by which it is identified as human, the development out of which would undercut its created being, or whether he leaves room for the causal formula to permit ongoing development, so that one defining criterion of humanity (as with all living creatures) would be a potency for new shape, color, motion, and so on. The latter possibility seems to me at least as likely as the former.

47. LMG VI.17.28

48. "When [miracles] happen they are not happening against nature except from our point of view, to which the course of nature appears from a different angle, but not from God's point of view, since nature for him is simply what he has made" (LMG VI.13.24).

49. Furthermore, although we cannot explore it here, Augustine leaves room for God, while not causing evil, to make creative use out of evil, to bend it into goodness, to bring life out of death. The goodness of decaying forms of matter can be affirmed in the life that often springs from their decomposition. Indeed, Augustine does not understand all animal death to be evil. He thinks that certain animals were simply created to be carnivorous, and that recognition of the sometimes-brutal cycle of animal life, wherein certain lives exist just for the sake of dying for others, is of heuristic value for the soul; see LMG III.15–16.

50. For Augustine's treatment of Gen. 1:24, see LMG III.11–12.

51. See LMG III.14.23.

52. LMG III.20.30.

53. LMG VII.12.19.

54. Just in LMG he takes it for up for several pages in Books VI, VII, and X. See also CG XIII.

55. LMG X.2.3.

56. For a helpful, text-centered discussion of the places that Augustine adjudicates possible origins of the soul, as well as of some of his main arguments, see Gerard J. P. O'Daly, "Augustine on the Origin of Souls," in *Platonismus und Christentum: Festschrift für Heinrich Dörrie*, ed. Horst-Dieter Blume and Friedhelm Mann, Jahrbuch für Antike und Christentum 10 (Münster Westfalen: Aschendorff, 1983), 184–91.

57. LMG VII.28.43.

58. LMG VII.28.43. These conclusions reflect dissatisfaction with alternatives, e.g., the Manichee notion that the soul is of the substance of God, Tertullian's view that the soul is corporeal, and the Neoplatonic concept of a transmigration of souls.

59. LMG VII.16.22.

60. LMG VII.16.22.

61. LMG VII.15.21.

62. "Just as God, after all, surpasses every kind of creature, so the soul by the very worth of its nature surpasses every bodily creature;" LMG VII.19.25.

63. LMG VII.19.25.

64. LMG VII.19.25; italics added.

65. *Conf.* XIII.ix.10.

66. Bynum, *The Resurrection of the Body*, 95–96.

67. It is as if Augustine operates with two conceptions of what is "natural" to the human. On the one hand, it is of humanity's essence to be conformed to the will of God, to grow and develop in keeping with and fulfillment of its causal formula, and on the other hand, it is natural for the human to live without growth and development, to realize a state of being that is perfectly grown and developed.

One might reconcile the tension by construing Augustine as an early dialectician: he wishes to hold the unchanging, absolute perfection of the causal formula as it exists in the divine mind in constructive tension with the relative perfection of the transforming soul as it exists in creation. The only problem with this is that the dialectic proves to be fatally out of balance, for the perfection of transformation turns out to be imperfection next to the perfection of eternal stasis: the first is entirely consumed by the second.

68. CG XXII.14–15, 524–25.

69. Augustine's exegesis is caught between two trajectories: a forward-moving reading of Gen. 2–3, such as I have endorsed throughout, which correlates creation, providence, and redemption, and locates authentic humankind in a future-ward fulfillment, and a backward-moving literalism, which breaks apart creation, providence, and redemption, situating each along a linear timeline, and locates authentic humanity in a rearward, fixed "state" of being.

70. Certainly, consciousness of creaturely self consists in part of maturation, we might even say of aging to a zenith then deteriorating. This particular element of consciousness seems to be constructed through reflexive assimilation of corporeal development. Baby teeth make way for adult teeth, more in number and endurance, yet adult teeth decay and fall out. The bald infant develops hair as a boy, which grows thicker and longer, yet turns grey in middle age and thins. The brain accumulates information, holds it at the ready, then becomes calcified, tangled, and subject to dementia. The body, including its organs, traces an arc from potential to actualization to deterioration.

Insofar as this arc structures creaturely life and human consciousness, resurrection hope affixes on a meridian, a noon of species time, and freezes it. Eschatological vision makes permanent an apex *adam*—full set of teeth, thick hair, strong muscles, supple skin, quick mind—and restores the deteriorated *adam* to it. But the shortcomings of this paradigm are severe.

What, for instance, makes a set of teeth forever and in every setting "full" in size, shape, structure, and number? The frozen apex model of eschatology works from the assumption of given norms for each species. But norms are always predicated upon environmental suitability (e.g., number and size of teeth betray adaptation over time according to available food). The assumption of normativity artificially absolutizes boundaries between species. Evolution's "descent with modification from common ancestry" relativizes them. The human exhibits a range of muscular ability, hand-eye coordination, hair number and thickness, distance and clarity of eyesight, auditory acuity, memory capacity, analytical competency, sensitivity of taste buds, and many more adaptations that have enabled survival. Deviation from the ranges can either aid or compromise the human, depending on environmental conditions. Her hope, then, is not to be restored to some pinnacle, but to enjoy ever-renewed adaptability.

Restorationist eschatology is suspect because it disguises an intrinsic ephemeralness beneath the mask of permanence: the ideal to which humanity is held turns out to be aspectual. Large collections of humans might, for a season, agree on particular ranges of normality, but no total collection of humans have or will agree on all such ranges. Certain zeniths are matters of taste: skinny or beefy, hairy or smooth, dark or light, short or tall—in the end, there can be no static ideal with regards to such matters.

Restorationist eschatology assumes that we already know what it means to be fully and authentically human, on the basis of extrapolation from our own (I-referenced, linearly past-present-future) existence. We project an unreflective, subjective ideal into a timeless eternity. Augustine seems to perceive this subjective shortcoming, then to fall victim to it. In keeping with his own initial commitments, authentic eschatological existence should mean continuing in the upward-spiraling movement of life before God, but in a refined way. It should mean something like Nyssa's ἐπέκτασις (cf. Phil. 3:13): perpetual victory over sin, and thus ascent, and this, I would add, within generational identity.

71. Bynum, *The Resurrection of the Body*, 66. Bynum rightly cautions against pressing the "genetic code" comparison too far, as such anachronisms often introduce a false measure of precision into pre-modern thinking. Besides this caution, I should add the further qualifier that the human body is always more than its genetic code.

72. For a summary of the "reconstructed statue" and "seed" metaphors, see Bynum's treatment of Methodius and Origen in ibid., 63–71. The critical questions are these: if the resurrected human continues to be susceptible to change, which is the condition not only of its pleasure but also of its pain, not only of its glory but also of its death, then why desire resurrection at all? On the other hand, if the resurrected human is not susceptible to change, then in what sense is it still *human*?

73. The qualifier "in a certain respect" is critical: Origen's broader-scope Neoplatonism, including, e.g., emanation-remanation schematic, adds nothing, in fact detracts from Augustine's eschatological insistence on the constant integrity of the soul.

74. Augustine's treatment of evil is by no means a single, uniform construction. Indeed, it can only be an interpretive reconstruction from across several writings. At the heart of Augustine's account is the conviction that evil takes rise out of the free operation of the human will. This conviction is not abstractly occasioned; it derives concretely from Augustine's opposition to the Manichaean heresy, which as already noted attempted to locate evil in the very essence of material creation.

So, in his earlier writings, Augustine finds the cause of evil in the freedom of the will. "All sins are included in this one class, viz. turning away from things which are divine and truly abiding, and turning to things which are changeable and uncertain. They are right enough in their own place, and have a certain beauty of their own. But it is the mark of a perverse and disordered mind to pursue them to the point of becoming subject to them. ... Unless I am mistaken, reason has demonstrated that we [turn to inferior things] by the free choice of the will;" "On Free Will," in *Augustine: Earlier Writings*, ed. J. H. S. Burleigh, The Library of Christian Classics Ichthus Edition (Philadelphia: Westminster, 1953), I.xvi, 34.

Augustine retained the belief that the essence of evil amounts to turning from higher to lower-order goods, and becoming fixed on them, but he tempered to a degree his view that this turn is *caused*, in any *efficient* sense at least, by a free will. That is because Augustine's rigors with respect to the Manichees exposed him to later criticism from the Pelagians. If the will's freedom is responsible for evil, then presumably the same freedom is responsible for righteousness; if the will's freedom allows the soul to alight on lower-order goods, presumably the same allows the soul to alight on the higher-order goods as well. In his *Retractions*, Augustine acknowledged that "Pelagius has made use of this quotation in one of his books," namely, summarizing what he wrote in "On Free Will," III.xviii, 50, "Who commits sin by an act which he could by no means avoid? If sin has been committed, therefore it could have been avoided" (ibid., 102).

In order to ensure that his focus on the will as the cause of evil is not turned around and made also into the cause of righteousness (but rather, against the Pelagians, grace causes righteousness specifically in confronting and correcting the will), Augustine nuanced his causal reasoning concerning the will and evil. In the end, as is discussed below, Augustine stressed that there is in fact *no* positive cause of evil. Evil arises from a defective will, or as *deficient*, not *efficient* cause. (For an earlier discussion of causation, which suggests for the will a more positive role in originating evil, see ibid., III.xvii, 47–49. There, Augustine straightforwardly states that "will is the cause of sin," and again "will is itself the first cause of sin." However, it should be noted that in context, Augustine is really trying to avoid a regressive search for a "cause behind the first cause," so to speak; he is trying to say that we really cannot get behind the will to account for evil, since that would presuppose an earlier will, or, by definition, the absence of evil. This discussion anticipates his more mature conclusions, even as it remains inchoate and somewhat at odds with them.) I have endeavored to relate Augustine's thinking about evil in a manner that reflects his mature concerns.

75. CG XI.22, p. 21.

76. LMG VIII.14.31.

77. *Conf.* VII.xiv.22.

78. LMG VIII.14.31. In keeping with our effort to translate Augustine's thinking out of its Neoplatonic background into a more thoroughly existential and actualistic frame of reference, we must say that it is not the changelessness of God, which represents the highest good/that to which humans ought to cling. Rather, it is the constancy of God's fidelity to the covenant, the uncompromising way in which God places God's self as Life-giver among lifeless creation, which the human ought to emulate. It is as the human reiterates in its own way the constancy of God's self-giving love that it actualizes its intended existence.

79. CG XII.6, p. 41.

80. CG XII.6, p. 42. The language of *efficient* cause should not throw us. Augustine does not parse out alternatives for the initiation of sin (say, a teleological cause). By disallowing an efficient cause, he is content to suggest a certain warrantless-ness to sin. It is antithetical to created existence, a bona fide contradiction in being.

81. CG XII.7, p. 43.

82. CG XII.7, p. 43.

83. CG XII.7, p. 44.

84. "The evil will has its origin not in the fact of [human] nature but in the fact that his nature was created out of nothing;" CG XII.6, p. 43.

85. LMG VIII.4.8.

86. LMG VIII.5.11.

87. LMG VIII.6.12.
88. LMG VIII.6.12.
89. LMG VIII.6.12.
90. LMG VI.19.30.
91. LMG VI.21.32.
92. LMG VI.25.36

93. It bears stressing that Augustine's views often developed over time. This particular conclusion that Adam and Eve would have procreated even without having sinned is a later deduction.

94. Scope does not afford us the chance to unpack all that Augustine has to say about death. Suffice to note that the body dies when it loses its animation, which is to say, when its soul departs. The soul, similarly, experiences death (even though it never fully ceases to exist) in the form of God's withdrawal from it. See for starters CG XIII.

95. LMG VI.24.35.
96. LMG VI.24.35.

97. That is, not the Garden of Eden per se, but what the Garden was intended to have been in view of resurrected communion with God.

98. LMG XII.6.15.
99. LMG XII.9.20.
100. LMG XII.24.51.
101. LMG XII.14.30.
102. See LMG XII.13–15.
103. LMG XII.14.29.

104. LMG XII.14.29. Edmund Hill, O. P. rightly contends that Augustine's argument here, proceeding as it does by self-serving categorical definition, is "not ... very convincing" (LMG XII, n. 24, p. 479).

105. LMG XII.14.29.
106. LMG XII.26.54.
107. LMG XII.34.67.
108. LMG XII.35.68.

109. Beatific vision is, of course, for those who are baptized into the faith of the church. Those outside the means of grace who persist in disobedience will receive the "reward" of hell, or a spiritual vision that is the inverse of the beatific vision:

> Although it is not bodily sights but sights resembling bodily ones that souls divested of their bodies are affected with ... what they see is both real joy and real affliction, made from spiritual substance. After all, even in dreams it makes a great difference whether we find ourselves in joyful or sorrowful circumstances. ... And it is of course not to be doubted that the things said about hell are much more vivid than such dreams. ... So there is then most certainly a substantial reality to hell, but I consider it to be of a spiritual, not a bodily nature" (LMG XII.32.61).

Chapter 5

Evil as Event between Humanity and Creation

וַיֹּ֣אמֶר יְהוָ֧ה אֱלֹהִ֛ים לָֽאִשָּׁ֖ה מַה־זֹּ֣את עָשִׂ֑ית וַתֹּ֙אמֶר֙ הָֽאִשָּׁ֔ה הַנָּחָ֥שׁ הִשִּׁיאַ֖נִי וָאֹכֵֽל׃

וַיֹּאמֶר֩ יְהוָ֨ה אֱלֹהִ֥ים ׀ אֶֽל־הַנָּחָשׁ֮ כִּ֣י עָשִׂ֣יתָ זֹּאת֒ אָר֤וּר אַתָּה֙ מִכָּל־הַבְּהֵמָ֔ה וּמִכֹּ֖ל חַיַּ֣ת הַשָּׂדֶ֑ה עַל־גְּחֹנְךָ֣ תֵלֵ֔ךְ וְעָפָ֥ר תֹּאכַ֖ל כָּל־יְמֵ֥י חַיֶּֽיךָ׃

וְאֵיבָ֣ה ׀ אָשִׁ֗ית בֵּֽינְךָ֙ וּבֵ֣ין הָֽאִשָּׁ֔ה וּבֵ֥ין זַרְעֲךָ֖ וּבֵ֣ין זַרְעָ֑הּ ה֚וּא יְשׁוּפְךָ֣ רֹ֔אשׁ וְאַתָּ֖ה תְּשׁוּפֶ֥נּוּ עָקֵֽב׃ ס

אֶֽל־הָאִשָּׁ֣ה אָמַ֗ר הַרְבָּ֤ה אַרְבֶּה֙ עִצְּבוֹנֵ֣ךְ וְהֵֽרֹנֵ֔ךְ בְּעֶ֖צֶב תֵּֽלְדִ֣י בָנִ֑ים וְאֶל־אִישֵׁךְ֙ תְּשׁ֣וּקָתֵ֔ךְ וְה֖וּא יִמְשָׁל־בָּֽךְ׃ ס

וּלְאָדָ֣ם אָמַ֗ר כִּֽי־שָׁמַעְתָּ֮ לְק֣וֹל אִשְׁתֶּךָ֒ וַתֹּ֙אכַל֙ מִן־הָעֵ֔ץ אֲשֶׁ֣ר צִוִּיתִ֔יךָ לֵאמֹ֕ר לֹ֥א תֹאכַ֖ל מִמֶּ֑נּוּ אֲרוּרָ֤ה הָֽאֲדָמָה֙ בַּֽעֲבוּרֶ֔ךָ בְּעִצָּבוֹן֙ תֹּֽאכֲלֶ֔נָּה כֹּ֖ל יְמֵ֥י חַיֶּֽיךָ׃

וְק֥וֹץ וְדַרְדַּ֖ר תַּצְמִ֣יחַֽ לָ֑ךְ וְאָכַלְתָּ֖ אֶת־עֵ֥שֶׂב הַשָּׂדֶֽה׃

בְּזֵעַ֤ת אַפֶּ֙יךָ֙ תֹּ֣אכַל לֶ֔חֶם עַ֤ד שֽׁוּבְךָ֙ אֶל־הָ֣אֲדָמָ֔ה כִּ֥י מִמֶּ֖נָּה לֻקָּ֑חְתָּ כִּֽי־עָפָ֣ר אַ֔תָּה וְאֶל־עָפָ֖ר תָּשֽׁוּב׃

וַיִּקְרָ֧א הָֽאָדָ֛ם שֵׁ֥ם אִשְׁתּ֖וֹ חַוָּ֑ה כִּ֛י הִ֥וא הָֽיְתָ֖ה אֵ֥ם כָּל־חָֽי׃

וַיַּעַשׂ֩ יְהוָ֨ה אֱלֹהִ֜ים לְאָדָ֧ם וּלְאִשְׁתּ֛וֹ כָּתְנ֥וֹת ע֖וֹר וַיַּלְבִּשֵֽׁם׃

The LORD God said to the woman, "what is this you have done?" And the woman said, "the serpent deceived me, and I ate."

So the LORD God said to the serpent, "because you have done this, cursed be you among every behemoth and among all life of the field; upon your belly you shall walk and dust you shall eat all the days of your life.

I put enmity between you and the woman and between your seed and her seed. They will bruise your head and you will bruise their heel."

To the woman he said, "I will severely increase your pain in pregnancy; with toil you will bear children. Your lust will be toward your man, yet he will rule over you."

And to the human he said, "because you have listened to the call of your woman, and you ate from the tree that I commanded you, saying,

'you are not to eat from it,' cursed be the ground on account of you. In
pain you will eat from it all the days of your life.
Thorn and thistle it will sprout for you when you eat herbs of the
field.
By sweat of your face you will eat bread until you return to the ground,
because from it you were taken. For dust you are, and to dust you
return."
And the human called his woman's name, "Havvah," because she
became mother of all the living.
And the LORD God made leather tunics for the human and his woman,
and he clothed them (Gen. 3:13–21).

"But in these cases," says Macbeth, "we still have judgment here, that we but teach bloody instructions, which, being taught, return to plague th' inventor. This evenhanded justice commends th' ingredience of our poisoned chalice to our own lips."[1] Shakespeare understood that ruinous designs cannot be hatched for another, even an evil other, without involving ourselves in the malediction. In turning against the other as proper object of hatred, as suited for it, we already take part in the evil that we deplore, for we affirm a self-consciousness of relational opposition, perceiving animosity as fit and right. We do not perceive the possibility of interdependence with this other as good and beautiful, or recognize the truth in seeking reconciliation, but the opposite; we pursue a history, a timespan constructed with regard to this other outside the freedom of responsible communion—a history of self-justification. We thereby contribute to a world of relational fracture, against its covenantal nature, and sooner or later will suffer the consequences of residing in this place.

Augustine reminded us last chapter that evil is not a thing external to humankind, but an event transpiring within the human soul, or as I argued, within human self-perception. Evil transpires as betrayal among humans, and as we will discuss in this chapter, between humanity and the broader creation. The very consciousness of Self betrays a predilection to externalize evil, to make oneself victim of nature's wiles, but as we will see, this amounts to an act of self-deception and manifests a constitutional treachery. In betrayal, the human betrays himself: he reveals his self-interest and harms his own nature that is properly one with nature. By turning against the world, the human instances a tension that is to his own compromise; he takes part in the affliction from which he would distance himself, including its consequential suffering.

Nothing in the world is evil unto itself. Evil emerges within human consciousness as part of a descriptive act that centers on the human. As the human describes affliction in terms of Self, calling nature's forces "destructive" in a way that personalizes their effects—how winds or waters or disease-agents *threaten* habitat or means of sustenance—the human creates within time the cadence of *malevolence*, the identifiable meter and rhythm of "evil." And as he does this, he immediately locates himself within that same time; by according forces and elements a quality that they in no way have unto themselves—for indeed, they otherwise are essential to the promotion of life—the human makes the world after his own Self-reference. He valuates the world according to a consciousness of danger, which obliges a corresponding manner of behavior, a danger-avoidance that pits him against nature's forces and elements.

Now, conscious effort at survival in the face of nature's forces is not entirely without warrant; it is not of itself evil. Hurricanes do take life. But affirmation of Self against nature as threat opens the door to evil. As the human only perceives the hurricane as potential life-taker, as she fails to graduate from this self-perception to one that identifies her life as partaking of the hurricane's own elemental properties, indeed, as so entwined with nature that her life-acts contribute to environmental conditions that influence the intensity and frequency of hurricanes, she perpetrates the evil against which she tries to identify herself as victim.

Not only this, she perpetrates the deeper wickedness of deception. She exercises her valuative capacity in a false way. She discounts the good of others to pursue the good of Self by ignoring nature's interconnectedness, how the input from a species bent on its own survival can be to the detriment of other species. She deems her survival "good," or identifies "goodness" with her survival, without reference to the consequence of its pursuit for the health and vitality of others or for the broader goodness of the whole, and so she falsely characterizes the success of her survival. She calls "good" what is in fact, "evil," or at least contains an element of evil. In this, she takes part doubly in evil.

Evil, then, is an event of human perception, and so is its corrective—that which defeats evil in the event of its closeted enactment by bringing its happening to light. The human is confronted with an alternative perception, a view on the self that shows its constitutional treachery as erroneous, something away from which to turn. As revelation teaches the human to perceive his lot as one with the world, that he shares in the world's convulsions and its creations, more exactly, as he learns to perceive himself to be a subject of the world, a part of world-forces and -elements that he may control but not master—from which he always must find a measure of derivation, therefore against which he cannot finally define his life—the human perceives the truth of evil in himself. Because the human must continue to learn this truth, because it must take residence in and give structure to his consciousness in each moment, thereby creating an alternative time within the time of evil, the achievement of a world without evil must wait. It is wrapped up with the eschatological achievement of the human in an actualistic, moment-by-moment, upward-spiraling vision as interdependent, what we might call the uninterrupted reverberations of revealedness.

And because God has purposed to have life in and through the redemption of the human and the salvation of the world, in the time of interdependence (negating the time of evil), the eschatological achievement of creation is the teleological determination of the divine. God *is* only as God *will be*; Creator is only as Redeemer and Sanctifier. God exists in the Spirit of creation's goodness, in the negation of evil and its consequences.

The science of cancer provides a point of reference for these conclusions. We will see that *this* malediction bears the features of creation's curse generally, and thus supplies important guideposts along the way to understanding evil. These guideposts find philosophical correlation in the work of Paul Ricoeur on language. Together, they show us that evil takes the shape of potent anti-covenantal force, which God returns to its factual impotence in and through the (re)turning (in the sense of perpetually-turning-again) of humanity Eden-ward.

EXEGESIS OF GEN. 3:13–21

Creation suffers the pain of unfulfillment. That is its fate, its curse insofar as it is dependent upon the human whose authenticity is yet before him. The creation is subjected to inconsistency and infertility, producing fruit only with thorns and only through struggle; struggling against humanity even as humanity has a hand in its destiny.

Creation's thorniness is not evil. Its struggle against the human occasions evil insofar as it rises to the level of life-denying or life-taking. Among a world of thorns the human perceives threat and places his life against it, falsely characterizing his fight against creation's thorns as *good* without reference to a broader reality impacted by the fight. Creation's thorns thus become a curse, but occasion a much wider curse in which the human takes part.

The woman dismisses the guilt of her transgression as the man previously did, but the very effort involves her, as it involved him, in deception.[2] To act as if the serpent's rationale was not her own, as if its account were not within the realm of her understanding, her self-consciousness, is artifice, the echo chamber of pretense booming back own-made noises. The serpent being struck down from its conceit serves as a metaphor for unmasking and judging sinful self-perception. It is not a spell cast on a once-tall-standing reptile against which the human stands. In fact, the self-positing of the human against the reptile proves the curse's occasion or manifests the treachery that is named in the curse.

"This curse does not mean the serpent once walked upright with legs anymore than [the text] wants the reader to assume the serpent will now literally eat dust as opposed to its previous fare," Arnold writes. "Rather, these are idioms for humiliation."[3] God does not cripple one of God's creatures and in contrast to God's own creative intentions forever change its constitution (or deviate from his causal formula, as Augustine would say). Rather, the cutting down of the serpent functions as an idiom for disgraced existence in which, again, the human participates. By cutting down the serpent, the text exposes the deficiency of its account of the consequences of violating the divine prohibition; it enacts the very judgment that the serpent refuted.

Thus, the curse of God upon the serpent is really commentary on the curse of the serpent—of sin—upon humankind: וְאַתָּה תְּשׁוּפֶנּוּ עָקֵב ("and you will bruise their heel"). The serpent/sin really does harm the human. Disobedience of the divine prohibition is not without effect; it poisons. It brings about an anti-way, a way defined by opposition to the other, not covenantal, "yes," but anti-covenantal, "no." This anti-way has infiltrated the human bloodstream. She can resist it but she cannot escape its toxin. She will commit the sin that she describes as being committed upon her.

The human may contend with self-deceit and vie against it, and in the wrestling may even strike a blow—יְשׁוּפְךָ רֹאשׁ ("they will bruise your head")—yet sin inflicts its injury.[4] Sin obliges the human to succumb to its fatality—to surrender to the emptiness of the Self in its very occurring, to be the victim of antagonism in its very perpetrating, to exist in the form of a discarnate substitute, cast down from the storied provision of the Garden and pushed from longing into craving into coveting, unable by the force of sheer effort to halt the transgression of these boundaries, simply inhabiting the movement between them and only fleetingly perceiving its regret.

This is the case even as the woman, conceding to the transience of her own-made existence, looks to secure her illusive future in the realm of progeny. The woman breeds, but insofar as she does so out of self-interest and not as willing participant in life's from-for goodness, she brings forth life only under the dispiriting shadow of death. The curse of sin issues with the child, ironically within the biochemistry of its very formation. The bent to inevitable nothingness incubates within the lust staining human procreation. Sin is seminal, not exactly in the sense of being passed along in the male seed, as Augustine and others thought, but close to this, in the sense of being congenital: resident in the storehouses of ancestry, co-spawned with the genetic code, and no less adaptively persistent.[5]

Sin admixes the agapic designs and erotic desires of each partner with improper craving for self-gratification, with envy and power. Conceived in this way, in love lust-stained, the child can only take life (be born) as life-taker, as Cain in the ensuing Genesis story. The entangled nature of human existence finds trenchant expression in the description of woman's and man's relational accursedness: הֵב־לְשָׁמִי אִוּחְן, וַהְתְקוֹשֵׁת רָּשִׁיא־לָאֵן ("your lust will be toward your man, yet he will rule over you"). In making sense of the biblical portrayal of woman's desire for man and man's rule over woman, I have found the insights of Sarah Coakley to be particularly instructive.[6]

Coakley has ably challenged insufficiently reflective notions of relational "power." Against unexamined associations with *control, dominance, mastery,* Coakley argues in behalf of a more nuanced connotation, which involves proneness and submission—what she calls a "paradox of power and vulnerability."[7] She defends what we might think of as a Christo-morphic account: in the *kenosis* (Phil. 2:8), we perceive "the normative concurrence in Christ of the non-bullying divine 'power' with self-effaced humanity."[8] That is not to say that in the hypostatic union, and more narrowly, the *communicatio idiomatum* (communication of attributes between Christ's divine and human natures) the divine ontology takes on the attribute of self-effacement.[9] Rather, in the Incarnation, we see deity exercising a constant self-command *"never to have* 'worldly' forms of power."[10] In Christ, God makes real and models among us the power of self-displacement, willful self-giving in order to create space for another; we see "God" in the act of refusing the lure to stand over the other, or in the other's place.

Coakley argues not only against masculinist, hierarchical structures of submission (the claim of a natural, imbalanced dominance-role between men and women) but also against feminists who would challenge such structures *on their own terms,* that is, who would unmask patriarchy only to replace it with an identical sort of matriarchy.[11] When it takes the form of control, even if by the once-controlled, power-grabbing amounts to inhumanity. To the contrary, Coakley commends the self-displacing practice of contemplative prayer.

"At the heart of any Christian doctrine of creaturehood must surely lie . . . the notion of a radical, and qualitatively distinct, *dependence* of the creature on God."[12] To be human is to be absolutely, existentially dependent on God, and contemplative prayer supplies the occasion and framework for self-conscious enactment of this dependence:

> We can only be properly "empowered" here if we cease to set the agenda, if we "make space" for God to be God. Prayer which makes this "space" may take a variety of forms, and should not be conceived in an élitist way; indeed, the debarring of "ordinary" Christians from "contemplation" has been one of the most sophisticated—and spiritually mischievous—ways of keeping lay women (and men) from exercising religious influence in the church. . . . This practice is profoundly transformative, "empowering" in a mysterious "Christic" sense; for

it is a feature of the *special* "self-effacement" of this gentle space-making—this yielding to divine power which is no worldly power—that it marks one's willed engagement in the pattern of cross and resurrection, one's deeper rooting and grafting into the "body of Christ."[13]

It is beneficial to read v. 16b in the light of Coakley's "Christic" conception of empowerment, and of participation in "the pattern of cross and resurrection." The woman's vulnerability, covenantally considered and eschatologically realized—that is, her uninterrupted, willed rejection of other-dominance even to the point of self-sacrifice—amounts to that active participation in Christ according to which "God" is teleologically determined. Vulnerability per se, then, is *not* her curse.

What is accursed is the *mortal* vulnerability of non-covenantal existence, the inability to sustain life in pursuit of the Self, which recurs in the sinful imbalance between the power of willful dominance and coerced submission. This can be seen in the male-female power relation insofar as man does not incline to Christic vulnerability and does not value it. Besides the woman's desire for man and man's rule over woman referenced in v.16b, it is worth considering man's second act of "naming" the woman in 3:20. Previously, in 2:23, the act involved reflective acknowledgment of the inherent mutuality between man and woman—she is *ishah* and only as such is he *ish*—but now, the man names the woman without concern for their interdependence, in a way alike to that which he named the animals: וַיִּקְרָא הָאָדָם שֵׁם אִשְׁתּוֹ חַוָּה ("and the human called the woman's name, 'Havvah'").[14] He gives her a name according to what he perceives as a defining characteristic: childbearing. Man thus relates to woman in terms of externally applied, non-reciprocal designation just as he does with the beasts.[15]

The woman's curse may be understood as having to bear this burden of unyoked power, but in drawing this conclusion we have to stress that the Genesis account functions descriptively and not causally. It depicts things as they are, not as how they should be. To the extent that woman bears the curse of imbalanced power in the form of submission before man's dominance, her life becomes a testimony akin to the witness of Christ's life against the *wickedness* of patriarchy, against the *inauthenticity* of man's turning away from interdependent vulnerability. God intends for man and woman to complete one another as each submits to the other or finds his and her true self fulfilled in the other. But the curse is such that man and woman, who may exist as self-complete in the other, find themselves pitted against each other in conflicted orders of "power." Exactly in the primal relationship whereby authentic humankind ought to be realized, it finds itself compromised. "It is quite clear from the description of woman in 2:18, 23," Sarna writes, "that the ideal situation . . . was the absolute equality of the sexes. The new state of male dominance is regarded as an aspect of the deterioration in the human condition that resulted from defiance of divine will."[16]

The woman's empowerment may, in turn, be understood as the graced capacity to refuse the kind of power typified in the man, although the text does suggest that the false power of the man presents itself to her consciousness as viable and desirable. She is not immune to the man's quintessential impulse to "power over"; the language of "lust toward your man" need not indicate only urge for relationship but also desire for the place of the man. "He will rule over you" also describes the bitterness of living in unfulfilled will to power. In this, we are reminded that the sin of humankind cannot finally be differentiated according to observational distinctions between the sexes. The man turns against the woman, but the "turning against" is not proper to the maleness of the man; the woman also turns against the man. Just as authentic existence cannot be rendered according to abstracted qualities of masculinity and femininity, neither can inauthentic existence.[17]

The "curse" of the serpent is condemnation of the serpentine character of inauthentic humanity. The figure of the serpent brings to consciousness the arrogating self-deception present to humanity and the primal power-relations after which it procreates. This point is further made by one more tonal echo with the words translated as "shrewd" and "naked."

We saw in last chapter that the text associates the shrewdness of the serpent and the nakedness of the human by deploying the similar sounding עָרוּם and עֵירֹם, respectively. Now the LORD God pronounces the serpent אָרוּר ("cursed").[18] The poetic trace suggests something like, "thus you are, thus you shall be. As you have deceived and are deceiving, be perceptually deceived. Let your own-made artifice take hold and become what it is." The curse certifies the naked shamefulness of sin's shrewdness.

Condemnations cascade in chiastic inversion of each creature's appearance; after "cursing" the snake, God turns to woman and then man.[19] To woman, God pronounces sentence against her bearing children.[20] Most significant is the parasitic nature of the sentence: the woman can only enact her distinguishing biology in the midst of affliction that hurts and threatens it. In *toil* and *pain* (עֶצֶב and עִצָּבוֹן), she brings forth children. Because she would be who she is without permission and in disobedience to the divine command, the woman can only give life at a cost. Because she does not accept her place in the from-for succession of life, but attempts to be life-dispenser in abstraction and isolation from the communion in which she is made to exist, her bringing forth offspring always takes place under the shadow of death. She must give life, yet she must do so under the sign of life's dissolution. The woman herself must be imperiled in life's begetting.

The same is true of the man. Human life can only endure by consumption. We must be fed even when our feeding amounts to exploitative feeding-off rather than sustainable cultivation. The man, too, must engage his proper role as man (now, perhaps, Adam, as the accursed man opposite Havvah). He must tend and till the earth. Yet he does this tending and tilling not in confirmation of his place in the created order, but rejecting it and grasping after another place over the created order where he, too, is subject to עִצָּבוֹן.[21] The same word used to describe the life-bearing work of the woman in v. 16 is used to described the life-cultivating work of the *adam* in v. 17.[22] In this, the shroud cast over the scene presented in Gen. 2 becomes fastened down. "The vista of thorn and thistle is diametrically opposed," Alter observes, "to the luscious vegetation of the garden and already intimates the verdict of banishment that will be carried out in vv. 23–24."[23]

It must be stressed that the anguish of human labor, both in giving birth and producing food, is not a corrosive additive sowed into the idyllic human land. God does not vengefully poison humanity and creation. The curse of humankind is not a life of futility set in motion by a sullen deity.[24] It rather describes what *is* in the light of what is *to come*. Precisely in life amid death the human finds herself pitched forward. In disclosure of sin's self-enclosing, the human can *only* look forward. She can *only* be human in the existential posture of *hope*. The humanity of sinful humankind can only be a future-ward condition, a promised participation in the victory of "God," which is already secured and made actual by the self-constancy of such a Creator who has life in relation also to the sinful creature.

God exists "with-us," as LORD, not just in the harmony of Genesis 2, certainly not if this is taken as a backward state, so that, until Eden is eschatologically restored, for the meantime of Gen. 3, God is "without-us" (except for the occasional and mysterious vision, miracle, or angelic whisper). No, God *is* "with-us" also in the fallen condition of Genesis 3, no less creatively. If we treat the canonically-second creation story, as much of the tradition has, as backward-oriented, as calling the reader to a rearward paradise, a sinless condition before its factually sinful state, then we miss the real hope that the myth contains. We do not treat 3:21 as climax, but as "anticlimax."[25] We place the decisive stroke on the protevangelium of 3:15, over-interpreting this verse to prophesy a chosen one who will come and crush the serpent's head, as it were, on the cross, and look forward to restoration of pre-serpentine existence. We do not see our actual, sinful selves as objects of God's self-relating. We do not see God as God actually is, the one whose glory is such that he can and will relate to us in our sin, so that our sinfulness does not nullify God's God-fulness.

The decisive stroke ought to fall on 3:21. Already, God creates the conditions to cover humanity's shame. Already, God exists as the propitiating one, the one who palls humanity's sinfulness and in just this covering opens humankind to the possibility of its authenticity. "Giving clothes to man is a modest yet mighty sign of God's forgiveness," Westermann concludes. "Life which has been freely given to humans who then forfeited it, is life which is made possible only by God's forgiveness. . . . Thus verse 21 is a modest and restrained indication of the goal of the story which began with man's creation."[26]

THE INTRICATE CONNECTION BETWEEN HUMANITY AND FAULT: CANCER AS PARADIGM

It is not correct to think of sin as a bacterium or foreign agent, which infected the cells of "normal" humanity at some historical stage, and which in turn has been passed along the ancestral line ever since, the salvation from which involves its eradication and restoration of humanity's normality. On the contrary, the impulse to sin is inbred from the start; Gen. 2–3 indicates that humanity never has been absent this impulse. Salvation is not the removal of a foreign agent, but triumph over the action and consequences of an internal disposition. Authentic humanity is already and not yet.

Accounting for evil presents a *special* logical conundrum—there is such thing as an intractable "problem of evil"—when one makes the exegetical blunder of rearward reading, of thinking of such things as error, misdirected will, and wrong choice as *alien* to a once-perfect humankind. In that logic, the appearance of fault becomes difficult, perhaps impossible to explain, because neither the goodness of the Creator nor the goodness of the creature should admit it. Augustine comes closest, perhaps, to giving a defensible explanation for evil from within a restorationist calculus, but as we noted, even his account falls short, or at least would be more consistent and satisfactory within the logic of a transformationist scheme.

In coming to grips with the reality of the human condition, we need to learn to see human existence as a contradiction from the outset, the resolution for which lies ahead. We need to learn to see sin and evil as part of our reality from the beginning, which as such cannot be removed, exactly, but which because of God's work in Christ by the Spirit can be defeated.

To make sense of the human contradiction, I have found it helpful to reflect on the particular malediction of *cancer*. Cancer supplies a useful focus because it offers quintessential expression of the human situation as it has always been, all the way down to its most minute constituents. Cancer is the "emperor of all maladies"[27] precisely because of its enduring, interlaced association with creaturely life. It is a collection of diseases so intrinsic to the evolutionary nature of what it means to be human that it causes us to reconsider the appositeness of seeking a final cure,[28] the constitution of *normal* and *abnormal*, and especially the utility and content of the descriptions *good* and *evil*. Cancer is an eventuality of biochemical life, an anti-human event correlated with the event of being human.

Mel Greaves has demonstrates that:

> Cancer doesn't just parody evolution. It is a form of evolution played by the same Darwinian ground rules as apply to evolution in general and particularly for asexually propagating species. The essential game plan is progressive genetic diversification by mutation within a clone, coupled with selection of individual cells on the basis of reproductive and survival fitness, endorsed by their particular mutant gene set. It's evolution in the fast track.[29]

Considered microbiologically, a human being is an intricate collection of cells replicating according to coded instruction and responding to environmental stimuli. Beginning with the single zygote (fertilized egg), cells replicate to a staggering total of 30-plus trillion in the "typical" body. Early on—just four days-worth of divisions—the self-cloning cells begin to differentiate or specialize, first into a blastocyst, or ring of cells with an inner cell mass, which eventually implants in the uterus where it is nourished and protected. The inner cell mass develops by continued division and specialization into an embryo, and so on. From the beginning of life and throughout its growth, differentiated cells enter into a kind of interdependent arrangement with each other; they perform certain functions for certain periods to promote the growth and vitality of a total organism, all of which is regulated by the genes that they carry.[30] At a basic level, cancer is a breakdown of this multicellular agreement[31] by a clonal mutant, the "revenge" of a somatic cell against the somatic compact,[32] but one whose biology is entirely in keeping with the evolutionary properties underlying cellular multiplication and development.

As cells replicate and differentiate, their particular shape, grain, function, and potential is regulated both by higher-order gene expression[33] and by epigenetic factors that influence this expression.[34] DNA sequences instruct cells how they are to divide, how many times to do so, how to operate once divided (both parent and daughter), and how to interact with other cells. And they (DNA sequences) do so in communication with other molecules within and without the cell nucleus, which can mute or intensify their instruction. Moreover, with each division the DNA itself is copied, not always perfectly. Given the number of replications necessary to produce our 30-plus trillion cells, the degree of error is impressively low—within cell functioning are repair mechanisms and "kill switches" of sorts that correct or eliminate miscopied genetic material in order to safeguard the integrity of the multicellular totality.[35]

Still, some genetic mutation escapes the safeguards. Together with the natural difference in gene expression caused by epigenetic input, downstream variation at the cellular level is inevitable. Mutation is intrinsic to the system.[36]

Of itself, cell mutation is not unwelcome, or to anticipate our later discussion, it is not "evil." In fact, it is necessary. Insofar as humans exist in a world of finite resources, competition for the means required to survive is, as Darwin noted, inexorable. Certain mutations will produce the traits that, by chance, enable survival in a given context better than others do. Over time, the organisms that have these mutations will endure and breed more successfully than those that do not, so that the "fittest," or at least those who find themselves best cellularly suited, will persist. In an evolutionary world, the human species needs cell mutation to exist.

When Greaves contends that cancer "is a form of evolution played by the same Darwinian ground rules as apply to evolution in general," he means that it is a microcosm of what takes place at the species level. Cancer is cell persistence by favorable trait inheritance via mutation. As cells produce variant daughter cells, particularly those that obtain mutations in the copied DNA, a fraction will manage to endure beyond all of the safeguards that work against their proliferation. They will luck into the adaptations needed to survive *over against* the multicellular agreement.

There are two basic categories of such mutations: those that promote cell replication and growth (what Greaves calls "the stuck accelerator pedal metaphor") and those "resulting in loss of some important penalty imposition or restraining functions (the faulty brake metaphor)."[37] A daughter cell develops characteristics that allow it to reproduce more freely than other cells. For instance, a cell that ought to remain geographically local might develop wider motility, or the capacity for spontaneous, independent movement, combined with additional mutation for invasion (of otherwise distant and foreign tissue). Such variations might further be companioned with the ability to mask their very existence—a mutation to mask mutation!—whereby the cell's signaling does not arouse immune recognition of an alien entity. Now the cell has both the ability to glob on to resources for growth and to avoid detection that would lead to its death.

Mark Pallen notes that motility, cell migration and invasion, and immune tolerance are all part of the "tool kit" of cell processes necessary for propagation of life.[38] Cells (of the trophoblast) must migrate and invade the maternal endometrium in order to form a placenta. Embryonic cells generally must develop a measure of immune tolerance in order not to be rejected by the mother's host environment. Hence, when a to-be-cancerous cell adopts these mutations, it is not adopting classes of modifications foreign to normal cellular existence. They are rather taking on characteristics essential to that existence, but in such a way as to promote that cell's own survival over against the multicellular composite. The cell has no intentionality toward this end. It is, like evolution generally, blind to consequences. The cell enjoys mutations that on a broad level have proven to promote survival of the total human organism, but at a narrow level affords the cell's own survival at the expense of the organism.

For a "malignant" cancer to form, a cellular lineage must develop what Greaves terms a "full house" of mutations.[39] Cells of all sorts need oxygen and nutrients to live. Besides the mutations just mentioned, an invasive cell collection might further develop the capacity to signal other cells to form a vascular network around them, which supplies them with blood (and the oxygen and nutrition that it carries). This process of angiogenesis, like motility, invasion, and immune tolerance, is a critical feature of multicellular life. When a tumor induces it, it amounts to "corruption, in the clonal cause, of a normally innocent or physiological process that has evolved to facilitate inflammation and wound healing as well as tissue assembly in the embryo and function of the cycling ovary and placenta in mammals."[40] Here again, a cell takes on a genus of variation that is otherwise innocent or "good," supportive of human life.

Once more, the odds of a cell developing the full house of mutations needed to survive at the expense of its own larger organism are almost impossibly long. Immune response, proteins that trigger apoptosis, genes that detect and initiate repair of chromosomal damage, and the genetic shuffle of sexual reproduction are among ways that the human species has downgraded over time the potential of rogue cell proliferation. But this is where the second staple of evolution kicks in: chance mutation is accompanied by the operation of *law-like numeric certainty*: "If the first mutation generates a clone of, say, 10 million cells, it only requires one out of these 10 million to incur a second hit or 'appropriate' mutation to generate the next quasi-species or subclone which then becomes the expanded venue for hit number 3. And so on for hits 4 and 5 up to the full house for malignancy in a single cell."[41]

In an organism of 30-plus trillion cells, a potentially harmful cellular variation that might have only a 1 in 10-million chance will, at some point, occur. It is a statistical inevitability. Many variations will get wiped out in the next cellular generation. But it takes only one cell of that next generation to survive and to adopt a second mutation, which gets passed along to the third generation, and so forth until just one cell out of hundreds or even thousands of millions emerges with the full house of cancerous mutations and begins to divide.[42] Considered mathematically, across the arc of human lifespan cancer is, ironically, "a-long-shot-sure-thing." It is a self-compromising application of processes learned over millions of years, which have been passed along to ensure survival, and which as such are at work in all of us at this very moment.[43]

Cancer in humans is at once a byproduct of our evolution and a form of that evolution itself. It arises from the mutative inheritance of our cloning cells and operates according to the same chance and necessity that brought about our cells in the first place. This obviously must complicate our understanding of "evil." Insofar as cancer falls under that designation, it challenges us to understand evil as something bound up with us, as part of the very nature of things in which we take part. It is not alien to our lives, and so we cannot simply imagine ourselves to be victimized by it. The very operations that bring forth and sustain human life are laden with its undoing or un-creating. Within the "biogenic principle"[44] by which life organizes and persists lies the susceptibility, even the startling penchant for death.

Characterizing cancer as breakdown of what Michor calls the "covenant of multicellularity" (see n. 31) invites a series of observations. Although we of course have to be careful about implying some kind of willed intentionality operating at the microbiological level—Michor gives no such suggestion—the language of "covenant" nonetheless captures a crucial element of biochemical life. This kind of life is not only *cooperatively* structured but also characterized by *promise*.

As for cooperation, beginning at the level of DNA we encounter a complex, emergent compliance.[45] This acid is a result and reiterative process of bonding. Its doublet backbone is a lengthy composite of carbon molecules bound covalently (i.e., by sharing valence or outer electrons), and its inner "coding" mechanism is made of a series of nucleotides (adenine, guanine, thymine, cytosine) connected by hydrogen bonds. The latter bonds are noteworthy in that they represent a weaker sort of connectivity, akin to the attraction between persons. (By contrast, we might think of covalent bonding like the interlinking of a chain.)

There is an inherent, in fact, vital separa-bility at work in these nucleotide pairs. They must remain zipped as a default (in storage and in being passed along), yet allow for unzipping in the right places at the right sequence, in con-sequence with multiple other unzippings. An enzymatic (catalytic) form of the oxygenated complementary acid, RNA, must transcribe and translate segments of these pairs (i.e., "genes") in the right order to give rise to proteins, then cell-structures, tissues, organism. There is, in other words, a kind of rhythmic harmony to the emergence and development of biochemical life; genes are not uniform packages unwrapped in a one-code, one-trait assembly line wherein the organism is built as if by bricks, but much more richly, they are performers in a symphony of potential arrangements interfacing with each other, with their own output (!), and with the audience (broader environment).

The storing, passing along, transcription, and translation of DNA all take place within the cell. The molecule is housed in the cell nucleus (for us eukaryotes) in the form of forty-six chromosomes (twenty-three pairs), tightly wound assemblies of DNA, the structural integrity of which affects the molecule's functionality. (For instance, translocation trisomy 13 is an "abnormality"—a word that again belongs in scare quotes to indicate that we are not thinking of a once-existing, perfect prototype—in the thirteenth chromosomal pair, in which a partial third copy attaches to another chromosome, giving rise to a series of potential downstream consequences, including forms of cancer.)[46] Upon copying out an assigned genetic sequence, RNA translates its coded message in the cell's cytoplasm, which process involves interaction with other molecular agents contained there, especially, ribosomes.

Translation is an intricate procedure.[47] The ribosome, itself a molecule comprised of RNA and proteins, reads, as it were, the messenger RNA molecule. The reading involves signaling progressions: starter codons (units comprised of 3-nucleotide pairs) indicate where the functional, output-producing nucleotide sequence begins, and terminator codons indicate where it ends. This is a kind of repeat of the process that took place in the cell nucleus with transcription, where the DNA signaled to the RNA molecule where to begin and end its copying. We see a dynamic back-and-forth at work in gene expression. The products of genetic material, from proteins to traits, are consequent not only upon the content portion, so to speak, of the transcribed message, but also upon "right" shape and function of signaling regions, which is to say, beckoning and marking as well as receiving and following taking place between DNA, messenger RNA, and ribosomes.

The output of this intricate cooperation, the molecules known as amino acids, which are chained together to form proteins of various three-dimensional shapes and to perform distinct roles, instance (and assume) further cooperation. Some proteins have immunological function; they bind to foreign agents (viruses and bacteria) to neutralize and remove them. Others are enzymatic; they catalyze and facilitate chemical reactions, some of which, as we have seen, involve translation of DNA to result in further proteins—a self-generative contribution, as it were. Others transmit signals between cells and tissues. Others store and transport atoms and molecules (like carbon, hydrogen, and oxygen taken in by digestion of food to be metabolized into energy). Still others form the structural components of cells themselves.

In short, even at the microbiological level, biochemical life is an interconnected whole. Cells transport and their energy, function, and content actualize the DNA that originates, structures, and gives determinative function to cells. This gene-cell holism did not always exist, but having now come to exist cannot be productively thought of otherwise than as it is. Neither genetic nor cell science can profitably proceed independently of the other.

Moreover, via proteins we have an equally interconnected cell–cell holism. The product of the cell is not only further cells (uniquely differentiated) but also the agencies by which these cells symbiotically interact. The interaction is astonishingly compound. Mechanistic paradigms fail to capture it. Allocation of cell energy expenditure is not only for production but also movement and binding; it takes place relative to signals sent and received by cell output (proteins); this output and interface is timed relative to the output and movement of other cells; the output-signaling-movement interaction takes place, as indicated, on the order of trillions of cells in the adult human; the descriptor "adult" reveals that all of this happens in a forward-looking development—the yield of tissues and organs, which now as cell-collectives interface with each other, and which over time express degrees of functional precision and imprecision (breakdown); the somatic totality, in turn, not only enacts its own agency in the world but also receives, determinatively, from other agencies, including other somatic totalities and environmental inputs (viruses, radiation, gases, chemicals), rendering an agent-and-agency that is intrinsically open-ended, ready, disposed to more.[48]

That brings us to the second crucial element of biochemical life captured by the language of "multicellular covenant:" *promise*. However scientifically satisfying it may be, it is logically unsatisfying to reduce biochemical life *entirely* to chance emergence from a non-distinct primordial stew. Doing so fails to recognize the key fact that the cooperative arrangements just described can now, in the light of their achievement, only be properly understood as entities themselves,[49] which is to say, as once-futures that have become the condition of as-yet-futures.

Evolution is as brutal as it is beautiful. As indicated in chapter 2, it assumes, in fact *requires* the zero sum postulate that resources are limited, thus that some species will find themselves to have more extensive or easier access to the earth's resources than others do and, consequently, enjoy greater likelihood for survival. It is this kind of upward pressure that seems to have occasioned the multicellular covenant in the first place. Division of labor proved itself to have been a useful adaptation. But that means, when we consider multicellular existence, that we cannot be reductionists; we cannot consider as sufficient those explanations of multicellular life, which reduce it to mere conglomeration of individual cells. The intricate cooperation between cells alone demands that they be viewed (and scientifically studied) as a unit, but more than this, we have to view their unitary character as *survival*, not over against an imagined non-collective alternative but over against *nothing*.[50]

Multicellular life is an event of emergence, as if out of the void, over against non-life. It hangs by a thread over the abyss, always moving, ever evolving, or it is eliding into nothing and not into a less-refined version of itself. There is no fixed point; not even we humans can arrest and preserve our humanity, for human being, alongside all other known being, is in process. *Life just is process. Non-process is non-life.* We have to say that to be a creature, considered from the standpoint of multicellularity, is to enjoy a *power* to become new again, not just relative to the old but also to nonexistence.

Let me come at this another way. Competition for the resources to survive may be overt and violent, as males literally "lock horns" to attract female breeding partners, or as a carnivorous pride guards its kill with the threat of more killing. It may be covert, even incidental, as successive years of rain lend a certain length of bird beak competitive advantage in the acquisition of food. In every case, it is those who chance into the traits that, according to the law of averages, offer greater odds of survival whose lineage will endure and overtake the lineage of others. There can be no qualification here. Every attempt to blunt the blow of evolution's brutality by appeal to some "higher" goal elides into non-scientific wishful thinking and, ethically, denies justice to "lower" forms of life.[51]

There is no life as we know it, which does not come to exist alongside, indeed, in important respects through death. I take this to be the point of the curse of woman and man discussed above, the "pain" that is ever-present in life's reproduction and production. Life's ending is in important ways ingredient to life's beginning. This is true in the sense that the death of a tree opens room for other lives - its removal from an overcrowded grove makes space for other trees to receive sunlight and nutrients. It is true also in the sense that the death of one life can itself provide nutrients for others, as in the form of predation or fertilization. And it is true, in the sense that biochemical existents must pass through the trial of death in order to prove themselves fit to survive. Extant biochemical forms are *extant* by having endured the reign of death (extinction). Death has ravaged other lines of existents as well as the ancestral members of this line, and it will ravage every current member of the line, but by taking other lines and members of this line, death has given shape to the conditions by which this line continues to survive. It endures by enjoying the adaptations (mutations) that support life in this environment.

Surfacing here is a sublime paradox of life both through and against non-life; a fashioning of life out of the nothing against which life struggles. Biochemical *being* turns out to be only a *becoming*. Biochemical life can never be affixed to any as-such, since every as-such was at some point a not-yet, only having come through and existing under the sign of no-more, which precisely as-such (having come through and existing under the sign of no-more in order to be-thusly) must give way to another as-yet-not. It is in its DNA, quite literally—this the only essence to which it might be affixed—to be-open, ready for something other.

Here is the point: we need a definition and description of "evil," which attends carefully to the paradoxical reality that life and death are closely interconnected. Cancer renders impotent any understanding of evil that lacks such sophistication. It is, as noted, a form of somatic cell *life*, which enjoys the mutations that promote its endurance in this environment, its continuance in the face of apoptosis or cell *death*, which will result eventually in the *death* of its host organism and, ironically, itself. It is not an incursion into human (or creaturely) existence, but an expression of that existence from the outset. It cannot, then, be *removed* in the sense of restoring humanity to a world without cancer (i.e., a world without the kind of cell mutation that promotes resistance to death in an environment but which, ultimately, will die), for doing that would be to remove humanity from itself, to extract it from the evolutionary processes whereby it is. But it might be possible to *defeat* cancer in the sense of developing therapies (stem cell, immunological) that stunt its growth and undermine its power. In this regard, cancer may serve as a paradigm for sin and its defeat as a paradigm for the eschatological victory of the Spirit. Paul Ricoeur's notion of "fallible man" allows us to fill out this conclusion a bit.

PAUL RICOEUR ON FALLIBLE HUMANKIND

Ricoeur argues that the human condition "consists in a certain non-coincidence of man with himself."[52] And this self-contradiction is unique to humanity: "[man] is the only reality that presents this unstable ontological constitution of being greater and lesser than himself."[53] Humanity's paradoxical intermediacy is fundamental: "Man is not intermediate because he is between angel and animal; he is intermediate within himself, within his *selves*. . . . His ontological characteristic of being-intermediate consists precisely in that his act of existing is the very act of bringing about mediations between all the modalities and all the levels of reality within him and outside him."[54] The human, as such, places reality in conscious medium, in thought, will, and behavioral intention, and this placing involves restriction and unrestriction at once, that is, it involves relations of possibility, of being determinatively set with regard to an other, yet also being open to newness as the human thinks and wills and acts in relation to this other. In this, the human manifests both finitude and infinitude.

Concerning thought, and for the sake of scope, we will restrict ourselves to this register as representative,[55] finitude is manifest in the perspectival nature of perception. The human manifests limitation with regard to her comprehension of sense objects. "The perspectival limitation of perception . . . causes every view of . . . to be a *point of view* on."[56] The human does not enjoy exhaustive perception of any object, but only a perspective. Her knowledge of things is always an attempt at coherent estimation of images as they present themselves: "I never perceive more than one side at any given time, and the object is never more than the presumed unity of the flux of these silhouettes."[57]

For understanding to require the presumption of unity among silhouettes means, of course, that the human can be wrong in her perception. Reflection upon the object teaches the perceiver of the limitation inherent in her perception. "It is upon the object that I apprehend the perspectival nature of perception, which consists in the very inadequacy of the percept, that is, in the fundamental property that the sense outlined may always be *canceled* or *confirmed*, that it may reveal itself as *other* than the one I first presumed."[58] Sensory honesty obliges noetic humility.

We are aware that our perspective is just that, *ours*. Our perception of reality is incorporated into a specific positioning. "The otherness of the silhouettes . . . makes me become aware of the unnoticed aspects of bodily mediation: my perceiving body is not only my openness onto the world, it is also the 'here from where' the thing is seen."[59] I become aware that my own bodily situatedness constitutes something of a shifting "zero origin";[60] the coordinates from which reality is mapped are fluid.

In this, it is not bald reception of the object, but also my kinesthetic relationship, which comprises understanding. "Kinesthetic sensations have the remarkable intentional property of designating my body as a motivating circumstance of the course of perception: *if* I turn my head, *if* I extend my hand, *if* I move about, *then* the thing appears in such and such a way."[61] Self-awareness informs one of kinesthetic input alongside of sense intake, and that is of the essence: I must know myself as a perspectival knower: "We see, then, in what sense it is true to say that the finitude of man consists in receiving his objects: in the sense that it belongs to the essence of perception to be inadequate, to the essence of this inadequacy to refer back to the one-sided character of perception, and to the essence of the one-sidedness of the thing's profiles to refer back to the otherness of the body's initial positions *from where* the thing appears."[62]

The perspectival knower takes a perspective even on her knowing. This is important, for it means that she can know her knowing relative to what it was and might be, and thus transcend it in its very occurring. It is of the very constitution of the human as knower to bypass her knowing in its happening, or, to manifest an inherent infinitude in her finitude, and this is the occasion of her self-contradiction:

> The very act of declaring man finite discloses a fundamental feature of this finitude: it is finite man *himself* who speaks of his *own* finitude. A statement on finitude testifies that this finitude knows itself and expresses itself. Thus it is of the nature of human finitude that it can experience itself only on the condition

that there be a "view-on" finitude, a dominating look which has already begun to transgress this finitude. . . . The complete discourse on finitude is a discourse on the finitude and the infinitude of man.[63]

Inquiring more deeply into the nature of this self-contradiction, Ricoeur contends that it condenses into the descriptive power, that is, to *speech*. "The transgression of the point of view is nothing else than speech as the possibility of expressing, and of expressing the point of view itself."[64] The human has the power to bring its perspectives to articulation, to public perspective, as it were. And in this it experiences a kind of self-enlargement; not that its perspectives are shared, but that it exercises a linguistic intentionality whereby it makes its views the subject of other views.

We should note at this point, for the sake of clarity and to sync up with previous, similar deductions drawn in this book, that the linguistic capacity for self-enlargement is not sinful per se. This quintessentially human operation is, as I made clear earlier, a gift to humanity, which humanity might rightly offer to creation. (Humanity's gift for knowledge expansion through theoretical postulation can promote creative stewardship as easily as malicious technocracy.) But Ricoeur will reiterate our previous point that sin does lurk within this capacity.

Language evinces a kind of ever-broadening quality. In that it *signifies*, language exhibits a faculty of standing-out (an ec-static functionality); it brings knowledge to the receptivity, consideration, and subsequent signifying of *all*. "In the sign dwells the transcendence of the λóγος of man: from the very first word I designate the self-identity of the signified, the meaning-unity which another discourse of mine will be able to recapture and which the discourse of another person will be able to catch hold of in flight and return to me in dialogue."[65]

In naming the thing perceived, I "capture" the totality of senses conveyed by its silhouettes. In "a cup" are contained all of the senses of cup-ness. The sign invites the full range of such associations as it is put into discourse. It unifies them. In this, the speaker transcends her perspectival viewing, both in reception and body-positioning, as she brings its object forth. "We need the 'name' to give a ground to the meaning-unity, the non-perspectival unity of the thing, the one which is announced to and understood by another and which he will verify in his turn and from his position in a sequence of converging perceptions."[66]

Speaking is the non-perspectival interaction of perspectival knowing, and in this, the limitless pole stands across from human finitude. "The dialectic of 'name' and 'perspective,' therefore, is the very dialectic of infinitude and finitude."[67] So, the human manifests both perspectival restriction and non-perspectival un-restriction in speech. But how is this an *unstable* intersection?

In what way exactly does the fact of her in-between condition make her susceptible to *fault*?

Ricoeur notes that the action-form of language, the "-ing" of nam*ing*, invites fault. As verbal supersedes nominal, predication tilts meaning in a particular direction: "the verb, Aristotle says, is a noun-meaning shot through with an added meaning . . . and even by a two-fold supra-signification. On the one hand, the verb designates tense. . . . On the other hand . . . the verb adds to the noun-meaning that it already has the attribution to the subject. 'Socrates is walking' means that the walk 'exists now' and that the walk is '*said of*' Socrates."[68] The verb takes the nominal sign and affixes it to something. And predication or affixing entails modification; the verb not only describes the action (Socrates is walking) but also invokes associations with the thing acting (Socrates is known as a walking-thing).

It is in the verb's twofold potency that humanity's fallibility first arises. For in this kind of speech, the human does not antiseptically render an object for public perspective, but also modifies it. He makes a judgment about it, construes it to be such and such a thing. "In the verb's twofold intention the human sentence finds at once its unity of signification and its capacity for truth and error. The verb is what makes the sentence 'hold together' . . . [and yet] by asserting being, it introduces the human sentence into the ambiguous realm of the true and false."[69]

The verb in a sense lifts the speaker into a position of authority relative to objects of speech, endowing him with a power to enact truth or falsehood. It does this by holding a subject and predicate in equative relation, and thus, by facilitating apposite and non-apposite signification. In the verb lies the capacity to articulate "a false negation, a false affirmation, a true affirmation, and a true negation."[70] The perversion of the human λόγος comes with the verb. In and by it comes false perception, accidentally and deliberately, which is to say, the verb is both evidence and means of misshapen self-consciousness.

Speech "designates the *occasion*" of fault.[71] The human is not faulty for being a speaker, but fault originates in the speaker, in that he is "reconciler of the extreme poles of the real," and as such "also the weak link of the real."[72] The human links the finite and infinite in the synchronization of perspective and name, yet also unlinks them by wrongly negating or affirming, unintentionally or intentionally. Right, harmonious linking of reality in the human is far from guaranteed, for the linkage point is always susceptible to breaking.

But that false speaking should come to knowledge as falsehood, of course, requires the human to recognize his own movement from fallibility into failure. He must, as Ricoeur likes to say, take responsibility or "avow"[73] his role in instantiating evil. This is the critical part that symbol plays in the anatomy of evil. Religious myth lifts the role of the human to consciousness, ensconcing the human in the history of evil as it is manifested verbally.

As we have been saying, it is the work of revelation to situate humankind in both its potency and error, its possibility and un-realization, and therefore within the revolution of divine promise and fulfillment. Evil originates with humanity, but its full reality cannot be humanly appreciated without help. Evil hides itself to the human. It is only in the light of "God," of life in its primal Source, that evil is understood (as the antithesis of life, the anti-god or "ungodly"). Otherwise, apart from God, verbalizing even death as "evil" simply misconstrues this fundamental element of biological and linguistic life. We create a false equivalence and so instance the very evil that we would publicly identify.

Evil originates with the human, but the human only knows this after the fact: "fallibility is the *condition* of evil, although evil is the revealer of fallibility."[74] Even more strongly, picking up the key element of human responsibility, "to say that man is fallible is to say that the limitation peculiar to a being who does not coincide with himself is the primordial weakness from which evil arises. And yet evil *arises* from this weakness only because it is *posited*."[75] In the knowing of evil per se, the "sag"[76] back into it becomes cyclical; the knowing itself serves evil's occasion in the form of *temptation*.

In fact, then, we cannot trace a single, *chronological* point of origin for evil. We can say that it arises with the *adam* as the *adam* develops into itself, or, per Ricoeur, enacts its primal affirmation. For the latter, the adamic myth (revelation) gives rise to the thought whereby the human avows her role in the emergence of evil historically, and whereby she knows herself presently and futurely as evil's occasion, i.e., as a sinner. The human only comprehends herself in the slide from innocence to fault, to which slide she is cyclically enticed as she once more takes her evils into view.[77] Revelation makes good who and what the human factually is exactly as, once more, it turns the human to what it might be.

In revelation, there is discontinuity between humanity's is and can be; the human is *untrue* or, once more, at odds with himself. The hope of revelation, the *divine* λόγος, which frames inauthentic humanity in the light of authenticity, or which draws the human into another time-framing even as divine judgment establishes the human in his fallen time, is that humanity's *is*—its *perception*—is brought into conformity with its *ought* or *might be* through *witness*.

Ricoeur has moved us along in our effort to learn from Augustine and yet translate him into a more existential and actualistic frame of reference. With the bishop of Hippo, Ricoeur finds evil to rise somewhat mysteriously with the free exercise of that agency by which the human is most human. In this, he likewise refrains, rightly, from indicting the human for its finitude. Being finite is not humanity's problem. It is, more exactly, by manifesting both finitude and infinitude, so that the human becomes a sort of linkage point of reality, that evil is given occasion. For Ricoeur, then, human existence takes existential shape, which eventuates evil, yet which might at once eventuate evil's defeat.

CONCLUSION

Humanity is at odds with creation not only in the sense that it lives at odds with the broader creaturely world, although that is often true enough. More profoundly, humanity manifests a fundamental contraction within creation, the contradiction between infinitude and finitude. The human uniquely experiences this in the conflict between perception and speech, but this uniquely human struggle merely concentrates the wider conflict between the persistence of life and the threat to life. Within biochemical, creaturely life more broadly are the ingredients of living and dying, pregnancy and cancer. In its uniqueness, then, humanity may take responsibility for the wider contradiction. It may learn to verbalize it truthfully, in right affirmation and negation, and in this, take accountability for the tragedy: the human alone is that creature who can name evil, and in naming it, name himself as evil's occasion as well as the locus of its defeat.

For cancer to be described as malediction (i.e., for it to be verbalized truthfully) and rightfully struggled against, consciousness must first associate it with I-referentiality. The human must come to construe cancer as self-compromising pursuit of life against the covenantal facts, as part of the falsehood of abstracted isolation over against the rich truth of life in communion.[78] Correctly perceived and described, cancer may, in turn, be struggled against. The human may pray and work for its overcoming: not the dissolution of her evolutionary cell structure, but the rendering certain of its infallible reproducing. Sin and malediction cannot simply be made vacuous, but their occasioning can be subdued and prevented.

The spirit of humankind can become galvanized against evil. Reanimated in her perception by God's perception, by God's perspective-on the human condition, the human may make profitable (not exploitative) use of creation in behalf of creation. The human may manipulate the genetic code not for individual gain, but for the benefit of all creatures. The human can set the evolution of other-centered, fertile reproduction over against the evolution of I-centered, infertile reproduction (cancer), from-for procreation over against Self-preservation, and devise instruments that promote the one and obstruct the other. But only as spiritually reanimated can the human hope to do this with any consistency; even within its grandest understanding and most brilliant science, the human cannot hope to avoid falling victim to its contradictory self by relying only on native self-perception. The human can only take part in the healing of creation's curse as the curse of his self-perception is cured—as God unites the falling human spirit with God's Spirit. The event of evil's defeat is covenantal, and as ever, the (re)creative covenant depends upon the readiness of God to renew it, to eventuate creation's newness as the teleological determination of God's very existence.

NOTES

1. Shakespeare, *Macbeth*, ed. Stephen Orgel, The Pelican Shakespeare (New York: Penguin, 2000), 21 (Act I, Scene 7, Lines 7–12).
2. "She remains equal to the man, in her guilt," Gowan writes, "for like him she can do no better than find someone to blame"; *Genesis 1–11*, 56.
3. Arnold, *Genesis*, 68.
4. It is only in this vein that the prophetic interpretation of Gen. 3:15 with respect to the work of Christ (originating, it seems, with Irenaeus) makes sense. Christ triumphs over sin only as he, having assumed its full extent and consequence, is mortally victimized by it. And in this same vein, we may think of Mary as an Eve-figure: she is "life-giver" in that she births a human that lives the human reality perfectly: that unrelentingly wages battle against sin, which is to say, that resists sin's temptation precisely in its most extensive, most complete form, and so strikes the most decisive blow against it. This perfect life thereby becomes the champion of all life, the existence in which all existence may (dialectically) participate in struggle, defeat, and counter-defeat, until, in the "end," humanity's counter-defeat of sin is existentially certified: what is already made certain in Christ's death is tangibly made certain among those caught up in Christ's life.
5. Evil is not a gene or a genetic trait, but an event coordinated with, even consequent upon at least part of the survival-instinct of the genes.
6. See especially Coakley's collected and edited essays, *Powers and Submissions: Spirituality, Philosophy, and Gender*, Challenges in Contemporary Theology (Oxford, UK, and Malden, MA: Blackwell, 2002).
7. Ibid., x, 34 n. 70. In the latter reference, Coakley acknowledges that this theme stretches back to lectures delivered in 1991 and 1992 and signals its importance for her then-planned (now-published) constructive project, *God, Sexuality, and the Self: An Essay on the Trinity* (Cambridge: Cambridge University Press, 2013).
8. Coakley, *Powers and Submissions*, 31. More narrowly, Coakley wishes to locate Christ's operative center in the (Antiochene) humanity and not the (Alexandrian) *logos*. She sees this as a necessary augmentation of the seventeenth-century Giessen school of Lutheranism (see 16–18), which otherwise rightly construed the divine emptying as willed self-refusal to grasp worldly power.
9. Concerning the *communicatio*, in her usually careful manner Coakley distinguishes between six historical options for understanding the relationship between Christ's natures (see ibid., 3–19). One of these, which she identifies with the thought of early twentieth-century theologians like John Robinson, sees a communication of weakness to the divine nature, or sees weakness as being equated with the divine nature. One problem with this, as I perceive it, is that it threatens to de-actualize the

divine constancy, which is to say, it suggests a fixed, even substantialist form of vulnerability that, in view of the Incarnation, must in a sense govern divine operation. God just is restricted (and so, perhaps, in process). By preferring instead the willed refusal of God to grasp after disfigured creaturely power, Coakley allows for an understanding of God in which God exercises self-command moment-by-moment to take on servanthood. The kenotic act of God remains just that: an *active* coordination of the divine life with the divine will. The upshot of this for a renewed feminism is that the woman is not coerced into the role of servant by the force of (patriarchal) religious conviction, but rather, she undertakes, in a manner reflective of Christ Jesus, the coordination of her life with the redeemed will for an other-centered flourishing.

10. Ibid., 31; italics in original.

11. Coakley argues for a distinct kind of feminism, in which the goal is not to displace men from the posture of dominance only for women to find themselves victim of the same dominating. Instead, she articulates an entirely different version of power: an agency of self-direction precisely in the event of willed submission. Coakley is fully aware of the dangers posed to women by such a vision given the long history of subjugation by men through pretentious idealization of personal sacrifice; she states them honestly and forcefully. And she rightly applauds more "traditional feminists," if the phrase may be used inoffensively, for taking up the fight against them. Still, Coakley argues on biblical and philosophical grounds that "there is another, longer-term danger to Christian feminism in the *repression* of all forms of 'vulnerability', and in a concomitant failure to confront issues of fragility, suffering or 'self-emptying' except in terms of victimology. And that is ultimately the failure to embrace a feminist reconceptualizing of the power of the cross and resurrection" (ibid., 33). For Coakley, "an inalienable surrender ('submission') to God . . . must remain the secret ground of even feminist 'empowerment'" (ibid., x).

12. Ibid., 55.

13. Ibid., 34–35.

14. Sarna observes that in 2:20–23, over against the animals, man gave "woman" only "a generic, not a personal, name, and that designation is understood to be derived from his own ["man"], which means he acknowledges woman to be his equal"; *Genesis*, 23. But in 3:20, like the animals, "she acquires a personal name" (ibid., 29). And obviously enough, this personal name, although expressing "her nature positively and sympathetically" (ibid.), has no reciprocal bearing on him.

On the other hand, it is worth noting that some commentators see in the naming ("life-bearer") of 3:20 "a positive development in the midst of the judgment, anticipating that life will still go on"; Fretheim, *The Book of Genesis*, 364. Fretheim asserts that "a negative assessment of this verse incorrectly associates naming with subordination" (ibid.). In light of strong evidence to the contrary, I can only take Fretheim's assertion to derive more from worry about those who would exploit subordination between the sexes in the text in order to support such subordination today, than from warranted historical considerations. Such a worry is regrettably well-founded. It must be stressed that the *adam* now acts *as a sinner* in naming Eve (having disobeyed the divine command), and so his actions are not to be taken as exemplary.

15. Although he thinks it "improbable" himself, Wenham relates the suggestion made by "early Jewish commentators and some twentieth-century writers," based on similarity between the Hebrew *hawwah* and Aramaic *hiwya*, which means *serpent*, that the man "was rebuking his wife for deceiving him by calling her, 'serpent'"; *Genesis 1–15*, 84. The explanation that the name was given "'because she would become mother of all the living,' is then seen as a punning reinterpretation" (ibid.) "On the contrary," Alter wonders, "might there lurk behind the name a very different evaluation of the serpent as a creature associated with the origins of life" (*Genesis*, 15)?

16. Sarna, *Genesis*, 28.

17. Such characteristics may predominate and give the appearance of being humanly constitutive, but human existence is more dynamic and multidimensional than that. The woman can take part in the sin of the man, and the man can also become victim of power imbalance in the form of submission before domination. Acquiescence to mortal vulnerability is not her singular failing as woman, as some have suggested. Conversely, interdependent vulnerability is no more woman's given constitution than man's; it is rather a condition to which she, too, must be conformed.

18. The same is said of the ground in v. 17, which limits how far I would press this line of interpretation (for the deceit of the ground in the promise of harvest is hardly willful).

19. As a kind of interlinkage among them, Arnold observes that each curse is both "functional and relational"; *Genesis*, 69–71. That is, the serpent is both made to crawl, and to stand at enmity with the woman's seed; the woman's natural childbearing is interrupted by pain, and she relates painfully to the man; the man's toil for food is burdened and his relation to the soil is painfully structured.

20. "The OT authors, most of whom were probably men, were obviously deeply impressed by the pain their wives experienced in childbearing, for they frequently refer to it"; Gowan, *Genesis 1–11*, 58.

21. Alter indicates the shared character of woman's and man's accursedness by using the word "pangs" in translation both of 3:16a and 3:17b: "I will terribly sharpen your birth pangs," and "with pangs you shall eat from [the soil]"; *Genesis*, 14–15.

22. And it is used again when the curse of the ground is recalled in 5:29. There, the perfect offspring of humanity is prefigured. The tenth in line from Adam and Eve is born: the son of the seventh day's "rest," Noah, who eases the effects of the curse and brings peace between humanity and the ground. Noach (which name means "rest") is the son of covenant, the child of God's promise, the one with whom God enters into agreement not to allow death any further rule, any more ground, which is to say, not to infest the *adamah* any further, but instead to preserve the earth and its inhabitants.

23. Alter, *Genesis*, 14.

24. Commenting specifically on the thrust of 3:14–15, Gowan rightly concludes, "the author now describes reality as we all know it, and makes it the consequence of the human inability to accept absolute dependence on God"; *Genesis 1–11*, 57. But reality as we all know it, or humanity's inability to accept absolute dependence on God, is not a new situation.

25. As Westermann rightly noted; see *The Genesis Accounts of Creation*, 33.

26. Ibid., 34.

27. Siddhartha Mukherjee's phrase; see *The Emperor of All Maladies: A Biography of Cancer* (New York: Scriber, 2010).

28. Leonard Hummel and Gayle Woloschak argue that cancer is best considered in asymptotic relation to biological life: it exists as a form of and threat to this life, yet through cancer research, the multicellular human comes closer and closer to overtaking this unicellular adversary. In time, it may be hoped that such research will in a sense defeat the threat of cancer, without canceling the microbiological structures by which the human just is human. See *Chance, Necessity, Love: An Evolutionary Theology of Cancer* (Eugene, OR: Wipf & Stock, 2017).

I am especially indebted to Hummel for insight and guidance offered while I was in residence at the Lutheran Theological Seminary at Gettysburg during the 2015–2016 academic year. My conclusions are close to his. I am also grateful for his many suggestions for reading and research; I was directed to several of the works cited here by the bibliography for his class, "Chance, Necessity, Love: A Pastoral Theology of Cancer."

29. Greaves, *Cancer: The Evolutionary Legacy* (Oxford: Oxford University Press, 2001), 39.

30. Mark Pallen calls this a "contract" among cells, which from an evolutionary standpoint exists in order to pass along the germ line; see "Bio380 Lecture 5: The Phylogenomics of Cancer," YouTube Video, 45:44, November 11, 2011, https://www.youtube.com/watch?v=OaR1YLTgQVo.

31. In a pregnant turn of phrase, to which I will return below, Franziska Michor speaks of a "covenant of multicellularity"; see "Franziska Michor at TEDMED2012," YouTube Video, 15:01, May 10, 2012, https://www.youtube.com/watch?v=blsk0AOAung.

32. The grabbing lyric of Baba Brinkman; see "Revenge of the Somatic: Gangster Rap from Cancer Cell's Perspective from Baba Brinkman at #DSMIS13," YouTube Video, 4:26, September 28, 2013, https://www.youtube.com/watch?v=rrwMRF-CqqM.

33. By "higher-order gene expression" I mean the operation of a given segment of the genome from within the total genome. Most of the body's cells (red blood cells excepted) contain the total genome, but of course, as they become specialized, their protein production and binding to other cells and so on is a consequence of the transcription and translation of a very narrow snippet of the DNA molecule. Although liver cells, for example, contain the coding for cells that will produce skin, muscle, and lung tissue, expression of the latter is shut off; indeed, the shutting off of all but that which supports the growth and function of liver tissue just is the essence of cellular differentiation.

34. "Epigenetics" broadly refers to that which is outside the genes, but which acts upon and with them, that is, to factors within the cell packaging of the DNA, which enter into a kind of causal interplay with the very genes that will instruct cell division and growth and thereby determine the phenotype. More specifically, "epigenetics refers to all those inheritable changes that occur in chromosomes that bring about changes in the phenotype without any changes occurring in the DNA nucleotide

sequence"; Denis Alexander, *The Language of Genetics: An Introduction*, Templeton Science and Religion Series (West Conshohocken, PA: Templeton, 2011), 197. As we will see, not only the DNA itself, but also the chromosomal structure of its storing and passing along, influences gene expression.

Two such epigenetic influencers are methylation, or the addition of a methyl group to a particular gene sequence, which tends to depress expression, and histone acetylation, or the addition of an acetyl group to an amino acid in the histones around which DNA is packaged, which tends to enhance or intensify expression. For an instructive and highly readable overview of each, see Nessa Carey, *The Epigenetics Revolution: How Modern Biology is Rewriting Our Understanding of Genetics, Disease, and Inheritance* (New York: Columbia University Press, 2013), 54–74.

The point is that the cell nucleus is not an inert container, but an interactive habitat, so that there is a kind of feedback between the genes and the "world" in which they function. Importantly, the genes per se are unchanged (base pair sequencing is unaffected); rather, the way in which genes are expressed and therefore received is impacted by factors outside the genes.

35. One such genomic custodian is the protein p53, which in the presence of corrupted DNA initiates apoptosis, or programmed cell death. Obviously enough, when the gene responsible for production of p 53 (*TP53*) is itself corrupted, the risk of uncontrolled mutant cell development, that is, of cancer, substantially increases.

36. It is worth noting that sexual reproduction assumes what Pallen calls the "intrinsic mutability and recombination capacity of DNA"; see "Bio380 Lecture 5: The Phylogenomics of Cancer." In the formation of the gametes (sperm and egg cells), each chromosome is a hybrid of DNA contributed randomly by dad and mom. This means, on the one hand, that the potential for the DNA molecule to become altered and corrupted is intrinsic to the nature of the molecule (to be cut, spliced, copied, and translated). On the other hand, the shuffle of genetic material makes it statistically less certain that any one gene-variant will get passed along to offspring (as the child is neither a direct replica of either parent).

37. Greaves, *Cancer*, 54.

38. See "Bio380 Lecture 5: The Phylogenomics of Cancer." Other characteristics that cancer cells might co-opt, which are also in the tool kit of processes needed for life, are stem cell readiness for replication, and chemotaxis, or movement in response to a chemical stimulus.

39. Greaves, *Cancer*, 61–68.

40. Ibid., 56. Exactly how many mutations make up a full house is not completely certain, and varies between cancer types.

41. Ibid., 62.

42. Such a cellular parent will obviously enough have developed extraordinary resilience. Killing it and its offspring and only it and its offspring among the lot of cells still functioning in agreement presents one of the great challenges of cancer therapy.

43. As cancerous cells invade tissues and grow, they interrupt the normal functioning of that tissue. Generally speaking, cancer kills by interfering with vital organ and tissue operation. In most cases, of course, by cancer's effecting our death it effects,

indirectly, its own. This might suggest that the evolutionary framework breaks down: selective pressure toward survival would seem to eliminate the possibility that cancer could be construed as evolutionary in character, in that its persistence ensures death and not survival. A cancer cell cannot be considered to have adapted sufficiently to survive.

But survival is, also at the species level, relative to environment, and it is not synonymous with "immortality" even by way of unending species propagation. Cancer survives just as all evolved species do, within a definite space/time or generation. Should a participant in an environment, by unchecked proliferation, compromise that environment and sow the seeds of its own demise, that does not undermine the integrity of its evolution. If humankind overpopulates the earth and undercuts its very survival in so doing (by over-consumption of resources, multiplication of toxin output, etc.), that does not render it somehow un-evolved or disconnected organically from its environment. Left to itself, an evolved species well might destroy all life—its environ and all lives in it.

44. I am borrowing this terminology from Holmes Rolston III, *Three Big Bangs: Matter-Energy, Life, Mind* (New York: Columbia University Press, 2010), 14 *passim*.

45. We can begin smaller. Atoms are themselves composites of electrons, protons, and neutrons, the latter two of which are comprised of quarks (fermions), until we are left simply with a kind of pull toward composition, or the propensity of unobservable nature to take on mass (Higgs boson). At its most elemental level of existence, there seems to be at work a movement toward order and life in the face of disorder and death (although, as discussed briefly below, such a conclusion can only be a post-facto judgment of meaning by a life-form determined to explain things thusly, even though the things themselves are not).

46. See for starters, "Chromosome 13," http://ghr.nlm.nih.gov/chromosome/13.

47. For an overview, see Suzanne Clancy and William Brown, "Translation: DNA to mRNA to Protein," *Nature Education* 1, no. 1 (2008), 101, http://www.nature.com/scitable/topicpage/translation-dna-to-mrna-to-protein-393.

48. The descriptive language of "zygote" is worth observing. From the Greek, ζῠγόω (verb) / ζυγόν (substantive), it means *to yoke* or *join*. The single cell from which a human agent-and-agency will take rise is itself a yoking of gametes, of course. But it also prefigures the inter-joining that will occur at an almost bewildering number of levels, which will identify this existent among others, and differentiate it as such.

49. Here I must make a critical qualification. By identifying various non-reducible stages in human development, I am not implying or defending a design argument. I must implore those familiar with the literature *not* to hear in what I have written echoes of "irreducible complexity," the signature claim of the Intelligent Design movement; see, for example, Michael Behe, *Darwin's Black Box: The Biochemical Challenge to Evolution* (New York: Free Press, 2006).

The critical failure of ID, as I see it, is the attempt to turn an observational, descriptive presentation into a prescriptive argument. That is, it reads into the factual holisms of emergent biochemical life a retroactive necessity: all prior processes (both temporally, in earlier life forms, and by degree, at "lower" stages of development) are understood as taking place *in service to* a particular totality (say, the cell structure, or the eye as organ of perception). The whole comes to be viewed as *outcome*, a *telos* unto itself. But that is pretty much the definition of *post hoc ergo propter hoc* logic.

If we maintain a more appropriately comprehensive view, we have to see every whole as a part, every end as means to a further end. Products are in fact processes, too; one cannot simply freeze any product and wonder at the complexity of its apparent sub-processes to yield such a purposive finality, for it is itself a process within the larger world-event of biochemical existence, which as such remains susceptible to continuing evolution.

50. This line of thinking coincides, in the frameworks of modern physics, with relativity and quantum processes. It is simply inadequate any longer to think and speak of reality strictly in the older reductionistic terms of isolated, localized, independent particles and systems. As physicist/priest John Polkinghorne has concluded, "nature fights back against the supposition of the ontological adequacy of a purely atomistic point of view. The history of twentieth-century physics can be read as the story of the discovery of many levels of intrinsic relationality present in the structure of the universe"; "Introduction," in *The Trinity and an Entangled World*, ed. idem. (Grand Rapids: Eerdmans, 2010), vii. Such discoveries include the mutually-determinative interaction of subatomic particles in quantum fields; the unity of Einsteinian space-time as the comprehensive field of existence (rather than space *and* time as discrete, Newtonian containers), and with this the unity of matter/energy; the unification of theories—for example, electricity, magnetism, and radioactive decay; quantum entanglement and the principle of non-localizability; chaos theory (the infamous "butterfly effect"); indeterminacy and multiple causation; the increased complexity in systems and the emergence of consciousness; and the homogeneity of the universe—the local reflects the universal, and interfaces with it; see Polkinghorne, "The Demise of Democritus," in ibid., 1–14.

In short, "the older style of scientific thinking started with isolated systems and then asked how they might be conceived to interact with each other. We now see that this is too simplified an account, which needs supplementation by an adequate recognition that holistic effects are also active in the physical world. . . . It is clear that atomism has to give way to some intrinsically more relational form of the structure of physical reality" (ibid., 7). It will no longer do to work from the assumption of localized beings, processes, and events to their "larger" relation. We must learn to move in the opposite direction. We must see that the *relation* just is the basic "essence" of those beings, processes, and events, or as I have been arguing, that the reality of beings, processes, and events just is a creation of organic and flexible, covenantal relation.

Part of what I hope to investigate more fully in volume 2 of this project is the quantum vision that entangled particles, when separated by distance, maintain the characteristic properties of their entanglement, so that we should not actually think of discrete particles, but of a totality, a triadic interconnectedness (a *t* between *p* and *p'*), which engulfs other particles and systems flexibly as *p* and *p'* move through space, but which maintains its integrity in so doing. This is especially exciting if, with theoretical physicist Argyris Nicolaidis, we consider ways of translating the logic of *p* and *p'* into the domain, or perhaps better, the scope of *humanity* and *objects in nature*. In that case, existence would not be a running narrative of individual subjects, but could only be thought communally: the "proposed interaction is so strong that it would be inconceivable to consider the involved entities as isolated subjects; conversely, the relation and the interaction itself establish their very existence"; "Relational Nature," in ibid., 94.

Nature, pace Einstein, cannot be rightly understood independently of its observer, indeed, of the act of observation. For, objects about the (human) observer are photon-emitters, which the observer receives and in the *light* of which she acts. And the human, too, is only experienced in an environment of photon emission. Natural existence, so far as it is conceived, takes place with the medium of its acquisition—its grasping or comprehension, the medium of knowledge and understanding—that is, light. Reality and its means of knowing are coordinated. Indeed, in certain cases, meaning can often only be assigned after the fact of observation; the meaning of a system is a function of time. "For example," writes Anton Zeilinger, "a later measurement can decide whether the data on the system already observed can be understood as implying entanglement with another system or not [i.e., observe the data once, then again to detect alteration]. Again, these experiments tell us that there is no meaning attached to individuals. The result from the individual measurement previously obtained has no meaning in itself; it cannot be understood on its own. The only way to understand it is in *relation* to other events that will happen in the *future*"; "Quantum Physics: Ontology or Epistemology?" in ibid., 37. From this and other arguments, Zellinger concludes that "relations are more important than individuals" (ibid., 36).

Finally, if entities separated in space demonstrate entanglement, exhibiting both a degree of predictability and indeterminacy (coordinated interface with the other and open-endedness or random readiness for yet further otherness), might it be possible to transport prefigured information, and compute further, possible configurations among them? Quantum teleportation and computing invite theological inquiry—what is "identity" in a world of such information reproduction and production; see for starters Jeffrey Bub, "The Entangled World: How Can It Be Like That?" in ibid., 15–31.

51. An ethics of what we might call "biological totality," wherein all life is viewed not in succession (so that the goal of "lower" existents is to serve the flourishing of those "higher") may escape this charge. What I have in mind is a process of multiple emergence, where different forms of life take the stage alongside each other and as such orient dynamically, in something of spiraling feedback loops, rather than linearly-stepping combat waged until one species stamps down the others—or for many, stamps them *out*. In this view, it may be the *telos* of what are generally considered "higher" forms of life to realize themselves in sacrifice, at least of some kinds of flourishing, in service to "lower" forms.

52. Ricoeur, *Fallible Man*, trans. Charles A. Kelbey (New York: Fordham University Press, 1986), 1. Republished with permission of Fordham University Press; permission conveyed through Copyright Clearance Center, Inc. This book is the second in a three-volume series, The Philosophy of the Will. We will take a glance

in the next chapter at the third volume in this trilogy, *The Symbolism of Evil* by Paul Ricoeur. Translated by Emerson Buchanan. Copyright (c) 1967 by Paul Ricoeur; renewed (c) 1995. Used by permission of HarperCollins Publishers.

53. Ibid.
54. Ibid., 3.
55. See ibid., 47–79, 81–132 for discussions of action and will, respectively.
56. Ibid., 20.
57. Ibid., 21.
58. Ibid.
59. Ibid.
60. Ibid., 23.
61. Ibid., 22.
62. Ibid., 23.
63. Ibid., 24–25.
64. Ibid., 26.
65. Ibid., 28.
66. Ibid., 29.
67. Ibid.
68. Ibid., 32.
69. Ibid.
70. Ibid., 33. Here, too, Ricoeur follows Aristotle's treatise, *On Interpretation*.
71. Ibid., 141.
72. Ibid.
73. See ibid., 143 passim; see also *The Symbolism of Evil*.
74. Ibid., 144.
75. Ibid., 146.
76. Ibid.
77. Not that the human does not or cannot be made to hate evil. The paradox of humanity extends to the fact that it may simultaneously abhor violence—either in the abstract or in concrete experience—yet love it (particularly as it appears in perception as means to some pleasure or gain).
78. One might wish to argue, to the contrary, that cancer is less a paradigmatic malady of self-giving humanity and more a threat to Self-establishing inhumanity. It is before the Self that cancer takes rise as obstacle; the eternal Self cannot take rise unless every threat like cancer is *removed*. But when one seeks to secure one's life apart from the from-for succession of life, one attempts to block the effects of all other lives, including cancer, which means denying to such lives the legitimacy of their I-referentiality on the ironic ground of an assumed legitimacy to one's own, which is to say the Self's same referentiality. One is no doubt blind to the fact that one does this; sin deceives the sinner firstly with regards to his own motivations. But that does not change the fact: condemning cancer on the basis of one's own Self-interest is innately arbitrary and confused. The Self cannot actually perceive cancer to be abnormal, as malady, for it is identical in its form of life to that of the Self.

If one is to perceive cancer as contrary to one's form of life, as abnormal, as malady, then one must identify one's will with an alternative way of existing. One must perceive and come to prefer an alternative form of life to the I-referenced if one is to condemn cancer. To be precise, cancer can only be condemned for its covenant *breaking*. One can only condemn cancer if one's will is not similarly inclined to covenant breaking, or conversely, only if one identifies covenantal existence as good, as proper indeed to oneself.

In turn, the defeat (not removal) of Self entails within it the seeds of cancer's defeat (not removal). For as one concedes to the from-for succession of life, one at once perceives the alienness of cancer. Cancer takes shape in consciousness as outside authentic existence, destructive to life not so much as it is, but *as it ought to be*.

Chapter 6

Evil as Event between God and Humanity

וַיֹּ֣אמֶר׀ יְהוָ֣ה אֱלֹהִ֗ים הֵ֤ן הָֽאָדָם֙ הָיָה֙ כְּאַחַ֣ד מִמֶּ֔נּוּ לָדַ֖עַת ט֣וֹב וָרָ֑ע וְעַתָּ֣ה׀ פֶּן־יִשְׁלַ֣ח יָד֗וֹ
וְלָקַח֙ גַּ֚ם מֵעֵ֣ץ הַֽחַיִּ֔ים וְאָכַ֖ל וָחַ֥י לְעֹלָֽם׃
וַֽיְשַׁלְּחֵ֛הוּ יְהוָ֥ה אֱלֹהִ֖ים מִגַּן־עֵ֑דֶן לַֽעֲבֹד֙ אֶת־הָ֣אֲדָמָ֔ה אֲשֶׁ֥ר לֻקַּ֖ח מִשָּֽׁם׃
וַיְגָ֖רֶשׁ אֶת־הָֽאָדָ֑ם וַיַּשְׁכֵּן֩ מִקֶּ֨דֶם לְגַן־עֵ֜דֶן אֶת־הַכְּרֻבִ֗ים וְאֵ֨ת לַ֤הַט הַחֶ֙רֶב֙ הַמִּתְהַפֶּ֔כֶת
לִשְׁמֹ֕ר אֶת־דֶּ֖רֶךְ עֵ֥ץ הַֽחַיִּֽים׃

And the LORD God said, "Behold, the human has become like one of
us in regard to knowing good and evil. So now, lest he send out his hand
and take also from the tree of life and eat and live forever. . . ."
So the LORD God sent him out from the garden of Eden, to work the
ground from which he had been taken.
He cast the human out, and he made him to dwell eastward of the
garden of Eden; the cherubim and the ever-turning, flaming sword to
guard the way to the tree of life (Gen. 3:22-24).

"Humankind has got what it wants," writes Bonhoeffer. "It has itself become creator, source of life, fountainhead of the knowledge of good and evil. It is alone by itself, it lives out of its own resources, it no longer needs any others, it is the lord of its own world, even though that does mean now that it is the solitary lord and despot of its own mute, violated, silenced, dead, ego-world [Ichwelt]."[1]

Humanity finds itself in states of contradiction. It is constitutionally suited for life among other humans, readied for conscious affirmation of interdependence, as having no life except in receipt of it, while free to participate in the giving of life by affirming its procreative potential. But it is at once a form of life that wills to take rather than to give, a life that arrogates to insular self-perception, seeing no life as necessary except its own, reflexing to the false view that it can possess such comprehensive understanding (divine

213

knowledge) as to be self-making. Similarly, it is constitutionally suited for life within creation, readied for conscious affirmation of interdependence among forces and elements of the world, as having no life except in receipt of an evolutionary heritage, while free to encourage the productivity of the world through personal sacrifice, practicing self-limitations that protect environmental viability for future generations. But it is at once a form of life that by its evolutionary heritage manifests tension with the world. It seeks its own survival against the survival of others in zero-sum competition for resources, and it instances molecular processes, which both propagate life and parasitically destroy it.

Now the wheel of the second creation story finishes its turning and presents the same circumstances with respect to the human and God. I have argued throughout this book that uninterrupted communion with God, signified by the Garden of Eden, represents humanity's authentic existence; Eden is humanity's true home. Eden is a dwelling into which humanity must move. It represents not past existence, but future, and this future gives shape to the present, framing the now after *hope*. I have further argued that it is the work of God as Creator to orient the human Eden-ward, to construct human existence according to the upward spiraling motion of promise and fulfillment, or according to the biblical pattern of redemption. God exists, in fact, in effecting this motion. The final turn of the wheel of the creation myth of Gen. 2–3 clarifies that this redemptive activity of God comes through the *judgment* of God against the human Self. God moves the human into Eden as God blocks humanity's opposite movement, its untoward Self-perception—as God banishes from Eden such human who would live there inauthentically (in disobedience to the divine command and disregard for the divine permission).

The Eden-ward movement of humankind presupposes refusal of the lapsing motion of sin, the turning away from covenantal life. God must be God in a *coordinated* activity: seeding the good *and* weeding out the evil, as I have said several times. It is in the latter that the present retains its sense of promise even in fulfillment; even as the Christ has fulfilled God's covenant, the Spirit of Christ brings the judgment of God to bear on the human spirit. The Spirit makes real within the history of each generation God's renunciation of anticovenantal humanity; the Spirit reiteratively refuses nothingness as alternative to God, and in so doing institutes humanity as authentic alternative, as God's willed partner. This eschatological "already" *and* "not-yet" of human existence, made real in the Spirit of God, gives teleological determination to "God."

Before each generation, God stands as both "No" and "Yes!" No to human betrayal and infidelity; no to such a human who would transcend creatureliness in pursuit of divinity; no to a "covenant" that reduces to a mere contract in which other humans, the world, and God must meet the demands of self-made *adam*. But yes—even more so, Yes!—to the human who perceives the rightness and fitness of from-for agency; yes to faithfulness and the way of creative self-giving; yes to human partnership with God in behalf of the world and other humans.

EXEGESIS OF GEN. 3:22–24

The shadow of judgment envelopes the concluding verses of Gen. 2–3. "Eden," Gowan writes, "is revealed to be no real part of human experience; it represents what ought to be, but is a place we do not know and cannot reach."[2] The Creator becomes a problem, an obstacle to the human.[3] The human "sends out" (וַיִּשְׁלַח) his hand and God "sends him out from the garden" (מִן . . . וַיְשַׁלְּחֵהוּ). In that very act whereby the human would assume the gifting of life as his possession, God removes that possibility from him. The repetition of שלח suggests immediate reciprocity. Corresponding almost pre-reflectively to the event of human sin is the event of divine action against sin, in precisely inverse form. As the human takes, God releases the human from the right and opportunity of taking.

God expels the human from the garden, and more, bars him from returning. The ever-turning fiery sword invokes the image of a blocked portal, which itself is guarded by a mythical sentinel (or sentinels), הַכְּרֻבִים.[4] The casting out of the garden describes humanity's sense of estrangement from its Maker in the event of inauthentic Self-consciousness. Gen. 2–3 do not concern a fall from grace in any chronological sense.[5] "Rather," writes Arnold (echoing Ricoeur), "Gen 2-3 situates humankind's position vis-a-vis God as one of opposition and estrangement, and gives explanation only for the common experience of all humans in alienation, guilt, and death."[6]

God confirms human mortality in the very instant that the human becomes aware of its Self, exactly as the human turns away from constitutional inter-dependence. Yet there is mercy in this *confirmatio mortalitatis*, this damning of such humanity that would perch against God, because the destiny of man-made-god is surely a fate worse than death itself. Humans' "likeness to gods gives them . . . the capability to introduce immense suffering into the world," Gowan concludes, "and if they could live forever, the suffering would become infinite. So the death of this would-be god is not solely punishment for hybris [*sic*]; it is also a blessing, delivering the god and those around from the great harm that is now potential."[7] Similarly, Arnold observes that "in ancient Mesopotamia, loss of immortal life is an almost comic tragedy and humans are ridiculed by the gods. . . . But in Gen 3:22-24, Yahweh God banishes the humans from Eden in an act of grace and mercy."[8] Arnold sees overlap between the calamity of Genesis 3 and ANE religious narratives, citing the Adapa myth, in which Adapa foolishly rejects a deity's offer of the bread and water of life. Yet he also finds a critical discontinuity between them: in the Genesis account, "God is also protecting humans from overreaching their grasp, almost as though God is ensuring their continuing humanity as opposed to a lesser option—that of becoming trapped in immortality."[9]

God moves humanity out of Eden, but we notice, "to the east" (מִקֶּדֶם), in the direction of the sun's rise, poised for the start of a new day. Fretheim concludes that "the ending of this chapter bears some remarkable similarities both to Israel's being sent/driven out of Egypt (Exod. 6:1) and to Israel's exile to Babylon, a banishment from the land (see Leviticus 26). The latter, in particular, may have been viewed as a parallel experience to this primeval moment in Israel's eyes."[10] The story of creation ends on the same juxtaposed, dark–light tone of the stories of Exodus and Exile, where the shadow of judgment is curbed by the dawn of redemption.[11]

God confirms human mortality only to *reissue* the gift of life, only to *confirm God's self* as Life-Giver. By upholding mortality as sin's consequence, God makes the realization of humanity an eschatological matter and assigns to God's life a teleological trajectory: the human will become what it was created to be, God's eternal covenant partner, and God will be who he is, the Giver and maintainer of the covenant from which life emerges and for which it exists, as self-giving love works its creative power also over sin. From the beginning, God takes the alternative to the creature and, indeed, the alternative to *God* into account. God makes God's life in the human history of alienation and estrangement, living responsively to humanity's need as if it was God's own need, as relevant also to God's existence, answering humanity's loss with empathy and compassion. Within the time of judgment, God institutes a concomitant temporality, a history of forgiveness. In the midst of existential decay, humanity receives a second wind or new spirit.

It remains only to expand a bit upon these conclusions in relation to those drawn in previous chapters. We will be led in this effort once more by Ricoeur: the movement from fallibility to fault, which we considered in last chapter, involves a condition of "before-God-ness," such that "sin" is understood covenantally and in fact takes place within the covenant. This is helpful, on the one hand, in that it demonstrates how a right conception of sin and evil can only surface for the sinning human in confrontation with prophetic and apostolic testimony to God's redemptive history. But, on the other hand, this covenantal embedding places fate and responsibility in a kind of equilibrium, which distorts the biblical portrayal. Sin is the responsibility of covenantal humanity, I suggest, but not its fate. In fact, sin for which the human takes no responsibility, to which the human feels fated and for which he makes no confession, breaks the covenant.

After consulting with Ricoeur, we will bring the book full circle and return to Schleiermacher and Barth. Schleiermacher's account of sin and evil echoes Ricoeur's but adds emphasis on the contrast between sin and grace. Yet even in this, Schleiermacher frames the event of sin within the covenantal constitution of the creature and so falls victim, in my judgment, to the same false equivalencies that Ricoeur does. Barth, therefore, gets the last word. In his account of sin and "nothingness," Barth restores appropriate concentration on human responsibility. Sin is not a feature of covenantal existence, but the anti-covenant against which God works in creating authentic humanity, in bringing harmony out of chaos.

PAUL RICOEUR ON THE SYMBOLISM OF "SIN"

For Ricoeur, "the transition from the possibility of evil to its reality, from fallibility to fault,"[12] involves progression from *defilement* to *sin* to *guilt*:

> "Guilt," in the precise sense of a feeling of the unworthiness at the core of one's personal being, is only the advanced point of a radically individualized and interiorized experience. This feeling of guilt points to a more fundamental experience, the experience of "sin," which includes *all* men and indicates the *real* situation of man before God, whether man knows it or not. It is this sin of which the myth of the fall recounts the entry into the world and which speculation on original sin attempts to erect into a doctrine. But sin, in its turn, is a connection and even a revolution with respect to a more archaic conception of fault—the notion of "defilement" conceived in the guise of a strain or blemish that infects from without.[13]

Ricoeur's method might be described as a phenomenological psychology, in which we "re-immerse" ourselves "in *our* archaism" as a "roundabout way by which we immerse ourselves in the archaism of humanity," in order to arrive at "a discovery, a prospection, and a prophecy concerning ourselves."[14] That is to say, we take up a "sympathetic reenactment in imagination"[15] of the religious experience of fault as a way of understanding the human condition and of making some prospective sense of ourselves.[16]

Because of its pivotal place between contamination and culpability (defilement and guilt), we will focus our analysis on Ricoeur's reenactment of *sin*, particularly, again, its covenantal character. But because sin expresses a more archaic notion of defilement, and gives way to guilt, comprehending Ricoeur's claims about sin compels some advance words about its before and after, or its objective and subjective sides.

The sense of *defilement* is "the idea of a quasi-material something that infects as a sort of filth, that harms by invisible properties, and that nevertheless works in the manner of a force in the field of our undividedly psychic and corporeal existence."[17] Human existence retains a sense of spiritual contamination from without, but as noted, this amounts to a holdover from our more archaic consciousness: "we no longer understand what the substance-force of evil . . . could be."[18] Partly, "our conscience no longer recognizes the repertory of defilement."[19] We no longer identify distinct powers of spiritual infection like, for instance, proximity to a gravesite. Partly, we have other categories than that of *contaminating exposure*, which give structure to our sense of wrong: "theft, lying, sometimes even homicide . . . become evil only in a system of reference other than that of infectious contact, [such as] in connection with the confession of divine holiness, respect for inter human ties, and self-esteem"[20] It is violation of divine law, or of social mores, or of healthy personal habit, not contact with a corpse (unless, of course, such contact is also forbidden by divine law or social custom or personal hygiene), which implicates us in evil. And partly, modern humanity cannot account for what seem like strange variations in the intensity of anti-defilement prohibitions: taboos "against incest, sodomy, abortion, relations at forbidden times—and sometimes places" are unchanging,[21] yet as noted, interdictions against lying, theft, and murder are subject to contextual norms. Thus, as a calculus of fault, sin transcends defilement even as it retains its core objectivity; a lingering, if vague, sense of harm from without.

Concerning *guilt*: "it can be said, in very general terms, that guilt designates the *subjective* moment in fault. . . . Sin designates the real situation of man before God, whatever consciousness he may have of it. . . . Guilt is the awareness of this real situation."[22] Guilt implies a reflective element, awareness of one's improper standing with respect to God as well as a sense of responsibility for it. Ricoeur traces the rise of the guilt-informed conscience, which is to say, of sin's internalization, to the "deepening" of the divine demand addressed to humanity:

> The Interdiction raises up a subjective pole of responsibility that can no longer be only one who answers for the sanction, one who is responsible in the elementary sense of a subject of punishment, but a center of decision, an author of acts. That is not all: the Interdiction . . . becomes unlimited as the demand for perfection which goes beyond any enumeration of duties or virtues. This call to "perfection" reveals, behind acts, the depths of *possible* existence. In fact, just as man is called to a unique perfection that surpasses the multiplicity of his obligations, he is revealed to himself as the author not only of his many acts, but of the motives of his acts and, beyond the motives, of the most radical possibilities which are suddenly reduced to the pure and simple alternative: God or Nothing.[23]

Guilt takes shape as the human comes to stand in its own consciousness as a responsible agent and not in the elementary sense of receiving punishment for transgressing taboos. The addition of divine command makes the human responsible as decider and actor for her relationship to God: the command calls for the "yes" of obedience. Even more, because the divine command knows no limit, the human becomes responsible for the motivations behind her decisions and acts and for the kind of existence that she desires—she is confronted with a decision between divinity and nothing. Before this unyielding standard, the human can only be guilty.

Although guilt stems from the limitlessness or perfection of the command, it is not absolute in itself, in the sense that it is without degrees, that is, that one is either at fault or not at fault. "The guilty conscience, on the contrary, confesses that its fault allows of more and less, that it has degrees of seriousness."[24] The responsible individual knows what effort, or lack thereof, she makes toward the limitless command, with what earnestness she answers the call to perfection and what relative success she achieves. This grading of her fault, in turn, commends a scale of penalties, or a *commensurate* order of punishment. The guilty get what they respectively deserve.

But a problem surfaces in the grading of guilt and penalty. Both ascribe to the guilty an authority of judgment vis-a-vis participation and propriety; that is, the individual's consciousness of sinfulness entails right assessment of her particular sins and of the fitness of penalty. Having a sense of her acts and their weight, the guilty party assumes jurisdiction over what counts as right recompense. This assumption serves as occasion for further fault: "the significance of guilt . . . is the possibility of the primacy of 'man the measure' over the 'sight of God.'"[25] The subjectivity of guilt threatens the external authority of God as guilt-pronouncer. Guilt results from sin (it is a sense of failure to meet the limitless divine demand) *and feeds back on it.* "With guilt, 'conscience' is born; a responsible agent appears, to face the prophetic call and its demand for holiness. But with the factor of 'conscience' man the measure likewise comes into being; the realism of sin, measured by the eye of God, is absorbed into the phenomenalism of the guilty conscience, which is the measure of itself."[26]

Guilt involves the threat of its own recurring through the subtle grading of fault and punishment. Preventing guilt from feeding back on to the sin from which it comes entails reestablishment of sin's communality and the objectivity of God's measure, which is to say, revealing the corporate condition of humanity before God. As the guilty party is put into her factual condition as one among many before God, her ability to justify herself over against the many is (mercifully) denied to her. If there is no "more or less" sinful than the neighbor, then there is no one "more or less" deserving of punishment, and no one "more or less" righteous. For Ricoeur, the Pauline experience of justification is requisite to the symbolism of Christianity because it shows the insidiousness of guilt-ridden Pharisaism. With this in mind, we may consider what Ricoeur has to say about *sin*.

"The category that dominates the notion of sin is the category of 'before' God."[27] At the pivot between defilement and guilt, between the external/objective experience of contamination and the internal/subjective experience of responsibility, is the objective-subjective condition of failing to keep the divine command in the specific sense of rejecting God or turning away from God. Human fault is not primarily forensic or blameworthy in character, but relational. "The initial moment is not the 'unhappy consciousness,' but the 'Covenant,' the *Berit* of the Jews. . . . It is . . . the prior establishment of the bond of the Covenant that is important for consciousness of sin; it is this that makes sin a violation of the Covenant."[28] Sin takes on meaning only in light of the *relational* ought of the covenant, how we are to live not in the abstract, but with regard to God and neighbor. "What there is in the first place is not essence, but presence; and the commandment is a modality of the presence, namely, the expression of a holy will. Thus sin is a religious dimension before being ethical; it is not the transgression of an abstract rule—of a value—but the violation of a personal bond."[29] In Pauline language, it is not just through general awareness of taboo or through philosophical principles of right and wrong that our conscience is formed, but *"through the Law* comes the knowledge of sin" (Rom. 3:20b). It is through the covenant-framing regulation given at Sinai that the human knows herself before God.

This is a promising observation, in that it affirms the importance of the covenant for right self-consciousness. Existential establishment of corporate guilt requires revelation of the creature in its shared fault before its Creator, its historical failure as part of a responsible people to keep the divine command. But making sin a function of the covenant would seem not only to describe the human situation but also to ensure it. The human would seem fated to sin precisely as covenantal, subject to falter in the gap between limit and unlimit written into the Law itself, fated to Israel's failure especially as it's Law-breaking is diagnosed by the prophets.

For Ricoeur, sin is something like the stretching of the covenant, a perilous tension that inevitably surfaces for the human confronted by God's demands: "the prophetic moment in the consciousness of evil is the revelation in an infinite measure of the demand that God addresses to man. . . . But as this infinite demand does not declare itself in a sort of preceding void, but applies itself to a preceding matter, that of the old Semitic 'codes,' it inaugurates a tension characteristic of all Hebrew ethics, the tension between an infinite demand and a finite commandment."[30] The form of demand, the commandment, say, against adultery, is perspectival and finite, yet the demand itself, particularly in its prophetic interpretation, is infinite (e.g., Jesus's interpretation of the commandment in Matt. 5:27–28), and this puts unyielding strain on the recipient of the commandment. "The prophet gives the man whom he calls to account a vis-a-vis, a neighbor, with whom he is never finished."[31]

The infinite-demand-finite-code interplay initiates what Ricoeur calls "the drama of the Covenant."[32] Human existence is played out before God and neighbor in the form of always-more-besides; the human perceives himself as following the will of God, yet never quite well enough, and so as sinner. "This tension between the absolute, but formless, demand and the finite law . . . is essential to the consciousness of sin: one cannot just feel oneself guilty in general; the law is a 'pedagogue' which helps the penitent to determine how he is a sinner; he is a sinner through idolatry, filial disrespect, etc."[33] The Law in prophetic understanding induces not guilt in general, but the specific, relational fault of idol-making (betraying God) and familial contempt (betraying neighbor).

The very mechanism of the covenant, the Law, would thus seem to work against the covenant by inducing un-covenantal fault in the responsible human creature. Or more exactly, even though it represents a step beyond the fatalism of defilement, it would seem to deliver the human of any real responsibility by fating her to a guilty existence before God and neighbor. At the very least, in his rendition of the prophetic interpretation of the Law, Ricoeur leaves covenantal humankind in the most tragic existence imaginable.[34] Might we gain from Ricoeur's insightful analysis of sin, and faithfully treat the prophets, without fating humanity to sin by virtue of its covenantal character?

Might we understand sin to transpire against the covenant, not within it, but ironically, as impossible rather than possible human existence? To be sure, the Self of sin appears possible and viable, a life to which the human can attain and even achieve. But is not the viability of the appearance, the serpentine lust of Self-perception, the ground of falsehood precisely in the Law's prophetic interpretation? Does Jesus not condemn betrayal of God and neighbor *in the heart*? If so, then the Law cannot simply induce human guilt; its primary role, in fact, would be to reveal human guilt in its recessed hiddenness.

In that case, the human is not subjected to fault by virtue of her covenantal character, for her fault is in perceiving an artificial, alternative character; her guilt is not in perceiving herself to have failed to keep the limitless command, but in wrongly perceiving herself to have done so. The Law shows her that she inherits this faulty perception, in the sense that she shares it with all humanity. But it shows her that this inheritance is conscious from the start, that from the beginning she instances a consciousness reflexively oriented toward an idolatrous, murderous, adulterous, covetous Self (as committing these and other sins in the heart). Prophetically interpreted, the

Law characterizes her as responsible for her share in sin by virtue of illicit preference for the anti-covenantal—born to sin but not fated to it. The life of "before-God-against-God," or sinful Edenic existence, is not a life to which the human is destined, but one from which the human is *banished*.

Insofar as the grace of God fulfills the Law, the human is fated, or much better, *elected* to responsible communion with God. Precisely because her existence is covenantal, sinful eschatological existence, however viable, is impossible, which is to say, unprophetic, not tragically prophetic.[35] By focusing on the role of grace in pious self-consciousness, Schleiermacher takes a step this direction, if only a step.

SCHLEIERMACHER ON IMPEDIMENT TO GOD-CONSCIOUSNESS

Schleiermacher structures the second part of *The Christian Faith* as an antithesis between sin and grace.[36] Each is understood, only and contrastively, in the light of the other. The consciousness of sin[37] takes place *as* opposition to the consciousness of grace: "it is the case that every Christian is conscious both of sin and of grace as always combined with each other and never dissociated."[38] There is no such thing as sin in general, which precedes the divine act of grace, because "sin" can only be understood as antagonism toward the benevolence of God. As in Ricoeur's account, it is the event of a hostile intuition *relative* to God.[39]

Schleiermacher uses the Pauline language of "flesh" and "spirit" to express the inner tension between sin and grace (Galatians 5). "The flesh manifests itself as a reality before the spirit comes to be such, the result being, that, as soon as the spirit enters the sphere of consciousness . . . resistance takes place, i.e., we become conscious also of sin as the God-consciousness awakes within us."[40] The sense of sin as existing before grace stems from the "*independence* of the sensuous function,"[41] or the unimpeded (free) operation of touch, taste, smell and so on prior to the rise of the feeling of *dependence*. But the human is not conscious of its sin until that feeling takes rise; the reflexive independence of the flesh can only be known in tandem with the spirit, as its counter-impulse. Sin is thus "original" to the human, in the sense that the fleshly impulse always shadows the spiritual; there is no point within human existence, or rather, within a human's religious self-awareness, when the feeling of dependence occurs without the contrary impulse to independence. God-consciousness is always experienced, at least in its initial manifestation, with impediment, non-spontaneously.

Schleiermacher argues that the happening of God-consciousness involves consciousness of "a complete incapacity for good, which can be removed only by the influence of Redemption."[42] Impediment to God-consciousness is progressively overcome by communication of the pure God-consciousness of Christ, which the human is capable of receiving. Incapacity for good does not entail incapacity for grace: "no improvement would be possible," Schleiermacher contends, without "the capacity to appropriate the grace offered to us."[43] The influence of redemption corrects human incapacity for good, but only by entering through the gate of a created human perfection. The creature *can* receive Christ's consciousness. Not all theologians of Schleiermacher's tradition have agreed with this logic. Some have argued for an *unqualified* human incapacity, and that God creates the capacity for grace in the act of its giving; it is of the very nature of "grace" to effect this wider restoration.[44] But pursuing this would take us off-topic.

Schleiermacher rightly stresses that original sin is not a force emerging from we know not where (or what), sinisterly descending upon the shire of human innocents. It is a consciousness of independence ever-vying against consciousness of dependence, flesh battling spirit. And it is not a strictly individual fault, but is "best represented as the corporate act and the corporate guilt of the human race."[45] The human inherits non-spontaneous God-consciousness through communal conditioning. Echoing what Schleiermacher taught us concerning the absoluteness of dependence in chapter 1—that any reflexive action on the part of the will vitiates the totality of the feeling of dependence, rendering it only relative—he argues that the absoluteness of original sin's inheritance is vitiated by the degree to which sin activates without external influence, *spontaneously*. "Original sin is purely a thing received only in the degree in which the individual is not yet spontaneously active, and it ceases to be such in the degree in which that activity is developed. Up to that point, and in that measure, it is rightly termed *originated*, as having its cause outside the individual."[46]

The human's sinfulness originates externally to the degree that her actual sinning (repression of piety) lacks reflexive immediacy. When that eventually happens, sin can be considered to have become internalized. On the way there, sin enters into a kind of feedback loop with its external origination through the operation of the will. "By the exercise due to the voluntary action of the individual, is there growth in congenital sinfulness."[47] Experiencing impediments to God-consciousness, the human gladly accepts and promotes them. The human is born into (a world of) sin, and gives birth to the same.

The sin of the individual is simply part of the sum of sinful humanity:

> The distinctive form of original sin in the individual, as regards its quality, is only a constituent part of the form it takes in the circle to which he immediately belongs, so that, though inexplicable when taken by itself, it points to the other parts as complementary to it. . . . And the aggregate power of the flesh in its

conflict with the spirit . . . is intelligible only by reference to the totality of those sharing a common life, and never fully in any one part. . . . The like holds good also of time. What appears as the congenital sinfulness of one generation is conditioned by the sinfulness of the previous one, and in turn conditions that of the later; and only in the whole series of forms thus assumed, as all connected with the progressive development of man, do we find the whole aspect of things denoted by the term, "original sin."[48]

The human exists within a community of sinful relations spatially and historically. Her existence is interwoven with social structures of behavior, given shape by public customs and expectations. She lives in a world of impeded, non-spontaneous God-consciousness and experiences herself within its conventions. Only as it is both originated and originating among humans living across time is sin "original" to humankind.

It is in this reference that Schleiermacher treats the sin of Adam and Eve. He expresses futility at trying to explain a one-time fall from grace. "All turns upon the endeavor to elucidate the genesis of sin in the first pair apart from an already existent sinfulness. But whether we take the narrative of the first sin literally or ascribe to it a universal significance, the attempt seems doomed to failure."[49] Schleiermacher reasons that if Adam and Eve were endowed with an absolutely potent, spontaneous God-consciousness, then they would have been immune to threat of sin externally (traditionally, to Satan) and internally (misuse of will), whether the story of Adam and Eve is read literally or is indicative of a universal human failure.

Schleiermacher rejects the view that sin originated out of sinlessness: "we must accordingly adhere to the position that the idea of a change in human nature entailed by the first sin of the first pair has no place among the propositions which rank as utterances of our Christian consciousness. . . . Incapacity was present in human nature before the first sin, and . . . what is now innate sinfulness was something native also to the first pair."[50] Adam and Eve participate in a broader incapacity for the good, which pious consciousness recognizes. Their story is very much our story:

We can use the story, as the early theologians did, in illustration of the universal process of the rise of sin as something always and everywhere the same, and it is in this illustrative quality that, for us, the universal significance of the narrative resides. There we find in Eve, on the one hand, a clear representation of the independent activity and revolt of the sensuous element that developed so readily upon any external incentive by way of opposition to a divine command. . . . On the other hand, in Adam we see how easily sin is assimilated by imitation even without any overpowering activity of sense, and how this presupposes some degree of forgetfulness of God, traceable possibly to mere lack of thought.[51]

Adam and Eve represent humankind in both the sin of the sensuous element—the freedom and readiness of the senses to seize upon external enticement contrary to divine will—and in the interconnected conditioning of the flesh—the assimilation of transgression among transgressors, which takes place by simple imitation. Individual flesh vies against spirit while existing among fleshes similarly vying. The fact that the biblical progenitors did not originate a change in human nature from sinlessness to sinfulness, but took their part in an originated–originating incapacity for good common to humankind, does not mean that God created humanity as sinful per se. It means that God created the human in a state of tension. Against the traditional view of a temporary perfection giving way to a temporary sinfulness, "we substitute a timeless original sinfulness always and everywhere inhering in human nature and co-existing with the original perfection given along with it," and "from the concomitance and development of the two there could issue no active righteousness properly so called, but at best a vacillation between vitiated spiritual efforts and increasing and fully matured sin."[52]

Schleiermacher thus leaves humanity in the same situation as Ricoeur did above, both fated to sin and responsible for it. As a fleshly creature among fleshly creatures, the human sins by instinct and by imitation from the very beginning. Sinfulness is as timeless to the human as is perfection (capacity for grace). We may take this analysis as a step forward because of the way that Schleiermacher correlates sin with grace: as the inverse of grace, sin does not give way to a fatalistic kind of guilt, to Ricouer's human tragically faltering before the limitless divine demand. Rather, sin comes to light within the promise of its undoing, as an incapacity that is already being overcome by very awareness of it, by rise of the spirit, thus as something to which the human cannot finally be fated. Consciousness of flesh only happens *as object of the spirit's contrary operation*. The struggle between original sin and original perfection, resistance to grace and the capacity for grace, is made known *by the influence of redemption*, by actualization of the capacity over the incapacity, thus *not* as indefinite tension but as prospective reconciliation. The sinner knows himself as sinner not necessarily, but provisionally (however much also potently). Although the experience of sin may be strong, even stronger is the experience of the overcoming of its resistance. Because the sinful human only knows his sin within consciousness of God, he knows himself under the sign of promise.

Still, the sinner knows himself as victim at least as much as perpetrator, if not subject to Satan then at least subject to a diabolical flesh, a sensuousness that conspires against him by virtue of its very operation. But it makes no more sense to construe the operation of sensuousness to be "independent" and therefore against piety than it does to construe the force of hurricane winds to be opposed to the goodness of creation. Sensory operation just is; "freedom" does not apply. Readiness of the senses to attach to external enticement, even enticements that lead away from awareness of dependence, does not constitute sinfulness, and suggesting that it does simply opens the door to externalizing fault, the heart's deception.

Schleiermacher is right to argue that sin only occurs within consciousness of grace, that "evil" is senseless except as it is perceived in contrast to God's life-giving will, but his account of sin does not carry this insight through consistently. He ought to have argued that sin is the inverse of grace not just as resistance or impediment to God-consciousness, but as event of self-destruction (interruption of the life-giving action of God in the event of obedience to divine command and acceptance of divine permission). It is the chaos asserting itself, the nothing opposite "God" vying for space-time in and through the human, which can only nullify the human. Instead of arguing that the human is created in a tension between timeless sin and timeless perfection, Schleiermacher should have contended that the human is made in a history of redemption, which actualizes the Creator's refusal of chaos and nothingness. Schleiermacher should have demonstrated that precisely as opposition to grace, sin is a radically destructive experience, which can only transpire within the sphere of human responsibility, and which God alone can overcome.[53]

BARTH ON SIN AND NOTHINGNESS

"There is in world-occurrence an element, indeed an entire system of elements, which is not . . . preserved, accompanied, nor ruled by the almighty action of God like creaturely occurrence. . . . This opposition and resistance, this stubborn element and alien factor, may be provisionally defined as nothingness."[54] Unlike Schleiermacher and Ricoeur, Barth does not locate sin within the covenantal fabric of creation. Sin and evil do not even "accompany" the creative action of God and so cannot be considered a polar tension within the life of the creature that God has made. Evil takes the quality of "nothing."

Because sin exists outside of God's action and "creaturely occurrence," Barth identifies no positive origin for it, no "timeless original sinfulness" or gap between finitude and infinitude. "There is that at work which can be explained neither from the side of the Creator nor from the side of the creature, neither as the action of the Creator nor as the life-act of the creature, and yet which cannot be overlooked or disowned but must be reckoned with in all its peculiarity."[55] Reckoning with "sin" for Barth means to start with its factual thereness, not with its theoretical origin. Like with Augustine, sin might best described along the register of defect (or perhaps better, defection) of the will, but Barth does not speculate about that. He simply describes sin and evil as *das Nichtige*, "the nothing," or "nothingness."[56]

Barth does not dismiss evil with such language. He writes profoundly of its reality within the human sphere; we recall that Barth's career spanned both the first and second world wars. But because evil does not originate with God or with God's creature, or as we have discussed, because it only takes rise *as artifice* within creaturely self-perception, Barth wishes to capture its essential, eschatological-protological negation. Evil really does threaten, but from the divine perspective, it is already defeated. "There is danger either of an uneasy, bleak and skeptical overestimating of its power in relation to God, or of an easy, comfortable and dogmatic underestimation of its power in relation to us."[57]

One way that the human overestimates evil's power is by confusing it with the many "absences" in creaturely existence that are actually good, that give definition and order to creation—things like absence of light (night), or absence of heat (cold). Nightfall and winter can mistakenly be taken as threats to God's creative work, a fraught association (like the association of hurricane wind with evil) not uncommon to religions of the ANE or to popular religious imagination, which implies an equally fraught association of divinity with daylight (sun gods) and harvest seasons (fertility cults). For Barth, such associations merely betray a reticence to relinquish mastery and a false sense of independence (fear of the dark because of its limiting qualities and of the winter because of the uncertainty it presents for next year's crops). In fact, however, such limitation is good and proper. "It belongs to the essence of creaturely nature . . . that it has in fact this negative side . . . that it is thus simultaneously worthy of its Creator and yet dependent on him, that it is not 'nothing' but 'something,' yet 'something' on the very frontier of nothingness, secure and yet in jeopardy."[58] Night and cold can signify creaturely limitation, but this is good, not evil; they can indicate to the creature the fact of her frontier existence—that she stands on the precipice of nothingness except for God's creative act, that she is utterly dependent on God—but they are not evil themselves and should not be related to as if they were. They have no part in *das Nichtige* against which God works in creating. (We will return to the "negative side" of creation in volume 2 when we consider Genesis 1).

If we are rightly to identify evil and not mistakenly associate it with creation's limiting qualities then we must understand it in the light of grace. As Schleiermacher did, Barth contends that sin and evil are meaningless apart from God's redemptive work:

> In plain and precise terms . . . nothingness is the "reality" on whose account (i.e., against which) God Himself willed to become a creature in the creaturely world, yielding and subjecting Himself to it in Jesus Christ in order to overcome

it. Nothingness is thus the "reality" which opposes and resists God, which is itself subjected to and overcome by His opposition and resistance, and which in this twofold determination as the reality that negates and is negated by Him, is totally distinct from him.[59]

By its very character, we might say, "nothingness" can only be construed as object of divine action, as the "on which" of God's creative work. It cannot preexist this action or that already would render it senseless, making it into an enduring something named "nothing." But that does not make it a mere foil, a mental placeholder endowing explanatory content to "God." It is a "reality that negates" God, a force of resistance to God, emergence of the anti-god or, as Barth elsewhere says, the "no-god." By making his life-act to be in opposition to nothingness, God affirms the genuineness of evil's threat, the sincerity of the impulse away from God that emerges within human history and must be dealt with there.

In a sublime paradox, God deals with evil on the human plane, which means by subjecting himself to it, indeed succumbing to its negation. This is what gives nothingness its fullest possible reality, as that which can destroy God. This victory of sin is what makes the serpentine alternative appear so viable to the human heart. But the sacrifice is effective, for it is the fullest possible gifting of life within the realm of life-taking. God makes real within the history of nothingness an alternative existence, a life that does not succumb to nothingness in the sense of its character; God does not give in to its Self-ishness, its anti-dependence. God's self-giving negates the effectiveness of the negation: "the issue in this whole [human] history is the repulse and final removal of the threat thus actualized. And God Himself is always the One who first takes this threat seriously, who faces and throws Himself against it, who strives with chaos, who persists in His attitude, who continues and completes the action which He has already undertaken as Creator in this respect, negating and rejecting it."[60]

God's active judgment against sin is simply part of God's active preservation of the covenant against the self-destructive force of nihilism. Preference for the autonomous Self; preference for the unlimited life; preference for self-serving exploitation of creature and creation; preference for the place of command-giver rather than life-receiver; preference for godlessness and neighborless-ness; all of this must be shown to the nihilist for what it is: baseless, useless, profitless. The lostness of meaninglessness must be made real, given a kind of meaning within consciousness even though, or precisely because, it is by definition devoid of meaning. That which is of the void must be voided; knowledge and ethics of the self-made one, of limitless personal design and privilege, must be known in its falseness and deception, its nothingness, and as such, it must be returned there.

Judgment is central to God's continuing act of creation, central to human redemption.

A right understanding of sin perceives its fullness in relation to God's act—as active dissolution of the covenant, which God actively disallows. The human cannot be fated to sin, for being anti-covenantal in nature sin can only take rise within responsible human agency. It can only surface as *preference* for existence apart from God and neighbor, for life above the world and not from it, let alone for it. Sin can only be the event in which the world is wrongly perceived as the realm of forces and elements hostile to the human over which the human constantly seeks mastery. Because the human is responsible for sin, or because sin only occurs within the agency of human response to God and world, God alone can be responsible for its defeat, or its defeat can only take place within the agency of divine response to the human in the world. God must make real an alternative perception, a new history within human history, into which the human can again live, or can regain the life he lost. God must negate the pull of nothingness, nihilistic allure, so that the creature might *not* be fated to it, but might be fore-destined to eschatological rebirth.

NOTES

1. Bonhoeffer, *Creation and Fall*, 142.

2. Gowan, *Genesis 1–11*, 61.

3. Westermann detects in Gen. 3:22 an "echo" of the common ANE motif of "the envy of the gods" (see *Genesis 1–11*, 273). But the verse is not so much concerned with what it means to be *God* as it is with what it means to be *human*. The text betrays the fundamentally Jewish assumption of the non-possibility of humanity becoming divine and populating the ranks of heaven with alternatives to YHWH; as elsewhere, the Jahwist critiques the very motif of which he makes use.

4. "Neither here nor anywhere else is there a clear cut definition or description of these beings. The use of the definite article presupposes a familiarity with them on the part of the reader, probably because they figured in popular legend and folklore" (Sarna, *Genesis*, 30). Fretheim describes the cherubim as "a human and animal/bird composite (a common phenomenon in the ancient Near East)" (*The Book of Genesis*, 364). He also notes, relevantly for this study, an association with the covenant: citing the cherubim on the Ark of the Covenant and around the tabernacle and temple, Fretheim notes that these creatures "assumed various functions, including guarding the sanctuary from unauthorized intrusion" (ibid.). The image, then, of guarding the entrance to the garden of Eden invokes the temple cult, and further suggests that Eden should be understood as the temple of creation, or as a depiction of God's covenantal presence in and with creation.

5. So Westermann: "one cannot cut [the narrative] down the middle and say that the first part, before the eating of the fruit, is the *status integritatis* beyond our

historical experience, but with the eating of the fruit the *status corruptionis* began. . . . The goal of the narrative of Gen 2–3 is not a state which is to be opposed to an earlier state, but the expulsion of the man and the woman from the garden and the consequent separation from God" (*Genesis 1–11*, 276–77).

6. Arnold, *Genesis*, 73.

7. Gowan, *Genesis 1–11*, 61.

8. Arnold, Genesis, 72.

9. Ibid.

10. Fretheim, *The Book of Genesis*, 365.

11. It merits observation, in this regard, that the immediacy of the death sentence threatened in 2:17 is set aside. "God drives [man and woman] out of the garden, but leaves them life, and by giving them a commission outside the garden, God gives meaning to their alienated existence" (Westermann, *Genesis 1–11*, 277).

12. Ricoeur, *The Symbolism of Evil* (Boston: Beacon, 1969), 3.

13. Ibid., 7–8.

14. Ibid., 13.

15. Ibid., 3.

16. Ricoeur engages in what he describes as a "phenomenology of confession," a mixture of observations and inductive inferences at the psychological level vis-a-vis religious expression of fault, in order to draw conclusions about human existence and its prospects. The phenomenological project is in service to a properly philosophical account of religious symbolism, particularly with respect to evil; for the latter, see ibid., 161–357. Our concern is with Ricoeur's phenomenology.

17. Ricoeur, *The Symbolism of Evil*, 25–26.

18. Ibid., 26.

19. Ibid.

20. Ibid., 27.

21. Ibid., 28.

22. Ibid., 101.

23. Ibid., 103.

24. Ibid., 107.

25. Ibid., 108.

26. Ibid., 143. Ricoeur contends that the most advanced "type" of guilty experience is Pharisaic "scrupulousness;" see ibid., 126–39. The Pharisee extends the Law and the preaching of the prophets into refined moral maxims, which he tags with *merit*. The scrupulous keeper of the Law is scrupulously rewarded, whereas the unscrupulous Law breaker, viewed within Pharisaic polarities as actively (scrupulously) opposed to the Law, is just as scrupulously held accountable for his misdeeds. Either way, there is inbuilt the most extensive kind of judgment of propriety.

27. Ibid., 50.

28. Ibid., 50–51.

29. Ibid., 52.

30. Ibid., 55–56.

31. Ibid., 56.

32. Ibid., 70.

33. Ibid., 59.

34. Scope prevents detailed treatment of Ricoeur's discussion of the tragic; for this, see ibid., 211–31 and esp. his consideration of the serpent figure in the Genesis myth, 252–60. Ricoeur closely echoes my exegetical conclusions drawn above in ch. 4, which regarded the serpent as a kind of metaphor for sin's deception, the way that humanity quietly pursues its own divinity: "the serpent, then, would be a part of ourselves which we do not recognize; he would be the seduction of ourselves by ourselves, projected into the seductive object" (ibid., 256). But making more than should be out of the fact that the Jahwist failed to demythologize this theogonic figure, Ricoeur contends that the serpent stands equally for the fact that sin *is* external to humankind, a reality to which the human is at once subject:

> There is thus an anteriority of evil to itself, as if evil were that which always precedes itself, that which each man finds and continues while beginning it. . . . That is why, in the Garden of Eden, the serpent is already there; he is the other side of that which begins. Let us go further: behind the *projection* of our lust, beyond the *tradition* of evil already there, there is perhaps an even more radical externality of evil, a cosmic structure of evil—not, doubtless, the lawfulness of the world as such, but its relation of indifference to the ethical demands of which man is both author and servant (ibid., 258).

The human finds herself in the tense condition of being cast into a cosmos of evil (a world indifferent to humanity's ethical demands), and "beginning" evil (seducing ourselves with false notions of innocence). Paradoxically, "the always-already-there of evil is the *other* aspect of the evil for which, nevertheless, *I* am responsible" (ibid., 259). But this appeal to the biblical depiction immediately distorts it. The Bible identifies the victim of sin as the perpetrator. Israel is not simply subject to the enemies of God; this son of God has himself become God's enemy and redemption from the impossible nothingness of *that* existence becomes God's defining work – this, especially according to the interpretation of the finite command by the prophets. There can be no equipoise, then, between fate and responsibility. The fate of humankind to sin is really just aversion toward responsibility, for which the sinner must also take responsibility.

35. Ricoeur does account for the experience of standing against God, but he does so as part of the "dialogue" in which the sinner confesses her position *before* God. Particularly in the psalms, "the 'unhappy consciousness' of the sinner discovers that its separation from God is still a relation" (ibid., 69).

36. Schleiermacher, *The Christian Faith*, 259–751

37. Schleiermacher treats the doctrine of sin in ibid., 259–354.

38. Ibid., 265.

39. To the extent that "we are conscious of sin as the power and work of a time when the disposition to the God-consciousness had not yet actively emerged in us," we are not, in fact, conscious of sin in its fullness (ibid., 273).

40. Ibid., 274.

41. Ibid., 273.

42. Ibid., 282.

43. Ibid.

44. Schleiermacher briefly acknowledges this possibility, but dismisses it as requiring the regenerated human to remain "absolutely passive," in which case, she would be passive through the whole process of salvation, including sanctification, so that (since it is in sanctification that the spirit completes the flesh) "redemption would become superfluous" (ibid., 283–84). The human would not actually *attain* the un-interruption of God-consciousness, or *progress* in the Spirit, but immediately possess it. But if the Spirit's work of regeneration entails reiteration of the quality of creation, particularly the refusal of disorder, then assertion of the need for absolute passivity in the event of redemption is unwarranted. Just as the creation of the human entails living reciprocity in and through divine breath, so does the re-creation.

45. Schleiermacher, *The Christian Faith*, 285.

46. Ibid., 286.

47. Ibid., 287.

48. Ibid., 288.

49. Ibid., 293.

50. Ibid., 298, 301.

51. Ibid., 302–03.

52. Ibid., 302.

53. So, Barth:

> It is now clear that the contradiction and opposition of man, his godlessness and inhuman-ity, his sin against himself, are not a little absurdity but one which is incommensurably great, provoking God and Lord. . . . What is made clear in the incarnation of the Word of God and the offering up to death of the Son of God is that evil is not an element in the orderly course of the world, but an element, indeed *the* element, which absolutely threat-ens and obscures it—the sowing of the enemy in the good field, the invasion of chaos, the nihilist revolution which can result only in the annihilation of all creatures. (CD IV.1, 411)

My correction to Schleiermacher may be read as endorsement of Barth's criti-cisms and conclusions; see for starters Barth, CD IV.1, §60, esp. "The Man of Sin in the Light of the Obedience of the Son of God," 358–413.

54. Barth, CD III.3, 289.

55. Ibid., 292.

56. Of course, the very act of assigning sin and evil a name accords them a kind of positive reality, even if the name is "the nothing," since doing so allows them to be treated as subjects and predicates of sentences, acting and acted upon ("the nothing" does this; that amplifies "the nothing"). I am not inclined to explore this rabbit hole and decide whether Barth undercuts his discussion from the outset by sleight of hand abstraction. I find value in the discussion as Barth has it, and as my ensuing analysis indicates, I think it possible to affirm Barth's intentions even under the restrictions of language.

57. Barth, CD III.3, 293.

58. Ibid., 296.

59. Ibid., 305.

60. Ibid., 352.

Conclusion

In this volume, I have begun to retell the biblical narrative and rethink Christian teaching on creation in terms of action and relation rather than states of being, along the register of *spirit*. I have tried to speak meaningfully of God's presence in a world increasingly disinclined to it—a self-absorbed world, or world of self-absorption in which creatures down to the level of biochemistry manifest contradiction, turning against their life-giving interdependency, manipulating and exploiting its processes for ephemeral and necessarily elusive gain. Contending for the curative and creative presence of the Spirit does not amount to deluded refusal to graduate from a prehistoric and mythical mindset to a modern and critical one. It simply, if also profoundly, means re-cognizing life's emergence and endurance to happen moment-by-moment in the event of eternal (never-ceasing) self-giving, that is, in the event of covenantal constitution reiteratively realized after the covenantal self-determination of "God." God exists, and so does the world, in a history of redemption, the upward-spiraling movement of promise and fulfillment inaugurated with Abraham and fulfilled in the Christ.

I have argued that we should not speak of the *being* of God in whom things relate, but of the *relation* of God in whom things come to be, in whom all things live, move and have being (Acts 17:28). Although neither register exists without the other, relation is a logically more basic modality than being, and "God" designates the primal event of relation in and through which things come to be. God *is* love. Only in the constancy of uninterrupted charity does "God" obtain substantival reference: only in giving and maintaining the covenant can we say, "he is."

God exists as Giver of Life. Giving life is not a thing that the being of God does, but the eternal act in which the relation of God is. God reiteratively establishes God's life by relating generationally—generating life within a proper time-framing. If our logic is the calculus of *relational event* and not *metaphysical being*, of coordinated living (συμβιόω) and not standing thingness (ὄντα) and sequential thingness-making (ὀντοποιέω)—the calculus of symbiology and not ontology—then "time" cannot be the output of Creator and container of creation. "Time" must rather be *the medium of the coordinated event of Creator and creation*. Time is that perpetual distending in which God firstly and creation secondarily have existence; cynosural, from-for durations of opportunity patterned after love. "In time" does not mean "in the container of sequentiality." It means "in the distention of self." Time refers to God's opening to another and that other's opening after God as *secunda* to *primus*, the movement toward otherness that initiates with God and culminates with authenticated humanity.

God comes to exist anew in the distention or timespan of each new generation, yet remains the same yesterday, today, and forever; this, by forming each generation's constitutive perception after its unique experience of dependence. In the event of self-perception, the human experiences her dependence and interdependence according to characteristics of her time, her history of love—her own from (receipt of the divine gift, genetics, and upbringing of her family, influences, and restrictions of her environment), and her own for (responsibly enacting the divine gift, supporting the procreative possibility if not actually taking part in it, and stewarding the environment). This is her authenticity.

In the biblical testimony to God's redemptive history, the human encounters divine command and permission. She may affirm her dependence on God and interdependence among creation by obeying God's command to stand in relation to God as God-effected partner (and not Self-effecting individual), and by accepting God's permission to stand in behalf her neighbor and the world, to exercise her perceptual agency responsibly. But to do this, every contrary impulse must be defeated, every fearful reflex to non-dependence and self-serving seizure of life-against-the-other must be stilled. Sin and evil must be overcome within the human. It is of God's essence as Spirit, as *living* Creator-Redeemer, to achieve this victory and authenticate human existence. God makes the eschatological achievement of the human to be God's teleological self-determination.

The redeemed human spirit, in conformity to that of its life-giving Spirit, at once desires time-with-another and freely pursues time-for-another. It takes the shape of love. Love longs for healing and growth—to seek and to find reconciliation and true companionship, to seek and to find yet-more-gracious charity and kindlier patience. The human born of love lives for renewal not only within but also without. She desires to be God's covenantal partner, indeed, the creaturely correlate to the Creator, the very image of God.

Bibliography

Alexander, Denis. *The Language of Genetics: An Introduction.* Templeton Science and Religion Series. West Conshohocken, PA: Templeton, 2011.

Arnold, Bill T. *Genesis.* The New Cambridge Bible Commentary. Cambridge: Cambridge University Press, 2009.

Alter, Robert. *Genesis: Translation and Commentary.* New York: Norton, 1996.

Augustine. *The City of God.* The Works of Saint Augustine: A New Translation for the 21st Century Volume I/6, 7. Hyde Park, NY: New City, 2012–2013.

———. *Confessions.* Translated by Henry Chadwick. The World's Classics. Oxford: Oxford University Press, 1992.

———. "The Excellence of Marriage." In *Marriage and Virginity.* The Works of Saint Augustine: A Translation for the 21st Century Volume I/9, edited by John E. Rotelle, O.S.A., translated by Ray Kearney, 31–64. New York: New City, 1998.

———. "Holy Virginity." In *Marriage and Virginity.* The Works of Saint Augustine: A Translation for the 21st Century Part Volume I/9, edited by John E. Rotelle, O.S.A., translated by Ray Kearney, 68–110. New York: New City, 1998.

———. "The Literal Meaning of Genesis." In *On Genesis.* The Works of Saint Augustine: A Translation for the 21st Century Volume I/13, edited by John E. Rotelle, O.S.A., translated by Edmund Hill, O.P., 155–506. Hyde Park, NY: New City, 2013.

———. "On Free Will." In *Augustine: Earlier Writings*, edited by J. H. S. Burleigh, 102–217. The Library of Christian Classics Ichthus Edition. Philadelphia: Westminster, 1953.

———. "On Genesis: A Refutation of the Manichees." In *On Genesis.* The Works of Saint Augustine: A Translation for the 21st Century Volume I/13, edited by John E. Rotelle, O.S.A., translated by Edmund Hill, O.P., 25–102. Hyde Park, NY: New City, 2013.

———. "The Spirit and the Letter." In *Answer to the Pelagians I.* The Works of Saint Augustine: A Translation for the 21st Century Volume I/23, edited by John

E. Rotelle, O.S.A., translated by Roland J. Teske, S.J., 139–202. Hyde Park, NY: New City, 1997.

———. "Unfinished Literal Commentary on Genesis." In *On Genesis*. The Works of Saint Augustine: A Translation for the 21st Century Volume I/13, edited by John E. Rotelle, O.S.A., translated by Edmund Hill, O.P., 105–51. Hyde Park, NY: New City, 2013.

Baden, Joel S. *The Composition of the Pentateuch: Renewing the Documentary Hypothesis*. The Anchor Yale Bible Reference Library. New Haven: Yale University Press, 2012.

Barth, Karl. *Church Dogmatics* II.2. Edited by G. W. Bromiley and T. F. Torrance. London: T & T Clark, 2004.

———. *Church Dogmatics* III.1. Edited by G. W. Bromiley and T. F. Torrance. London: T & T Clark, 2004.

———. *Church Dogmatics* III.2. Edited by G. W. Bromiley and T. F. Torrance. London: T & T Clark, 2004.

———. *Church Dogmatics* III.3. Edited by G. W. Bromiley and T. F. Torrance. London: T & T Clark, 2004.

———. *Church Dogmatics* IV.1. Edited by G. W. Bromiley and T. F. Torrance. London: T & T Clark, 2004.

———. *Protestant Theology in the Nineteenth Century: Its Background and History*. Valley Forge: Judson, 1976,

Behe, Michael. *Darwin's Black Box: The Biochemical Challenge to Evolution*. New York: Free Press, 2006.

Bernhardt, Karl-Heinz. "בָּרָא III Meaning." In *Theological Dictionary of the Old Testament Volume 2*, edited by G. Johannes Botterweck and Helmer Ringgren, translated by John T. Willis, 246. Grand Rapids: Eerdmans, 1974.

Biblia Hebraica Stuttgartensia with Werkgroep Informatica, Vrije Universiteit Morphology. Logos Bible Software, 2006.

Biel, Gabriel. "The Circumcision of the Lord (ca. 1460)." In *A Reformation Reader: Primary Texts with Introductions*, edited by Denis R. Janz, 51–56. Minneapolis: Fortress, 2008.

Bonhoeffer, Dietrich. *Creation and Fall: A Theological Exposition of Genesis 1–3*. Edited by John W. de Gruchy. Translated by Martin Rüter and Ilse Tödt. Dietrich Bonhoeffer Works 3. Minneapolis: Fortress, 1997.

Botterweck, G. Johannes. "בָּרָא II.3 *LXX*." In *Theological Dictionary of the Old Testament Volume 2*, edited by G. Johannes Botterweck and Helmer Ringgren, translated by John T. Willis, 245–46. Grand Rapids: Eerdmans, 1974.

Brinkman, Baba. "Revenge of the Somatic: Gangster Rap from Cancer Cell's Perspective from Baba Brinkman at #DSMIS13." YouTube Video, 4:26. September 28, 2013. https://www.youtube.com/watch?v=rrwMRF-CqqM.

Brown, Francis, S. R. Driver, and Charles A. Briggs. *The Brown-Driver-Briggs Hebrew and English Lexicon*. Peabody, MA: Hendrickson, 2000.

Bub, Jeffrey. "The Entangled World: How Can It Be Like That?" In *The Trinity and an Entangled World*, edited by John Polkinghorne, 15–31. Grand Rapids: Eerdmans, 2010.

Bynum, Caroline Walker. *The Resurrection of the Body in Western Christianity, 200–1336*. New York: Columbia University Press, 1995.

Carey, Nessa. *The Epigenetics Revolution: How Modern Biology is Rewriting Our Understanding of Genetics, Disease, and Inheritance*. New York: Columbia University Press, 2013.

Cassuto, Umberto. *A Commentary on the Book of Genesis Part One: From Adam to Noah*. Translated by Israel Abrahams. Jerusalem: The Hebrew University Press, 1989

———. *The Documentary Hypothesis and the Composition of the Pentateuch*. Translated by Israel Abrahams. Jerusalem: Shalem, 2008.

Childs, Brevard S. *Introduction to the Old Testament as Scripture*. Minneapolis: Fortress, 1979.

Christian, William A. "Augustine on the Creation of the World." *Harvard Theological Review* 46, no. 1 (1953): 1–25; Reprint, "The Creation of the World." In *A Companion to the Study of Augustine*, edited by Roy W. Battenhouse, 315–42. New York: Oxford University Press, 1955.

"Chromosome 13." http://ghr.nlm.nih.gov/chromosome/13.

Clancy, Suzanne, and William Brown. "Translation: DNA to mRNA to Protein." *Nature Education* 1, no. 1 (2008): 101. http://www.nature.com/scitable/topicpage/translation-dna-to-mrna-to-protein-393.

Clements, Keith W. Introduction to *Friedrich Schleiermacher: Pioneer of Modern Theology*, edited by Keith W. Clements, 7–65. The Making of Modern Theology: Nineteenth- and Twentieth-Century Texts. Minneapolis: Fortress, 1991.

Clifford, Richard J., S.J. *Creation Accounts in the Ancient Near East and in the Bible*. Catholic Biblical Quarterly-Monograph Series 26. Washington, DC: The Catholic Biblical Association of America, 1994.

Coakley, Sarah. *God, Sexuality, and the Self: An Essay on the Trinity*. Cambridge: Cambridge University Press, 2013.

———. *Powers and Submissions: Spirituality, Philosophy, and Gender*. Challenges in Contemporary Theology. Oxford, UK and Malden, MA: Blackwell, 2002.

Delitzsch, Franz. *A New Commentary on Genesis Volume 1*. Translated by Sophia Taylor. Clark's Foreign Theological Library 36. Edinburgh: T & T Clark, 1888.

Dierken, Jörg. "Synergismus." In *Theologische Realenzyklopädia XXXII*, 508–24. Berlin: De Gruyter, 1976–2004.

Dorner, Isaak A. *Divine Immutability: A Critical Reconsideration*. Translated by Robert R. Williams and Claude Welch. Minneapolis: Fortress, 1994.

Dozeman, Thomas B., and Konrad Schmid. *A Farewell to the Yahwist? The Composition of the Pentateuch in Recent European Interpretation*. SBL Symposium 34. Atlanta: Society of Biblical Literature, 2006.

Drever, Matthew. "Redeeming Creation: *Creatio ex nihilo* and the *Imago Dei* in Augustine." *International Journal of Systematic Theology* 15, no. 2 (2013): 135–53.

Edwards, Denis. *Breath of Life: A Theology of the Creator Spirit*. Maryknoll, NY: Orbis, 2004.

———. *The God of Evolution: A Trinitarian Theology*. New York: Paulist, 1999.

———. *The Natural World and God: Theological Explorations*. Adelaide, Australia: ATF, 2017.

Einstein, Albert. *Relativity: The Special and General Theory*. Translated by Robert W. Lawson. New York: Three Rivers, 1961.

Erasmus. *Discourse on Free Will*. Milestones of Thought. Edited and translated by Ernst F. Winter. New York: Frederick Ungar, 1961.

Feuerbach, Ludwig. *The Essence of Christianity*. Translated by George Eliot. New York: Harper, 1957.

Fichte, Johann Gottlieb. *The Vocation of Man*. Translated by Peter Preuss. Indianapolis: Hackett, 1987.

Fox, Everett. *The Five Books of Moses: Genesis, Exodus, Leviticus, Numbers, Deuteronomy: A New Translation with Introductions, Commentary and Notes*. The Schocken Bible Volume 1. New York: Schocken, 1995.

Fretheim, Terence. *The Book of Genesis: Introduction, Commentary, and Reflections*. The New Interpreter's Bible Volume 1. Abingdon: Nashville, 1994.

Greaves, Mel. *Cancer: The Evolutionary Legacy*. Oxford: Oxford University Press, 2001.

Hagoort, Peter. "The Uniquely Human Capacity for Language Communication: From *Pope* to [po:p] in Half a Second." In *Neuroscience and the Person*, edited by Robert John Russell, Nancey Murphy, Theo C. Meyering, and Michael A. Arbib, 45–56. Scientific Perspectives on Divine Action. Vatican City State: Vatican Observatory; Berkeley, CA: Center for Theology and Natural Sciences, 2002.

Hawking, Stephen. *A Brief History of Time*. New York: Bantam, 1998.

Hector, Kevin. "Actualism and Incarnation: The High Christology of Friedrich Schleiermacher." *International Journal of Systematic Theology* 8, no. 3 (July 2006): 307–22.

———. "The Mediation of Christ's Normative Spirit: A Constructive Reading of Schleiermacher's Pneumatology." *Modern Theology* 24, no.1 (January 2008): 1–22.

———. *Theology without Metaphysics: God, Language and the Spirit of Recognition*. Issues in Theology 8. Cambridge: Cambridge University Press, 2011.

Hill, Edmund, O.P. "General Introduction." In Augustine, *On Genesis*. The Works of Saint Augustine: A Translation for the 21st Century Volume I/13, edited by John E. Rotelle, O.S.A., translated by Edmund Hill, O.P., 13–22. Hyde Park, NY: New City, 2013.

Hugenberger, G. P. "Rib." In *The International Standard Bible Encyclopedia Revised Edition Volume 4*, edited by Geoffrey W. Bromiley, 183–85. Grand Rapids: Eerdmans, 1988.

Hummel, Leonard, and Gayle Woloschak. *Chance, Necessity, Love: An Evolutionary Theology of Cancer*. Eugene, OR: Wipf & Stock, 2017.

Janz, Denis R. "Late Medieval Theology." In *The Cambridge Companion to Reformation Theology*, edited by David Bagchi and David C. Steinmetz, 5–14. Cambridge Companions to Religion. Cambridge: Cambridge University Press, 2004.

Jenson, Robert. "Ipse Pater Non Est Impassibilis." In *Divine Impassibility and the Mystery of Human Suffering*, edited by James F. Keating and Thomas Joseph White, 117–26. Grand Rapids: Eerdmans, 2009.

––––––. *Systematic Theology Volume I: The Triune God*. Oxford: Oxford University Press, 1997.

––––––. *Systematic Theology Volume 2: The Works of God*. Oxford: Oxford University Press, 1999.

Johnson, Elizabeth. *Ask the Beasts: Darwin and the God of Love*. London: Bloomsbury, 2014.

Joest, Werner. "Synergismus." In *Die Religion in Geschichte und Gegenwart: Handwörterbuch für Theologie und Religionswissenschaft Volume 6*, 561–62. Tübingen: Mohr, 1957–1965.

Kant, Immanuel. "Groundwork of the Metaphysics of Morals [1785]." In *Practical Philosophy*, translated and edited by Mary J. Gregor, 37–108. The Cambridge Edition of the Works of Immanuel Kant. Cambridge: Cambridge University Press, 1996.

Knight, Douglas A. Forward to *Prolegomena to the History of Israel*, by Julius Wellhausen, translated by J. Sutherland Black and Alan Menzies, v–xvi. Scholars Press Reprints and Translations. Atlanta: Scholars Press, 1994.

Kolb, Robert, and Timothy J. Wengert, eds. *The Book of Concord: The Confessions of the Evangelical Lutheran Church*. Minneapolis: Fortress, 2000.

Lacugna, Catherine Mowry. *God for Us: The Trinity & Christian Life*. New York: HarperCollins, 1993.

Levenson, Jon D. *Creation and the Persistence of Evil: The Jewish Drama of Divine Omnipotence*. Princeton: Princeton University Press, 1994.

Luther, Martin. "The Estate of Marriage." In *Luther's Works 45* edited by Walther I. Brandt, 11–49. Philadelphia: Fortress, 1962.

––––––. *Lectures on Galatians 1535: Chapters 1–4*. Luther's Works 26. Edited by Jaroslav Pelikan. St. Louis: Concordia, 1963.

––––––. *On the Bondage of the Will*. Luther's Works 33. Edited by Philip S. Watson Philadelphia: Fortress, 1972.

––––––. "Preface to the Complete Edition of Luther's Latin Writings, Wittenberg, 1545." In *Martin Luther's Basic Theological Writings* 3rd Edition, edited by Timothy F. Lull and William R. Russell, 496–97. Minneapolis: Fortress, 2012.

Marty, Martin. *Martin Luther: A Life*. New York: Penguin, 2008.

McCormack, Bruce. "Divine Impassibility or Simply Divine Constancy? Implications of Karl Barth's Later Christology for Debates over Impassibility." In *Divine Impassibility and the Mystery of Human Suffering*, edited by James F. Keating and Thomas Joseph White, 150–86. Grand Rapids: Eerdmans, 2009.

––––––. *Karl Barth's Critically Realistic, Dialectical Theology: Its Genesis and Development 1909–1936*. Oxford: Oxford University Press, 1995.

Manschreck, Clyde L. Preface to *Melanchthon on Christian Doctrine: Loci Communes 1555*. Edited and translated by Clyde L. Manschreck. New York: Oxford University Press, 1965.

Melanchthon, Phillip. *Commonplaces: Loci Communes 1521*. Translated by Christian Preus. St. Louis: Concordia, 2014.

Michor, Franziska. "Franziska Michor at TEDMED2012." YouTube Video, 15:01. May 10, 2012. https://www.youtube.com/watch?v=blsk0AOAung.

Moltmann, Jürgen. *The Crucified God: The Cross of Christ as the Foundation and Criticism of Christian Theology*. Translated by R. A. Wilson and John Bowden. Minneapolis: Fortress, 1993.

Mukherjee, Siddhartha. *The Emperor of All Maladies: A Biography of Cancer*. New York: Scriber, 2010.

Nicolaidis, Argyris. "Relational Nature." In *The Trinity and an Entangled World*, edited by John Polkinghorne, 93–106. Grand Rapids: Eerdmans, 2010.

Niebuhr, Richard R. *Schleiermacher on Christ and Religion: A New Introduction*. New York: Charles Scribner's Sons, 1964.

Neusner, Jacob. *Lamentations Rabbah: An Analytical Translation*. Brown Judaic Studies 193. Atlanta: Scholars, 1989.

O'Daly, Gerard J. P. "Augustine on the Origin of Souls." In *Platonismus und Christentum: Festschrift für Heinrich Dörrie*, edited by Horst-Dieter Blume and Friedhelm Mann, 184–91. Jahrbuch für Antike und Christentum 10. Münster Westfalen: Aschendorff, 1983.

Olsen, Oliver K. "Flacius Illyricus, Matthias (1520–1575)." In *Theologische Realenzyklopädia XI*, 206–13. Berlin: De Gruyter, 1976–2004.

———. "Flacius, Matthias." In *Religion Past and Present Volume 5*, edited by Hans Dieter Betz, Don Browning, Bernd Janowski, and Eberhard Jüngel, 137–38. Leiden: Brill, 2008.

———. *Matthias Flacius and the Survival of Luther's Reform*. Minneapolis: Lutheran Press, 2011.

Ozment, Steven. *The Age of Reform 1250–1550: An Intellectual and Religious History of Late Medieval and Reformation Europe*. New Haven, Yale University Press, 1980.

Pannenberg, Wolfhart. *Systematic Theology Volume 1*. Translated by Geoffrey W. Bromiley. Grand Rapids: Eerdmans, 2009.

———. *Systematic Theology Volume 2*. Translated by Geoffrey W. Bromiley. Grand Rapids: Eerdmans, 1994.

Pallen, Mark. "Bio380 Lecture 5: The Phylogenomics of Cancer." YouTube video, 45:44. November 11, 2011. https://www.youtube.com/watch?v=OaR1YLTgQVo.

Pesch, Otto Hermann, O.P. "Existential and Sapiential Theology—The Theological Confrontation between Luther and Thomas Aquinas." In *Catholic Scholars Dialogue with Luther*, 61–81. Chicago: Loyola University Press, 1970.

Polkinghorne, John. "The Demise of Democritus." In *The Trinity and an Entangled World*, edited by John Polkinghorne, 1–14. Grand Rapids: Eerdmans, 2010.

———. Introduction to *The Trinity and an Entangled World*, edited by John Polkinghorne, vii–xi. Grand Rapids: Eerdmans, 2010.

Pope Francis. *Laudato si'* (May 2015). http://w2.vatican.va/content/dam/francesco /pdf/encyclicals/documents/papa-francesco_20150524_enciclica-laudato-si_en .pdf.

Preger, Wilhelm. *Matthias Flacius Illyricus und seine Zeit.* Erlangen: T Bläsing, 1859–1861.

Pylas, Pan. "Half Billion More People Face Poverty Due to Virus—Report." Associated Press. April 9, 2020. https://apnews.com/b219627e31d87779e5253f9 a072be4dc.

Rahner Karl. *The Trinity.* Translated by Joseph Donceel. New York: Herder & Herder, 1970.

Rasmussen, Larry. *Earth Honoring Faith: Religious Ethics in a New Key.* Oxford: Oxford University Press, 2013.

Reimann, Henry W. "Mathias Flacius Illyricus: A Biographical Sketch." *Concordia Theological Monthly* 35, no. 2 (1964): 69–93.

Rendtorff, Rolf. *The Canonical Hebrew Bible: A Theology of the Old Testament.* Translated by David E. Orton. Tools for Biblical Study 7. Leiden: Deo, 2005.

———. *The Covenant Formula: An Exegetical and Theological Investigation.* Translated by Margaret Kohl. Old Testament Studies. Edinburgh: T & T Clark, 1998.

Richter, Sandra L. *The Epic of Eden: A Christian Entry into the Old Testament.* Downers Grove, IL: IVP Academic, 2008.

Ricoeur, Paul. *Fallible Man.* Translated by Charles A. Kelbey. New York: Fordham University Press, 1986.

———. *The Symbolism of Evil.* Translated by Emerson Buchanan. Boston: Beacon, 1969; New York: HarperCollins, 1995.

Rolston, Holmes III. *Three Big Bangs: Matter-Energy, Life, Mind.* New York: Columbia University Press, 2010.

Sarna, Nahum. *Genesis.* The JPS Torah Commentary. Philadelphia: The Jewish Publication Society, 1989.

Schleiermacher, F. D. E. *The Christian Faith.* Edited by H. R. Mackintosh and J. S. Stewart. Edinburgh: T & T Clark, 1999.

———. "The Second Letter." In *On the Glaubenslehre: Two Letters to Dr. Lücke,* trans. James Duke and Francis Fiorenza, 64–67. American Academy of Religion Texts and Translations Series 3. Chico, CA: Scholars, 1981.

Schmid, H. H. "Creation, Righteousness, and Salvation: 'Creation Theology' as the Broad Horizon of Biblical Theology (1973)." In *Creation in the Old Testament,* edited by Bernhard W. Anderson, 102–17. Issues in Religion and Theology 6. London: SPCK; Philadelphia: Fortress, 1984.

Schmid, Konrad. "Schöpfung als Thema der Theologie." In *Schöpfung,* edited by Konrad Schmid, 1–15. Themen der Theologie 4. Tübingen: Mohr Siebeck, 2012.

Shakespeare, William. *Macbeth.* Edited by Stephen Orgel. The Pelican Shakespeare. New York: Penguin, 2000.

Shubin, Neil. *Your Inner Fish: A Journey into the 3.5-Billion-Year History of the Human Body.* New York: Pantheon, 2008.

Simpson, Cuthbert A. *The Book of Genesis.* The Interpreter's Bible Volume 1. Nashville: Abingdon, 1952.

Smith, Aaron T. *A Theology of the Third Article: Karl Barth and the Spirit of the Word.* Minneapolis: Fortress, 2014.

Smith, Mark S. *The Priestly Vision of Genesis 1*. Minneapolis: Fortress, 2010.

Spiegler, Gerhard. "Theological Tensions in Schleiermacher's *Dialectic*: Response and Discussion." In Robert W. Funk, *Schleiermacher as Contemporary*. Journal for Theology and the Church 7. Herder and Herder, 1970.

Stoeger, William R., S.J. "The Mind-Brain Problem, the Laws of Nature, and Constitutive Relationships." In *Neuroscience and the Person*, edited by Robert John Russell, Nancey Murphy, Theo C. Meyering, and Michael A. Arbib, 129–46. Scientific Perspectives on Divine Action. Vatican City State: Vatican Observatory; Berkeley, CA: Center for Theology and Natural Sciences, 2002.

von Rad, Gerhard. "The Theological Problem of the Old Testament Doctrine of Creation (1936)." In *Creation in the Old Testament*. Issues in Religion and Theology 6, edited by Bernhard W. Anderson, 53–64. London: SPCK; Philadelphia: Fortress, 1984.

Vriezen, Th. C. *Onderzoek naar de Paradijsvoorstelling bij de oude Semietische Volken*. Wageningen: H. Veenman and Zonen, 1937.

Walton, John. *Ancient Near Eastern Thought and the Old Testament: Introducing the Conceptual World of the Hebrew Bible*. Grand Rapids: Baker, 2006.

———. *Genesis 1 as Ancient Cosmology*. Winona Lake, IN: Eisenbrauns, 2011.

Welker, Michael. *Creation and Reality*. Translated by John F. Hoffmeyer. Minneapolis: Fortress, 1999.

Wellhausen, Julius. *Die Composition des Hexateuchs und der historischen Bücher des Alten Testaments*. Berlin: De Gruyter, 2012.

———. *Prolegomena zur Geschichte Israels*. Berlin: De Gruyter, 2001.

Wenham, Gordon J. *Genesis 1–15*. Word Biblical Commentary Volume 1. Waco, TX: Word, 1987.

Westermann, Claus. *Genesis 1–11: A Continental Commentary*. Translated by John J. Scullion. Minneapolis: Fortress, 1994.

———. *The Genesis Accounts of Creation*. Translated by Norman E. Wagner. Facet Books Biblical Series 7. Philadelphia: Fortress, 1964.

Williams, Robert R. Introduction to *Divine Immutability: A Critical Reconsideration*, by Isaak A Dorner. Translated by Robert R. Williams and Claude Welch. Minneapolis: Fortress, 1994.

Wirzba, Norman. *The Paradise of God: Renewing Religion in an Ecological Age*. Oxford: Oxford University Press, 2003.

Zeilinger, Anton. "Quantum Physics: Ontology or Epistemology?" In *The Trinity and an Entangled World*, edited by John Polkinghorne, 32–40. Grand Rapids: Eerdmans, 2010.

Zizioulas, John. *Being As Communion: Studies in Personhood and the Church*. Crestwood, NY: St. Vladimir's Seminary Press, 1985.

———. "Relational Ontology: Insights from Patristic Thought." In *The Trinity and an Entangled World: Relationality in Physical Science and Theology*, edited by John Polkinghorne, 146–56. Grand Rapids: Eerdmans, 2010.

Index

About the Author

Aaron T. Smith (PhD, Marquette University) is senior pastor of Trinity Evangelical Lutheran Church in Chambersburg, PA, and adjunct professor of theology at United Lutheran Seminary. He is the author of *A Theology of the Third Article: Karl Barth and the Spirit of the Word* (Fortress, 2014). Besides work on Barth, Smith's several publications have focused on the broad theme of divine action in the modern world through the person and work of the Spirit.